IN
CUBA

√

IN CUBA

ERNESTO CARDENAL

Translated by Donald D. Walsh

A NEW DIRECTIONS BOOK

Manufactured in the United States of America
First published clothbound and as New Directions Paperbook 377 in 1974
Published simultaneously in Canada by McClelland & Stewart, Ltd.

Library of Congress Cataloging in Publication Data

Cardenal, Ernesto.
    In Cuba.

    (A New Directions Book)
    1.   Cuba—Description and travel—1951–
2.   Cuba—Politics and government—1959–
I.   Title.
F1765.2.C2713   917.291′03′64   74–8493
ISBN 0–8112–0537–1
ISBN 0–8112–0538–X (pbk.)

New Directions Books are published for James Laughlin
by New Directions Publishing Corporation,
333 Sixth Avenue, New York 10014

Chronology

1853, July 26. Birthdate of José Martí, Cuba's greatest hero, killed leading the 1895 War of Independence. A century later (July 26, 1953) Castro began his rebellion against Batista.

1895, March 24. The Cuban War of Independence against Spain began.

1898, February 15. The U.S.S. *Maine,* anchored in the harbor of Havana to protect the lives and property of American citizens, was sunk, presumably by Spanish forces, and the United States turned the War of Independence into the Spanish-American War.

1901, June 12. Cuba's first Constitution included the Platt Amendment, which gave the United States the right to intervene to preserve Cuban independence and a stable government. The Amendment was abrogated in 1934.

1926, August 13. Fidel Castro was born in Mayarí in Oriente Province, the son of a landowner.

1933, September 4. Army Sergeant Fulgencio Batista led a revolt of students and soldiers that established him as Cuba's strong man for twenty-five years.

1934, August 24. A treaty between the United States and Cuba abrogated the Platt Amendment (1901) and gave the United States permission to lease land for a naval base at Guantanamo Bay.

1953, July 26. Castro's "army" of two hundred attacked Fort Moncada near Santiago in Oriente Province. This was the second largest Cuban military center, with a thousand soldiers. The attack failed and many of the rebels, including Fidel and Raúl Castro, were jailed.

1955, May 15. An amnesty freed Castro and his comrades. Two months later he went into exile in Mexico to establish the "26th of July Movement."

1956, December 2. Castro and eighty-one followers, after a disastrous six-day trip from Mexico in the yacht *Granma,* landed in Oriente Province and sought refuge in the Sierra Maestra in a second attempt to overthrow Batista.

1957, May 28. Castro's forces attacked and captured a Batista garrison at Uvero, in Oriente Province. The victory was widely reported throughout Cuba and greatly strengthened the Castro cause.

1959, January 1. Batista was forced to flee from Cuba by the rebel army.

1959, February 8. Castro's Fundamental Law of the Republic replaced the 1940 Constitution.

1959, May 17. The Agrarian Reform Law limited the amount of property that any individual could own.

1960, September 13. The United States banned all American exports to Cuba, except medicines and some foodstuffs.

October. All American enterprises in Cuba were nationalized.

1961, April 17–19. A force of Cuban exiles, trained and financed in Guatemala by the CIA, landed at two beaches, Playa Larga and Playa Girón, in the Bay of Pigs. The attempt at invasion failed.

1962, January. The Organization of American States excluded Cuba from its membership.

October 14. The United States discovered that the Soviet Union was shipping ballistic missiles to Cuba.

October 22. President Kennedy imposed a naval "quarantine" to prevent further shipments and asked Premier Khrushchev to withdraw the missiles.

October 28. Khrushchev gave orders for the missile withdrawal.

1967, October. Che Guevara attempted to persuade the Bolivian peasants to revolt against their government. The attempt failed and the peasants killed Guevara.

Contents

CHRONOLOGY   v
PREFACE   xi
Airport   1
Walking around Havana   6
Shopping with Margaret Randall   13
At the du Pont House   16
The Young Poets   19
Young Ordoqui   25
Haydée Santamaría   28
The Fishing Port   31
Supper at the Retamars   34
The People's Courts   39
A Conversation in My Room   49
At the Former Country Club   54
Supper at the National   58
Ernesto   63
The Casino Boy   71
An Excursion   74
Books   76
The Archbishop   78
Pablo Armando   83
Conversation in a School   87
With Catholics   97
Interview with Ernesto Cardenal   101
A Mass   104
A Teacher   112
Che's Pilot   116
In the Habana Libre   120
Sectarianism   122
The Psychiatric Hospital   125
The Isle of Youth   128
A Lay Theologian   139
The Chamberman   141
A Young Catholic   145
The Son of Batista's Lieutenant   149

Two Officials   152
A Seminarist   159
Letter from a Woman Guerrilla Fighter   163
Cutting Cane with Love and Grace   166
A College Girl's Story   172
The Mother of Camilo Torres   175
Millionaire Cane-Cutters   181
José Antonio's Will   186
With Lezama Lima   191
On the Highway   196
A Farmer   203
Two Party Militants   209
Sandino City   215
In a Hut   218
At the Central Committee   223
A Poet in the Factory   225
With the Nuncio   231
In the Social Disgrace Unit   236
Che's Orders   241
The "Venceremos" Brigade   244
A Sermon   250
With Young Catholics   256
A Religious   258
A Reformed One   262
A Television Program   267
With the Foreign Secretary   272
Communist Parties   275
A Catholic Leader   278
Waiting for a Bus   283
Frank   285
A Gathering of Poets   288
Three Friends   292
The 26th of July   297
The Speech   300
Airport   321
Epilogue. A Conversation with Fidel   325
APPENDIX: Some People, Places, Dates, and
    Other Data   334

List of Poets and Poems in Translation

Domingo Alfonso, "Intranscendental Biography"   94
Antón Arrufat, "The 1958 Exile"   109
Miguel Barnet, "Che"   119
    "Revolution"   24
Roberto Branly, "Sports Report"   207
Víctor Casáus, "Bárbara"   147
    "A Commentary to the Martyrs of the Revolution"   194
    "Volunteer's Poems"   178
David Chericián, "Loving Them, Naming Them"   184
Félix Contreras, "Let My Brothers of This Hour
        Hear Me"   171
Samuel Feijóo, "A Visit to the Trenches"   257
Nicolás Guillén, "I Have"   59
Rogelio Fabio Hurtado, "3700 Rockets Canimar
        Year '64"   213
    "Some Customs of the Soldier on Duty"   47
Fayad Jamis, "For This Freedom"   277
César López, "In Those Summers Things
        Kept Happening"   18
Fina García Marruz, "Prayer for the Dead"   137
Noel Nicola, "Let's Go, for This Is the Year"   266
    "My Generation"   52
    "A Small Housing Problem"   154
    "26"   296
Luis Rogelio Nogueras, "Poem"   26
Lisandro Otero, "The Generation of the '30s"   161
Heberto Padilla, "The Old Bards Say"   100
    "Placard for 1960"   238
Roberto Fernández Retamar, "Madrigal"   36
    "That We Shall See Ablaze"   298
    "With the Same Hands"   228
Silvio Rodríguez, "Playa Girón"   75
Cintio Vitier, "Cane-Cutting Notes"   246
    "Do Not Ask of Me"   3
    "Work"   221
José Yanes, "Havana Is a City in Waiting"   10
    "Not to Talk about It Ever with My Mother"   252

Preface

This report on Castro's Cuba is the result of two visits, one lasting several months in 1970 and the other a few days in 1971. The reporter is a widely read and much admired poet. Born in 1925 in Nicaragua, he was influenced religiously and poetically by Thomas Merton. He entered the Trappist Order at Gethsemani, Kentucky, as a novice in 1957. An avowed Marxist, Cardenal points out that the primitive Christian Church was much closer to Marxism than to capitalism.

Many of the chapters of *In Cuba* are reports of conversations with poets, priests, young people, both hippies and squares, bureaucrats, ardent *fidelistas,* equally ardent anti-Castro Catholics. Cardenal is an assiduous and perceptive interviewer, and the result of his labors is a book filled with insights, an account of the inspiring efforts and the occasionally tragicomic results of the governmental machinery of Fidel Castro.

If this translation reads well, as though the book had been written not in Spanish but in English, much of the credit should go to Donna Rowell Walsh, whose editorial expertise removed Hispanic traces in the vocabulary, the syntax, and the word order.

Madison, Connecticut   D. D. W.

*To the Cuban People
and to Fidel*

Airport

When the ancient Russian plane landed at the Havana airport, it was raining. And I remembered one other time that I had been in this airport (an unforgettable day for me, and the happiest day of my life). It was raining that day, too, and getting late, and I had seen Havana from the air surrounded by a halo of opalescent mist, as if wrapped in a great sadness. Some Yankees, sunburned and smiling, got on the plane loaded with Bacardi rum, and I felt that they were coming from a depressing world. Airline attendants carried their bottles to the landing stairs. It was Batista's Cuba. A cousin of mine who had been in Cuba had told me shortly before that a young man was fighting in the mountains and that his name was Fidel Castro. I was stopping off in Havana on a flight from Managua, Nicaragua, to Miami, but I was going to Miami only to enter the Trappist Monastery of Gethsemani. This flight I later described as "a true flight to Heaven rather than a routine Pan American flight." It was a flight to freedom. (And I remember that from the air I had seen far-off mountains and I had wondered where that fellow Fidel Castro might be fighting.)

Now, eleven years after the triumph of the Revolution, I was arriving at the same airport on the invitation of that Revolution as a member of a poetry jury, and again it was raining. What would this other Cuba be like? I had some reservations, especially because of the religious question. And yet I had already read a judgment of the Catholic writer Leopoldo Marechal: "The most fascinating socioeconomic experience that we have seen in this second half of the century."

On the plane there was no other reading material than *Granma* (the official organ of the Communist party). *Granma* in Spanish, *Granma* in English, and *Granma* in French. "Granma" was the name of the yacht from which Fidel landed in Cuba. And that issue of *Granma* was full of attacks against the Yankees for having kidnapped some Cuban fishermen. It also told how all the plasma in Havana had been given to Peru after the great earthquake. Thousands of blood donors were giving blood all over Cuba. Fidel and Dorticós had given

1

blood. The stewardesses were not especially beautiful, one was white, the other black.

When the plane stopped and the door opened, a soldier came in and said a name. A bald man sitting in front of me said "That's me," and he was hustled out of the plane in the rain. A CIA agent who had just been discovered and was about to be shot? At the entrance to the terminal he was smothered in embraces. He was a VIP getting a special reception.

I did not go through customs with the rest. I was taken to a small room where I was greeted by a delegation from the House of the Americas, among them my friend the poet Cintio Vitier. There were daiquiris and a photographer from *Granma*. Cintio said he also was a judge in the poetry contest arranged by the House of the Americas.

Cintio went with me in the car taking us to Havana. He talked gaily, recalling the time that we saw each other in Mexico. I suddenly noticed that the signs along the highway were not billboard ads: MAKE MAN'S LIFE PERFECT . . . AMERICA'S LAND OF FREEDOM . . . OUR BATTLE-FIELD COVERS THE WHOLE WORLD . . . WE'RE SHOOTING FOR TEN MILLION. . . Cintio tells me that they have just had a rude shock. They're not going to reach the ten million. The great sugar harvest of 1970 that had been announced for years, the ten million tons. Fidel had already admitted this at the giant meeting to celebrate the release of the kidnapped fishermen. Fidel confessed the failure almost in tears. Cintio wept when he heard it. It was not just a question of the economy, he said, it was above all a moral question. The economy was important: that goal meant the beginning of the breaking away from underdevelopment. But the whole national sense of honor was bound up in it, as Fidel had said. It was a battle that had been lost. (I was surprised to hear this, and I thought: Do you suppose that Cintio is talking that way so that the driver can hear it?) It was an excessive goal, he said. The biggest capitalist harvest had been seven million. Then it was done with wage-earning field hands, the pariahs of society. That caste no longer existed because all the people had become literate. The Revolution had wanted to show that it could reach ten million with mostly voluntary labor and with moral stimuli. In order not to interrupt the harvest the Christmas and New Year holidays had been postponed, moved to the 26th of July, the anniversary of the Revolution. Will

I be here on the 26th? They expect a very important speech by Fidel on that day. Cintio told the driver that Fidel's speech admitting to the failure of the harvest goal had been one of the most beautiful that he had made, really inspired. I thought: Can it be possible that they can force Cintio into being insincere? I'll find out what he thinks about all this when he talks with me alone in the hotel.

I knew that Cintio had not wanted to be part of the Revolution. But he had not wanted to be against it. He had stayed on the fringe. As a Catholic he had his reservations. When we talked in Mexico, in the first period of the Revolution, he had confided his fears to me because atheistic training was beginning to be dominant, and he had two young children. But he had realized that it was his duty to stay in Cuba. And they had never harassed him or removed him from his position as Director of the Martí Room in the National Library. I knew his poem—and it had seemed to me significant that it was published in Cuba—in which he says to a friend:

> Do not ask of me false
> collaborations, games
> of quibbling and confusion:
> ask me to carry my soul
> to its bleeding earth.
>
> Do not ask of me signatures,
> photographs, credence in an abominable
> spread of duplicity: ask of me
> that we be like brothers
> opening our hearts to one another until we die.
>
> Do not flatter my vanity, seek my strength,
> which is yours. Do not love me, with your daintiness
> that betrays me. Do not pretend
> that you are going to believe in my pretense.
> Let us not create another world of lies.
>
> Let us create a world of truth, with the truth
> split open like a terrible loaf for all.
>
> That is what I feel that each day, implacably,
> the Revolution demands of me.

—CINTIO VITIER

3

We drove through Revolution Square, and Cintio told me: "This is the monument to Martí. There is the platform where Fidel speaks, where he will speak on the 26th. There opposite is the Jose Martí National Library where I work." We passed by the huge building that had been the U. S. Embassy and was now the Embassy of Switzerland, which represents U. S. interests, and Cintio told me that it was there that the enormous protest demonstrations were held when the fishermen were kidnapped, a meeting of half a million people, and Cintio was amazed when I told him that nothing about this had been published abroad. He told me that there was great solidarity between Cuba and Peru. Twenty planes with plasma and other supplies had gone to Peru. They gave all the plasma in Havana, and there were more than a hundred thousand donors, all giving spontaneously; they gave more plasma than Peru gave; and Fidel gave his blood. I told him that *Time* announced that Cuban aid had been "a pint of Fidel's blood."

We reached the imposing National Hotel, where the House of the Americas judges were staying, and Cintio told me that it was the most elegant hotel in Havana. The sumptuous dining room was crowded with poets and other writers, all in shirt sleeves: Fernández Retamar, Lezama Lima, Mario Benedetti, Roque Dalton, Norman Brisky, Jorge Ruffinelli, Rodolfo Walsh, André Gunder Frank, and Foreign Minister Raúl Roa, who was also on the jury. There were several tables reserved exclusively for us. At other tables were other hotel guests: Vietnamese, Chinese, Russians, Koreans. On the menu there were lobster thermidor, frogs legs, French wine. Over the loudspeaker a woman's voice said: "Comrade So-and-so, go to the telephone, comrade." The uniformed waiters were not servile but companionable; they didn't call you "sir" but "comrade."

At the end of the long luncheon Cintio came to my room with me, and he said that he was now totally on the side of the Revolution. Three things had influenced his decision: The disputes between Fidel and the Soviet Union had convinced him that this was a wholly Cuban Revolution and not an imitation of Soviet communism. Fidel had fought three times with the Soviet Union and once with China. The example of Camilo Torres, who made him see that a Christian could work closely with communists. Finally, going out to cut sugar cane (he hadn't ever gone before) completed the job of identifying him totally with the people and the Revolution. Now he had become a militiaman. Now he had agreed to be a member of the House of the Americas jury, he signed all the manifestos, he was wholly integrated with the Revolution. This was after eight years of being on the fringe and in the wings through a scruple of religious conscience, which had now disappeared. This same process had been experienced by his wife, Fina, and the other Catholic poets, Lezama, Eliseo Diego, Octavio Smith. It had not been easy for him to be like this, he told me. All these years they had been showering him with invitations to congresses, to trips, to round tables, to give lectures, to contribute to publications, to sign manifestos, protests, petitions, to be a contest judge. He had refused them all. "And note, they never bothered me. They always respected my attitude, and I'm grateful for this." He smiled as he puffed on his Havana cigar and said: "And now we really are on the side of the Revolution."

Walking around Havana

Havana at night is a dark city because it has no billboards all lit up. The newcomer has the impression that there has been a blackout on the top floors of the buildings. The effect can be sad if one equates joy with neonlit ads, showcase windows, bustle, night life. To me Havana seemed very joyful. I said to Benedetti: "This is the most joyful city that I have ever seen. The only joyful city."

Everyone in the streets was well dressed, not some with haughty luxury and others in rags. And this seemed to me very joyful. In the vicinity of the great hotels, the National, the Capri, the Habana Libre, the streets were filled with people, but nobody was buying or selling anything. People were *strolling* through the streets. They were walking slowly, taking a walk; nobody was chasing after money. No face was strained by poverty. There were no taxi drivers cruising on the watch for foreigners, no prostitutes, no bootblacks, no beggars. And it seemed to me that a city like that ought to be called a joyful city. Around this city there was no encirclement of misery, and it seemed to me that this also made of Havana a very joyful city.

"Many probably say that Havana is sad," I said to Benedetti, "because here there is no bourgeois joy, but here there is true joy. Capitalist cities seem very joyful at the center, but for those who haven't a cent, they are a horror. Joy is only for the rich, and besides, that joy of the rich is false and it is another horror. Here I see the immense joy of a metropolis without poor people, without misery. And the joy of everybody being equal."

Little black children (who once would have been called "urchins") ran through the doors of the Habana Libre (the former Hilton), and the uniformed porters said nothing to them. They chased one another boisterously across the great marble-floored lobbies. Young proletarians, too, whites and blacks mixed, strolled in to chat there with the confidence once possessed by millionaires.

I thought: Thousands have left. But those who remain seem happy, and they are the masters of everything. It must be very joyful for these people to know that they are all proprietors, that there is not a single bejeweled lady or a tuxedoed gentleman. People don't try to outdress one another. They don't envy anything, and they don't envy anyone. There are no seductive advertisements of things that people can't buy. That must be the main reason why these people laugh, why we see so much joy in these groups of young people, blacks, whites, and mulattoes, and these couples that go by holding hands.

"You don't miss all the goods in the stores, do you?" asked Benedetti, the poet. I told him: "It seems to me most beautiful. I have withdrawn from the world to live on an island, because I loathe cities. But this is my city. I now see that I had not withdrawn from the world, only from the capitalist world. This is a city that is bound to please a monk, a meditator, anyone who in the capitalist world has decided to withdraw from the world."

Benedetti says: "In Uruguay they make a thousand ladies' handbags, and they are very expensive, and scarcely anyone can afford to buy them, and so the shops in my country are stuffed with ladies' handbags. Here when they make ladies' handbags they have to make four hundred thousand of them, and everybody buys them up, and so there are no ladies' handbags left. I mean, there are no handbags in the stores, because the people are walking around with them. Shirts are made all alike, alike in quality and price, but with different colors and styles. And nobody goes around dressed worse than anybody else, and nobody goes around luxuriously dressed; everyone wears clothes of the same quality. The problem is not money, it's goods. There's money left over and a lack of goods, and that's why the stores are empty. In our countries it's not that there are too many goods, but it seems that there are too many because there's no money to buy them, and so the stores are full of goods."

I said to him: "I see that no one is elegantly dressed here. Everybody dresses the way I like to dress. And the way that poets, artists, intellectuals, and students like to dress. And the way Fidel Castro likes to dress. And the way everybody ought to dress everywhere. The clothes are colorful and varied. And the girls' dresses are pretty, besides."

Opposite the Coppelia there was a line of people two or three blocks long waiting three or four hours to get into the famous ice-cream parlor that has more than sixty different flavors of ice cream. The line is so long because everyone can afford to buy that ice cream, which is surely the most delicious in the world. "The only limitation for the public is the long waiting line, and before shifting to an ice-cream parlor less good than this one you ought to think twice—or ten times," said Benedetti's wife.

I remember what Cintio said to me: "Everyone here has more money than he can spend. Money is no longer a problem. Money is no longer a concern to people." And what Fina said: "When people eat in the most elegant restaurants, sometimes they don't have enough money, although most of the time they have enough and more than enough. People earn more than they can spend." And what Margaret Randall said to me this morning: "It's very odd to hear you talk about a writer with financial problems (I was talking to her about a young Nicaraguan poet), very peculiar. And I remember now that it's like that, that there are people out there who are troubled by lack of money. But I had forgotten it, because it's years since I've heard anyone talk about a lack of money. Here there are other problems, but not a lack of money."

In a small room on the ground floor of the Habana Libre some students were rehearsing a play. Many people peered in from the sidewalk and some came in and sat down to watch the rehearsal. Also on the ground floor was a bookstore with glass walls, but we didn't go in because we could see that the bookshelves were almost empty. The books (I'm told) are bought up as soon as they arrive, and people stand in line at bookstores when there are new books. I remember Modern Poetry—which probably no longer exists—where Thomas Merton went in to buy books and discovered that it was a clothing store.* The same with Philosophy, which Merton also went to and which turned out to be another clothing store. I'm told that Twentieth Century Poetry is no longer in existence, and that was a great bookstore, but no private store exists now in Cuba, whether it's a bookstore or a clothing store. There

---

* Thomas Merton (1915–68) visited Cuba in the spring of 1940, on a pilgrimage to Our Lady of Cobre. It was, in fact, in Havana, at the Church of St. Francis, that he experienced his first mystical illumination. See his early autobiography, *The Seven Storey Mountain* (New York, The New American Library), pages 271–78, for a full description of the journey. —D. D. W.

are bookstores all over Havana and all over Cuba—they tell me—but like other stores, they are empty.

This is a city quite different from the one that Merton knew. Merton was in Havana thirty years ago, after his conversion to Catholicism and shortly before he became a Trappist monk. Merton became very fond of the Havana of that period, full of color and noise, shouts and smells—so different from the New York from where he had come—and for all of its sinfulness, Merton compared it to Heavenly Jerusalem. He tells us that blacks would go by smoking cigars and with bloody aprons carrying great hunks of meat, and that the streets were filled with bunches of bananas and papayas and coconuts and all kinds of fruits, and that there were enormous quantities of cigarettes and cigars piled up and heaps of books on the sidewalks, great wads of lottery tickets, countless magazines of all kinds. Many, many newspapers, and people shouting at you offering all kinds of things, shoeshines, lottery tickets, postcards, the latest Extra (a new Extra came out every minute, said Merton), and the street noises and laughter went into the cafés and the bars, and the music and the laughter in the cafés and the bars went out into the streets. And this "sinful Havana," said Merton, was, for anyone who knew how to live in it, "analogous to the Kingdom of Heaven." (Of course, the other Yankees who arrived in Havana did not read in it those signs that Merton read, nor did they know how to live in it as he did.) And I now wondered: What would monk Merton say of this other Havana, so different: still, dark, silent, austere? He would have liked it better, as he had liked his monastery, and he would not have missed the former analogy.

Near the Capri people were amusing themselves by looking at a gigantic illuminated sign about the sugar harvest, along one wall of a large building. The sign showed ten sacks of sugar representing the ten million tons. Dates lit up and the sacks filled with light until eight and a half were filled: that's as far as the harvest had reached. In the Capri there is still a night club, and there are shows Saturday and Sunday. But no, thanks, I have no desire to see the show. This Capri, I'm told, was a hotel to which American businessmen would phone from New York or Miami and ask for a room with a woman.

Farther along there was an exhibit of anti-imperialist caricatures. We went in. In one of them there were some pot-

9

bellied bishops next to some generals, sitting at a table and devouring the people. But most of the caricatures are anti-Nixon. Back in the street we watched the people walking by. Benedetti said: "There's a curious change in mentality produced in a people when you take away commercial advertising. They no longer desire to make unnecessary purchases. They no longer want to get ahead of others by buying more things or owning the best things. People know that they buy more or less what they need, and above all, that they buy the same things that everyone buys. This creates a very fraternal feeling among everyone."

Benedetti told us about the time that he went by a stadium all lit up and he went in: a baseball game had just ended, but with the baseball players now were playing Fidel, Raúl, and other Cabinet members. The public had stayed on to see this extra game, and they were shouting to Fidel and joking with him, and he was joking with the public and arguing about each play at the top of his lungs.

It seemed to me suddenly that I saw advertised in neon lights our Nicaraguan beer "Victoria." But no, it was a red sign on a building that said:

VENCEREMOS [We Shall Overcome]

»»»

HAVANA IS A CITY IN WAITING

—José Yanes

Each morning,
like people who come out of the ruins after a shelling,
the men of this city face life in any way they can:
with militant faith, hatred, pessimism reaffirmed.
They come out, walk through the dirty streets,
the rickety buildings with peeling paint
that they can't see now in the darkness of the dawn
but that they know by heart
covered with op art nouveau posters that demand:

Everyone to the Fields.
You, What Are You Doing for the Ten Million?
Give Your All in the Year of Decisive Struggle

Let This Not Be a Mere Slogan
A Sign Painted on the Walls
You Can Always Do More
Civil Defense Is *You*
What Interests Us Most Is to Fulfill the Revolution
    and the Party
Each Worker an Advance Guard Worker
  Facing the Fields
  More Revolutionary Offensives
  The Fighting Charge Is Always Fatherland or Death
  We Shall Overcome. The Cuban's Word Is Go Go.

The trash cans, the cigar butts, the cats,
the militiamen on guard, they receive these men.

That one who walks swiftly, he is a member of the Party:
he knows that the city is falling apart.
But yesterday he was on the Mayarí Plateau:
he saw the old dreams that seemed lost,
the elevated highways over the mountain, the hospitals.
He has had no breakfast. He extends his visit.
On a shut shop, the wind creaks on a worm-eaten sign:

Oquendo   The Minute Café

He thinks of other times, he rambles; there's no
    turning back.
He hears laughter. Several men climb on a truck
    with a sign:

Now With More Determination and Courage Than Ever
    We Must Change Defeat into Victory

That slow man with the black bag has not
    seen the dreams.

He has seen only the city, each day more broken.
This urban vision of life annihilates him.
An avenue lit up specially on an unusual night
has made him think hopefully that tensions are lessening;
he lives in a time that does not exist,
clutching at a city that does not exist.

He does not see the progress in those ruins.
This morning the world makes him more gray and
        more lost than ashes.

That lady who runs along like a mouse being chased
was too late for the bread line. She hurried in vain.
She is incapable of thought: at this moment she
        simply hates.
That young man with a knapsack is going to do his
        military service.
He used to study. Now he will cut cane. He has not slept.
His mother weeps at home and curses.

Havana is a city waiting for lights,
for food, for buildings, for automobiles,
for the men who will come sometime to rebuild her
and who are now scattered through the countryside,
in filthy huts, trying to raise up the country
        in the midst of horrors,
faith, hatred, love, and fits of despair,
dreaming of her because in the evening the neon lights
        are soft
and the mercury lights pale.

The sun rises over the buildings.
Now we can see clearly a sign that announces:

UNTIL VICTORY FOREVER.

Shopping with Margaret Randall

The poet Margaret Randall said, showing me her ration card: "This card is exactly alike all over Cuba. Food is scarce, as you can see, but the ration card is the same for a Cabinet member as for a farmer in the most remote village. I don't mind privations if I know that those privations will bring food for everyone."

She invited me to go shopping with her for provisions for herself and her husband, the poet Robert Cohen. She said: "So that you can see what shopping is like in a socialist country." The store that she had to go to was near my hotel. While we stood in line she said: "The finest thing about this Revolution is that we all receive the same amount. Every adult has the right to four eggs a week, three quarters of a pound of meat a week, a half pound of bread a day, six pounds of sugar a month, six pounds of rice a month. It used to be four pounds, but it has gone up to six because rice production is up. In this way the people understand the relation between the work of their hands and the products that they obtain. Bread is in greatest abundance (we can't eat all the bread that they give us). At the end of the day they give away all the leftover bread so that the next day there won't be any stale bread. There's a shortage of toilet paper. Cigarettes, five packages every three weeks. That's not much for a smoker, but since not everyone is a smoker, one can beg the ration of those who don't smoke. There is a special diet card for sick people and those over sixty-five (they get more eggs, two chickens a week, and so forth), and also for pregnant and nursing women. Children get three toys at Christmas all over Cuba: one big toy and two little ones. The children can pick them out in the stores. And the child of an important director and the child from the most remote canefield in Cuba get toys that have exactly the same value. There is a birthday party for each child, the same party for every single child in Cuba: a birthday cake for a hundred people and seventy-five bottles of pop. I went to get a cake for Gregory, who had his birthday last week, and it was so big —she opened her arms—that I could hardly get it on the bus. If you want to have the party in a playground—in the Havana Zoo, for example—they'll also give the child a pineapple and seventy sandwiches for his friends. When a girl has her fifteenth birthday she gets a big party, with beer, rum, and a dress. Every couple that's going to be married also gets a party with a buffet and a photographer. Wedding clothes are given to the bride and bridegroom. They get a car with a chauffeur and flowers. They have a honeymoon in a luxury hotel. Besides, all the workers in Cuba get a month's vacation every year, which they can spend at hotels or beaches that used to be exclusive. When a woman is about to have a child she gets a special ration card to buy clothes for the baby. When a child is born he does not bring scarcity into the home but abundance instead, an increase in the food allowance. At school, children get free clothes, shoes, and books. And two meals a day. All women have a ration book for the beauty parlor. Dress materials? We get twenty yards a year to make our clothes—every woman in Cuba has the same allowance. All medical services are free. Transportation is free or almost free. Telephones are free. When there is a death, the Government pays for everything: the coffin, five wreaths, and the hearse—it doesn't cost a cent to die. Taxes? There are no taxes in Cuba."

When we got to the counter we saw a sign that read: "If You Take Two of Anything You're Taking One Away from Someone Else." And I tell Margaret that it reminds me of what Thompson says about contemporary Mayans: "No one believes he should try to get more than his due because that would have to be at the cost of his neighbor." What Margaret got was very little, because she had almost no right to anything on that occasion. Her purchases: a pound of spaghetti, a can of tomato paste for the spaghetti, a large hunk of bread. The rest could wait until her turn came. "I don't need anything," she said, "because I have just got the other provisions for the week."

I said: "This system that delights you because you're a communist delights me because I find it evangelic. I also am fond of scarcity: I am a monk. I hope you will never have too much abundance. These rations are like what we have to eat at Solentiname." I asked her how they manage for special parties. "Parties? That's very hard. You have to save from your weekly ration in order to eat a little better that day. Either that or the guests help out with their ration cards." "And the drinks?" "Those parties are without drinks, because there aren't any. But there *is* liquor when there's a celebration of some kind in a factory or a worker's center: those are the real parties."

And what about servants? I wanted to know how they managed with the cooking and the clothes washing. "There are almost no maids or cooks, except in a few cases where a woman has stayed on out of affection serving a family. One usually has lunch in his work center, and the children also have breakfast at school. Clothes washing is done in laundries at the cleaners. And that's why there are no servants in Cuba. . ." Margaret works at the Book Institute. She went out to cut sugar cane with the whole staff of the Institute. She told me: "It is incredible how people in Cuba are reading now. After spending the whole day cutting cane all the employees read in their bunks (not just we writers), and they fight to get books."

On going back to my hotel I passed a park where there was a day nursery where mothers leave their children while they are at work. I went in. A young brunette was watching the children at play, black and white, and all bare to the waist (because it was very hot). She said to me: "Here the child does what he wants and not what we want him to do." There was a room filled with cribs where they took naps, and in each crib a blanket in case it was chilly. In one section were the Little Pals (children up to eighteen months). In another part the New People (from eighteen months to six years). Marvelous toys. Some children playing, others singing, others rolling over in the sand. A very black black child sprinkling sand with a shovel on the shoulders of a very white white girl. (The white girl, said the young woman, was the daughter of a German writer.) I remembered what Fidel had said: that racial discrimination could not be totally eradicated, even in a revolution, unless it was eradicated from childhood, in school and in day nurseries. And as I continued on my way toward my hotel, I was thinking: In Cuba the new name of charity is Revolution.

»»»

"... if we settle for the easy way and use material interests as the driving lever for socialist construction, if merchandise is kept as the economic cell, if the presence of money continues to be omnipotent within the new society, then egotism and individualism will continue to predominate in the conscience of men and we shall not succeed in creating a new man." Editorial from *Granma,* the official organ of the Communist party

At the du Pont House

On Sunday a drive to Varadero to the small palace of Mr. du
Pont. En route we passed the airfield (full of Russian MIGs).
Those who are leaving Cuba take off from there. On the
Miami radio they are called "freedom passengers," and here
they are called "stateless persons." The du Pont Beach is one
of the most beautiful in Cuba. Mr. du Pont had a tip of the
island of Cuba all to himself (where now the people come to
spend the summer), with a private airport, a golf course, docks,
yachts, seventy-five servants. One servant, who did nothing but
serve him daiquiris, is now in charge of the palace and shows
the millionaire's rooms to visitors. At first glance the house
seems to be a medieval castle, but what it really is is a luxurious piece of nonsense. From the highest terrace, as far as the
eye can see, we look out at the land that had belonged to Mr.
du Pont. The Revolution didn't have to take it away from
him; he gave it up voluntarily from the United States soon
after the victory. Before the Revolution he had lived here most
of the time and managed all his affairs from this house. After
the triumph of the Revolution he never came back to Cuba.
The ex-daiquiri-server told us that Mr. du Pont was not a bad
man. That is, that he was not personally bad, although of
course he was bad since he was a capitalist, and that they all
now realize that all capitalists are bad. He means—he explained—that in those days the servants considered him good
because he was generous with them, he had given each of them
a house of his own, he paid them salaries that were high in
comparison with the rest of the salaries in that system of exploitation that existed in Cuba, and so on. Now he sees things
in a different way from the way he saw them then, he told us.
Now he is a communist. At first he was afraid of that word
"communism," as everyone was in Cuba, but Fidel began to
talk about communism, and he said to himself: If Fidel is a
communist, communism is a good thing. A short time before,
Fidel was on that same terrace where we were talking. He has
come four or five times, and when he comes he likes to inspect
the estate.

Lunch was endless, as it would have been with the du Ponts,

with French wines, sea-food cocktail, lobster, in the ostenta-
tious dining room, paneled in precious woods, with a sea view,
at the immense mahogany table, with the du Ponts' own china,
and while a black sang to us accompanied by the organ that
had cost du Pont a million dollars and which was now, they
said, a little out of order. For a moment I forgot that I was in
a socialist country, and I saw in imagination our host Mr.
du Pont coming in and seating himself at the head of the table.

On the beach some children between ten and twelve,
many of them black, were surrounding the writer Rodolfo
Walsh, and when I arrived they were asking him what country
he was from, and when he said he was from Argentina they
said, "Che's country!" They asked me where I was from and
then said: "Sandino's country!" I asked the youngest one, a
little black of about nine, who Sandino was, and he said
promptly: "A Nicaraguan guerrilla fighter who fought against
Imperialism." They said they were from a school in Matanzas,
and that they were the best students in their class, and that,
as a reward, they had been brought to this Varadero beach.
They talked about the Tupamaros, about Vietnam, about
Laos, and suddenly they ran off to plunge into the sea.

One can imagine the humiliation it must have been for
children like these and for all poor Cubans, which is to say
for almost all Cubans, to see along the beaches, for thousands
of miles of coastland, signs saying: "Private Beach," "Restricted Spa," "No Admittance." With temperatures over a
hundred, the poor people couldn't go near the water. Many
Cuban peasants knew nothing of the sea, even though Cuba is
a long and narrow island surrounded by dreamlike beaches on
all sides. The Revolution opened up to the people some fifty
exclusive beaches, they tell me, and it has created many more.
Now any worker or farmer can go into the Havana Biltmore
Yacht and Country Club (which is no longer called that but
the Cuban Workers' Club) which used to be so exclusive that
Batista, to become a member, had to pay $800,000 in "public
works" for the benefit of the Club.

»»»

IN THOSE SUMMERS THINGS KEPT HAPPENING

—César López

In those summers things kept happening
(we know very well that in the city there are no seasons,
there's only heat and sometimes more heat;
but we'll insist on saying: in those summers . . .)
As an example to show how things were,
one among many only one.
(The number of deaths in the city, in that time of accidents,
made people in the areas affected move away from the sea.)
There's no need to remember Flebas, it's better to think of
Eugenia Solorzano, that shapely black woman, in
          a red bathing suit,
who drowned at the public beach and whose body
floated afterward among sargasso weeds and blobs of oil.
          A fish,
or many of them, nibbled at her breasts, her eyes,
while the slim young men watched astonished
from the racing yachts, their rather blond hair sea-blown,
protected beneath the insignia of the fashionable club.
          Water
was never a friend of the poor, of the blacks. It's a
          funny thing,
only at public beaches were there drownings.
One never heard of one anywhere else.

The Young Poets

Midnight. I was just going to sleep. The telephone rang: "We are two young poets who are downstairs and we'd like to talk with you, perhaps this isn't a proper hour, but we couldn't come earlier." I went down. I was interested in what they would tell me. I had been there three days, and I hadn't seen any young poets. I wanted to get to know the generation shaped wholly under socialism.

They were of this generation. I could see at once that they were revolutionaries. Their eyes shone with enthusiasm when they spoke of the Revolution. They were happy that I had come to Cuba. One of them was teaching at the University, in spite of his youth. The other was in the militia and was wearing his uniform. They showed me some poems and a short story. The story was by the militiaman and had some social criticism. I liked it, and he said: "But of course, you know, it can't be published in Cuba because of the repression." "Is there repression in Cuba?" I asked, lowering my voice. And the young poet answered, smiling sadly, and somewhat incredulous: "You didn't know?" "I thought that you were revolutionaries. . ." "We *are* revolutionaries, and there *is* repression. And the repression is not revolutionary. Repression, wherever it occurs, is counterrevolutionary. Although those who indulge in it call themselves revolutionaries, repression is always Batistan."

"Can't you speak out? Do they arrest you?" I ask, lowering my voice again, because we three are sitting on a sofa in the middle of the lobby and a lot of people are walking around us, hotel employees and guests. "They don't arrest you for talking. If they did, we wouldn't be talking here so calmly. You can shout against Fidel in a public park and they won't arrest you. The most that could happen is that a soldier might come to argue with you or to persuade you to shut up and stop disturbing the peace."

I had noticed that they didn't look around them as they spoke, to see if anyone was listening, nor did they lower their voices, as I did. I couldn't get over it: they were revolutionaries, and they were saying that there was repression, just as capitalist propaganda kept saying. They were saying that there was repression, and they weren't afraid. The teacher said: "We have come not so much to read you poems as to talk about Cuba. We want you to know all this and not to let yourself be influenced by propaganda. We want you to know all the bad things about this Revolution, because you must have been seeing the good things from the moment you arrived. And we don't want the same thing to happen to you that has happened to others who have come to Cuba; they became disappointed. We have had many who have come to give courses at the University, and who afterward have gone away unexpectedly, certainly disappointed. I think that's what happened to Cortázar, who has not come back to Cuba. And we think a lot of you, and we don't want you to be disappointed. We want you to understand this Revolution just as it is, with all its marvelous things and all its bad things. And we also want you to tell about these bad things. Tell about them, please; for love of Cuba and of this Revolution. We love this Revolution very much, and we would like it to be perfect."

The other one said: "They've probably told you that there is no prostitution in Cuba, haven't they?" "There are whores?" "There are whores. Not as an institution; that was suppressed. But you still find women who will sell themselves to sailors, if not for money, for nylon stockings. Of course there aren't many, but there are some, and they don't talk about it." "You probably haven't heard about the UMAP?" "What's that?" "Concentration camps." "They don't exist now," the militiaman said. "Fidel suppressed them. But nobody mentions them. How do I know about them? I was in one. Not as a prisoner but as a guard. Yes, a jailer. I saw the bad business, but we were just on guard. They told Fidel about what was going on. One night he broke into the camp and lay down in one of the hammocks to see what kind of treatment a prisoner gets. The prisoners slept in hammocks. They were waked with saber whacks if they didn't get up. The guards would cut their hammock cords. When one guard raised his saber he found himself staring at Fidel; he almost dropped dead. In another camp he saw a guard making a prisoner walk barefoot on pieces of glass. He ordered the guard to suffer the same punishment he was giving to the other man. In another place he turned up at breakfast time. And so he went around observing things. Afterward he ordered punishments. They say that there was even an execution."

"That's another of Fidel's exploits. Fidel is the man of the unexpected visit. He is a legendary figure who has captured people's imagination. But there's also the censorship of books. You know the Padilla case. He was a year without getting any work because his poems displeased some official. And there, too, Fidel had to intervene. A short while ago they gave the David Prize to a young poet, and afterward they found out that he was a homosexual. The book was already printed, and they reduced the whole edition to pulp. I know one of the censors who is merciless to homosexuals, and he's a homosexual himself. Long hair is forbidden. From time to time they round up the hippies, because they congregate in front of these hotels and the Coppelia, and they take them off to jail. A while ago in one of those roundups they carried off a director of Communist Youth who had long hair and they cropped it. The day after he got out of jail he turned up furious at Communist Youth headquarters to turn in his card. The persecution of homosexuals we feel is hateful and unnerving. Not that we're homosexuals. But there's always the fear that they'll think you are, because of the long hair or because you're an artist or a poet. It's dangerous for me to go out on the street because of my long hair. We're also criticized for liking jazz or certain styles of clothing. It's all repression. We like those things because we are young, not because we're against the Revolution. I am not a revolutionary: I am the Revolution. I and the others of my generation did not make the Revolution. We are its product, we were made by it. The others, there was a time when they weren't revolutionaries, and then they became revolutionaries; among them a trace of the Batista regime remains. Ever since we've been able to think we have been revolutionaries. We have never known anything but the Revolution. If you ask me what it's like to be a counterrevolutionary, I couldn't tell you, because I've never seen a counterrevolutionary. So I couldn't be a counter-revolutionary even if I wanted to. I have never known the middle class. They say that the new man is being created in Cuba, and I believe it, but the old men, how can they create the new man? Stalinism is always lying in wait to destroy the Revolution. Stalinism or the Batista spirit, which is the same thing. In the Writers' Union they wouldn't publish a poem of mine because in it I say that I go along the street and insult, deny, curse, and blaspheme. They didn't like the blaspheming. Because they imagined that I was blaspheming against the system; but no, it had a different meaning. There are poems that they won't publish because they consider that in them we are making some criticism of the Revolution. But I am sure that Fidel would publish those poems."

They tell me that there are writers who take advantage of the Revolution to obtain favors: "There's Guillén, who's been a communist all his life, and now he has a car with a chauffeur at his door and he's always running off to Paris. He doesn't like to live in Cuba. Or Retamar, who also is always traveling, he has a fine house and a splendid table." I ask them what they think about the Church in Cuba. They have no opinion about the Church because they don't know it. They are both atheists. "But we can say that it's not interested in social questions. And before, it was closely identified with capitalism, with the bourgeoisie, and with Batista. Now education is atheistic, and the new generation has no interest in the Church. We are a result of that training. In Cuba the Church committed suicide."

I ask if the militant Catholics in the University are revolutionaries. "There are no militant Catholics in the University. They don't admit them. I don't agree with that. One of the great martyrs of the Revolution was José Antonio, the student leader of the assault on Batista's palace; he was a militant Catholic, a director of Catholic Action. And this Revolution wouldn't now allow José Antonio to enter the University. What right would they have to prevent José Antonio from being a student, from being a student leader, from being José Antonio? What right would they have to prevent him from dying for the Revolution? If they don't allow a Catholic student to be a revolutionary, what is he going to be? A counterrevolutionary? To say what I'm saying will get me into serious trouble. But I think that this is what moved Fidel to rise up in the Sierra Maestra."

"And what do you think about the lack of freedom of the press?" "Freedom of the press is denied through fear and inability to give the news truly and completely without harm to the people and the Revolution. I believe that the Cuban people are now sufficiently politicized and mature to hear the news complete without being harmed. There is also a latent danger in the Revolution, and that is deification. The deification of Fidel. Not through any fault of his, but of the people. Up to now he has been able to manage it very well, with great skill, and he has kept it under control. He has even pointed out the danger. He has said that the starters of a Revolution have great prestige and great authority among the people, and that this can do great good, but it can also do great evil. And that we must hope that in the future no leader will have so much authority, because it is dangerous for him to have so much authority. He has also said that it's not necessary to see a statue on every corner nor the name of the leader in every town: that does not create a moral sense in the people; that creates an artificial moral sense by means of slogans and reflex actions. And he has denounced other socialist countries where the contact of the people with their leaders is contact with the statues of the leaders of the people. Fidel also has made a Law of the Revolution, which was one of the first laws of the Revolution, making it illegal to give the name of any living leader to any street, city, town, village, factory, or farm, and forbidding even official photographs in administrative offices, which has not been forbidden in any other country. Because, as he has said, a revolutionary can do many good things in his life and commit great atrocities at the end of his life. It seems to me that Fidel is not a leader but a teacher. Fidel is above all an educator. His speeches are long because they are lessons that he gives to the Cuban people. More than teaching with words, he teaches by example. At the time of the Peruvian earthquake, he went at once to a clinic and gave blood. He didn't say anything, he just gave the example. And the people immediately followed the example. There were more than a hundred thousand blood donations in about a week. This people has been formed by Fidel. But Fidel is also very Cuban. When you get to know what it's like to be a Cuban, you'll understand what I'm saying." And taking leave at two-thirty in the morning: "Forgive us if we've robbed you of your sleep. We wanted you to hear what criticisms this generation has about the Revolution."

»»»

REVOLUTION

—Miguel Barnet

Between you and me
there is a heap of contradictions
that pile up
to make of me the frightened one
with sweat on his brow
who builds you.

Young Ordoqui

Joaquín Ordoqui, at age seventeen, is one of the youngest poets in Cuba. He came to see me and told me that his father was a very important figure in the Revolution, although for some years his house has been his prison; he is in what Fidel has called "spiritual ostracism." He had been Organizing Secretary of the Communist party in the Batista era, and after the Revolution he was Vice-Minister of the Air Force. They accused him—his son said—of disloyalty, of having supplied certain information to the CIA (rather insignificant information, according to the accusers themselves) while he was in exile in Mexico during the Batista era. The father has always denied the charges, which moreover were not serious; if they had been serious he would have been shot. Fidel once publicly characterized the crime as "revolutionary weakness," nothing more. The boy told me that his father was in a hospital with terminal cancer. And he has always remained, in spite of everything, a supporter of the Revolution. In spite of having been, in a certain sense, a victim of the Revolution. He too is a revolutionary.

I asked the young man if Fidel knew him, and he said that he did, that Fidel had seen him several times after his father's downfall and that he had greeted him cordially. And also that his studies were not handicapped in any way. Afterward he said: "The Revolution demands a lot. And it costs a lot. It demands a great deal of sacrifice, but you have to give it." He was six years old when the Revolution triumphed. Before that he had spent his childhood with his parents in exile, in Mexico and Prague. He still remembers when there were commercial ads in Cuba. And he said: "For us, now, that is an anachronism, like something medieval, incomprehensible, although we know that it still goes on in capitalist cities. I still remember a very stupid song that they sang on the radio. I was very young but I still remember it: 'Proceso, Proceso, el mejor queso' ['Process, Process, the best cheese']. It was unbelievable that they forced people in that way to buy things. And also that a man could say to you that he didn't have a cent in his wallet or that he hadn't eaten in three days, we can't imagine that such a thing was possible. We know that things are like that in your countries because they have told us, but it seems to us unbelievable."

He told me that there was a lot of excitement about my arrival, and I asked him why. "For three reasons, or rather, four. First, because of your life, the testimony of your life as a religious and as a revolutionary. Second, because of your poetry. Third, because your coming had already been announced many times. They said in '63 that you were going to come, then they said it again in '65 and once again in '67. We had been waiting a long time for you." That was three reasons, not four. He went on talking: "At the University the students were interested in seeing what kind of clothes you would wear. Some thought you would come in civilian clothes, and others, with the religious habit. We see that you didn't come either way but dressed as a Nicaraguan farmer. There's also a lot of interest in Solentiname; that's one of the main reasons why I've come. . ."

In Cuba priests do not have a good image. The clergy before the Revolution were evil: bourgeois, retrogressive, Batistan. And yet Ordoqui had good Catholic friends. He was an atheist. His father and mother were communist atheists, and he hadn't even been baptised. He added: "But one thing I'm sure of: survival after death. I don't know why; but I'm absolutely certain about it." It was very hot, and we were walking in the garden of the hotel while we talked. Other strollers were "middle-class" ladies (in a classless society) and couples on their honeymoon, of no identifiable social class. The poet Ordoqui finally said: "A revolution is painful. It splits a country in two. It divides. All Cuba is divided. Even in Fidel's family there is that division, with his sister who fled from Cuba. There are many Cubans who love the Revolution and who have loved ones who are in prison or in exile or dead."

»»»

POEM

—*Luis Rogelio Nogueras*

They woke me that morning at six.
There was noise, shouting, I gradually

shut my eyes again until I was
sound asleep.

I dreamt that God was lowering
candy down to the deep-purple leaves of the trees
of the park,
which had a new pickup truck.

In the gulf,
the *Granma* advanced
slicing the fog.

Haydée Santamaría

She took part in Fidel's attack on the Moncada barracks, with her brother, Abel, and her fiancé, Boris. When she was in Batista's jail they brought her brother's eye to her cell. She told them: "If you tore out his eye and he wouldn't talk, there's even less reason for me to talk." Afterward they brought her fiancé's testicles and told her: "You no longer have a fiancé." Haydée said that after they killed her brother and her fiancé, she thought only about Fidel. Fidel, who must not die. Fidel had to stay alive to make the Revolution. If Fidel was alive, her brother, her fiancé, and all the others had not died, they would live in Fidel, who was going to make the Revolution.

"In Moncada there was so much suffering that a moment came when I was completely numbed. . . 'Abel is dead, Boris is dead, why don't I weep or feel anything? Why don't I suffer?' That's what I used to think. But I came to life when I saw Fidel. Melba and I were at the top in the bivouac when we heard an uproar, and she said: 'There's Fidel!' When I saw Fidel alive I reacted, and I began to cry, and I think I spent the whole night weeping. . . Moncada was terrible for everyone, because no one was prepared to have such horrible things happen." She also said: "Like when a woman is going to have a child: the pains make her scream, but those pains are not pains. That's the same sensation that I had in Moncada: a deep pain, but I felt as though something had been born within me, that I had stopped being a child and had become a woman. There is deep grief because of all that was left behind there."

Haydée Santamaría is the Director of the House of the Americas. She told us that recently she has also been working with her husband in a far corner of Camagüey Province. So far removed that beyond it there is no more land, only sea. She called this place "Macondo." But it is a socialist Macondo. It is a place so remote that it is astonishing. But it is a Macondo in which people are reading García Márquez, and in which there is a high school. Haydée wants García Márquez to come, and she has invited him so that he can see a Macondo, like the one he imagined, now transformed by the Revolution. She was brought up on a sugar plantation, in Las Villas, close to highways and everything. There was a little rural schoolhouse with six grades in the single room. In this Macondo there was no highway, and they have built one. Not even a jeep could get in. And now there are school centers, from pre-school up, and a room for each grade, and a high school, and three boarding schools.

Here there are no hotels. And no trees either. It is one of the few places in Cuba where there is no vegetation. "I always say: Here there is neither sea nor mountain. And to live without sea or mountain is a terrible thing. I say it's the only place in Cuba that doesn't even have palm trees. Often to console myself I used to say: I went to a little school with six grades all together, where there were benches and we all sat together. Many times we didn't even know what grade we were in because there was only the one teacher, and one day she taught all the subjects at the first-grade level and another day at the sixth-grade level. Here, this Macondo has a standard primary and secondary program, large school centers, and good boarding schools." Haydée told us that we must not idealize the Revolution: "Many will discover perhaps that it is not as fine as they thought. But this will help them, too, so that they can find out how hard it is to make a revolution. I urge them to see it all. Show them not only our Literacy Museum, show them all that we still have to do."

»»»

Notes from my notebook:

A woman member of the Party, who told her daughter that what she really regretted was not being able to go to Mass.

The poet José Yanes, one of the best young poets in Cuba: he learned to read during the literacy campaign. He was a worker in a sausage plant. He is now a member of the Writers' Union.

Laurette Sejourne tells me that at the University there is great excitement among the students because of my arrival.

What Arguedas said when he came to Cuba: that this

was where the Vallejo era had begun (the new man, and man as the brother of man).

Now a distinction is made between the people and the government of the U.S.A. (which didn't used to be made). Now you no longer see CUBA SÍ, YANQUIS NO.

You don't see any drunkards.

The houses of Havana, run down, paint peeling. Mud-covered trucks; and the broken down buses, with rotten floor boards. "Havana is an afflicted city," someone said. "No public works are in progress. All the progress is in the towns and in the country. They used to call Havana the brothel of the Caribbean, and it's a city that the Revolution is still punishing."

This Revolution, like Christ, has come to divide: "The father shall be divided against the son, and the son against the father; the mother against the daughter, and the daughter against the mother; the mother-in-law against her daughter-in-law, and the daughter-in-law against her mother-in-law" (Luke 12:53).

The Catholic poet Eliseo Diego: "Cuba was the first country in the world to help Peru during its catastrophe. It's really funny, here in Cuba there's a scarcity of everything, but when it's a question of giving help, we give away what we don't even have. There's a shortage of plasma in our hospitals but there were one hundred and four thousand blood donations for Peru in ten days. And there were twenty-two planes stuffed with supplies." Eliseo Diego speaks very softly and very seldom; he is very humble; he is deeply Catholic; and he is on the side of the Revolution. He smiles all the time.

The Fishing Port

They took us to see the fishing port of Havana, and at the entrance to one of the fish-processing plants a group of workers came out to receive us. One of them, quite young, came up and said he was waiting for me and that he wanted to talk with me. He pestered me with questions: What is Solentiname like? What kind of contemplative life do we lead? Am I still translating North American poetry? What's the news of Sergio Mondragón? What happened to *Corno?* Has it stopped publication? And is Henry Miller still writing? Ginsberg? Yes, he knew that they deported him from Cuba because he said that instead of confining homosexuals on farms they should use them as bellboys in hotels. He asked me what I thought of Borges and of *A Hundred Years of Solitude.* Was William Agudelo still at Solentiname? He was very fond of his poem about the hippy Christ with faded blue jeans and long hair and electric guitar, and also his poem to girls studying chemistry.

While we went up and down stairs and passed from one room to another he kept asking questions and answering my questions. He taught classes to the workers in this factory. He was twenty-three. The classes here went from literacy to the bachelor's degree. He was a poet, too. He was a volunteer in the militia until a psychiatrist gave him a medical discharge. Then he bummed around for two years. Yes, you don't have to work unless you want to, and he devoted two years to loafing. He thought that a certain loafing time can be good for a poet. During that time he visited libraries and read the new literary magazines. Later he felt that he ought to work for the community. His job was teacher on the Workers' Faculty of this plant, and he worked from eleven in the morning until two in the afternoon except Wednesdays, Saturdays, and Sundays. Other comrades who taught classes worked more hours, but all received the same wages. There were a thousand workers in this building. They were studying Spanish, but there were plans to teach them literature, too, in their fourth year. The Spanish classes consist of spelling, grammar, and the correction of Cuban weaknesses in Spanish, those peculiarities of

Cuban speech that are not an enrichment but an impediment
to the language and are an obstacle to communication within
the Spanish language. His father was a laborer, and his grandfather also.

At the entrance to a cold-storage plant I saw a sign: WHEN
A COMMUNIST IS BORN DIFFICULTIES DIE. The plants
were immense, each room the size of an enormous building,
with an arctic temperature inside. Frost and icicles covered
the walls and the ceilings. There were great heaps of sacks of
frozen fish and a penetrating smell of fish. We could go only
a few feet in because of the cold, and when we emerged the
heat seemed much more intense.

The young poet told me that he once wrote on the black-
board the poem about plums by William Carlos Williams that
Coronel Urtecho translated, and that the workers liked it very
much. (It is an extremely simple Objectivist poem in which
the poet tells his wife that he ate all the plums that she was
keeping in the refrigerator, and that they were very sweet and
very chilled.) He also told me: "I have written an epigram
that has been much discussed, because some people like it,
and others say that it is much influenced by you."

We went on to the wharfs and afterward to a shipyard
where boats are repaired. A technician gave us an interminable
explanation—without sparing us the slightest detail—of the
process of getting a boat out of the water, as if the whole
poetry jury of the House of the Americas had come to Cuba
just to learn about this. Step by step he described the complicated process until the boat reached the dry dock, like the
huge Soviet ship from whose hull they were about to remove
the barnacles before they repaint it. The heat was suffocating,
and Marta Lynch was almost fainting on a bench.

We were told that the fishing boats went as far as Africa
and Newfoundland to fish. At the wharfs about a hundred of
these little fishing boats were moored. We went closer to
inspect one that was being repaired, and we noticed that it
had a small library, with no books in it at the moment. All
fishing boats have libraries, we were told. Finally in a little
keg, they brought us orange soda. Some other teachers of the
workers came up, all very young. One of them, the math
teacher, twenty years old, said: "I can go back to the time
when people asked a blessing in Cuba. You asked a blessing,
when you went to bed, of your mamma or your grandfather."

Another one, as young or younger: "I can go back to the time when people prayed. They said some prayers at night, before they went to bed, for example. They said a prayer that was called, I think, Amen." (Laughter.) I understood that he meant the Hail Mary, but someone else corrected him, also laughing: "No, that prayer was called the Our Father. I remember it, too. They used to make you make the sign of the cross when you went to bed, didn't they?" "That's not done any more," said the math teacher.

At the entrance to a building that seems to be a workshop or warehouse, a sign: "Our goal: to increase production eight times."

Supper at the Retamars

Retamar invited me to his house at eight, and I thought he was inviting me for supper. I arrived a little before eight, and he opened the door chewing a mouthful. I could see he was surprised that I arrived so early. "Have you eaten?" he asked flustered. "No, but I'm not hungry." He made me sit down at the table even so. He was having supper with his two small daughters and his mother-in-law, who had cooked the meal. There was a fish croquette for each one, a potato, a little rice, a tiny dessert, and so I said again that I wasn't hungry, although I really was. They insisted that I eat something anyway: half a croquette, half a potato, the dessert. The girls asked me if I was the priest. Retamar said: "He's a poet and a priest."

Retamar's house was peeling paint. The paint was coming off everywhere. In a long corridor that led from the street door to the dining room there were great stacks of books piled on the floor for lack of bookcases. The living room sofa had two sprung springs. Later Margaret Randall arrived, and we drank parsimoniously a tiny quantity of rum. Retamar told me that the girls were very moved because they had met "the priest," and Margaret smiled and said: "In your case we have to make a psychological readjustment in the children. As I had created for my children a horrible picture of priesthood, they are surprised that we are friends, and now we must explain to them that not all priests are alike."

Other friends arrived. In reality it was a little celebration that Retamar arranged for me, although without food and without drink—except for that third of a bottle of rum that we savored in little sips. Retamar put on a record of Carlos Puebla: "Here remains the clear / the lovable transparence / of your beloved presence / Commander Che Guevara." It was a farewell to Che when he left Cuba. The capitalist press said that Fidel had killed him. The Cubans knew that he had gone off to make the Revolution somewhere else, although they didn't know where: "Your revolutionary love / leads you on to new endeavors."

In the Sierra, Che said that he would not live to be old,

that when the war ended he would go on fighting. "When we finish freeing Cuba, we shall have many other places to free," he told a farmer in the rebel army. And someone else said that Che had told him that when the Revolution ended he was going to make another revolution, and he thought Che was crazy. The last strophe of Puebla's song is a premonition of Che's death and that this farewell is forever: "We'll go on ahead / as we go on next to you / and with Fidel we say to you: / until forever, commander." Retamar told how Che, just before he left Cuba, borrowed a book by Neruda to copy a poem. After Che's disappearance they called Retamar from the Commerce Department to return the book, and he asked the secretary what poem Commander Guevara had copied; it was Neruda's sentimental poem, "Farewell."

I told Retamar an anecdote that I had heard about Che: when he was Secretary of Commerce some employees of the department complained of the rationing card and said that the food didn't last to the end of the week, and Che heard them and said that *his* food lasted. They said to him: "Commander, since you are a commander perhaps you have a different card from ours, and it's quite proper for this to be so." Che did not answer. The next day he summoned them and said: "You spoke to me yesterday about my ration card, and I kept quiet. But when I got home I found out that you were right, that my card was different. I have brought it here to tear it up in front of you, and I swear to you that I shall never again have a different one." And he tore up the special ration card.

Retamar already knew the anecdote. He told me that there were lots more like it in Cuba. When Che was still Secretary of Commerce he once went to work with a shovel for three weeks in a row, to remove rubbish from a place where there had been a fire. He was digging with his shovel under the blazing sun like any worker, and a neighborhood lady brought him a glass of milk. He asked: "Is there milk for everyone?" And the lady said: "We have no more, just this glass for you." And he said: "Then I won't take it." And he refused the milk.

And others said that in the Sierra Che was the last one to eat, because he was the leader. He would ask if everyone had been fed, and only afterward would he eat, a ration just like that of the others. He said that if any comrade was left without food, it ought to be the leader. And they also told how Commander Acevedo said that once there were three cans of condensed milk left, after the distribution to the troops, and a servile soldier had taken them to Che as "a little reserve supply for the Commander's headquarters." Che became furious and said to him: "You'll divide these among all the column, and even if we only get a teaspoon apiece, no matter; spread it as far as it will go. Here the leader eats what the troops eat, if there's enough to go around." And another says that Commander Luis Crespo told how if someone gave Che a piece of candy he would take a knife and cut it into three pieces to give it to three people. And they told how he was always sharing with the farmers. If they killed a cow, half of it was for the camp and half for the farmers, because he said that everyone ought to live the same. He didn't like special favors even for the sick. He said: "Everybody equal in everything." There were few canvas hammocks, and Fidel had said that they would be given as prizes to those who had slept beforehand in cloth hammocks that they made themselves. Che couldn't sleep in a cloth hammock because of his asthma, so he slept on the wet ground because he felt he had no right to ask for a canvas hammock. Finally Fidel found out about it and ordered that he get one. When he was Secretary of Commerce he used to go and work in the fields, and in 1964 they honored him for having done two hundred and forty hours of voluntary work in a semester.

When I said good-by, quite late at night, I had some trouble in returning to my hotel because Fernández Retamar, in spite of the high literary position that he occupies in Cuba, had no car. I told him, some days later, that some young poets had told me that he led a privileged life and that I had made it clear that this was not true. He said: "I live in the same old house in which I lived with my mother before the Revolution."

»»»

MADRIGAL

—*Roberto Fernández Retamar*

The petty bourgeoisie speaks,
the buying bourgeoisie,

the estate owners,
the proletariat,
the farmer,
other classes,
and you,
all atremble, all illusion.

»»»

A picture in colors in a double spread of *Bohemia:* A young mother nursing a child and the caption:
HE NEEDS IT: GIVE YOUR BREAST TO YOUR CHILD

»»»

The Salvadoran poet Roque Dalton said: "Fidel has often said that we must avoid falling into the collectivization and the uniformity of the socialist countries in the East. He says that this is not Cuban. Once he went past a bakery and saw that it just had a number as a name: Unit Number Such and Such, and he denounced this in a speech; he said that socialism should not do away with the Cuban tradition of picturesque names and reduce everything to numbers and acronyms. Apparently they pay no attention to him. There are a lot of very good things that Fidel has said in his speeches, and he ought to say them again because they pay no attention to him."

»»»

The political announcements at first seem to me unattractive, but I think that the commercial ads of capitalism are more unattractive and much more numerous. And afterward I think besides: The announcements here are always urging sacrifice, heroism, working for the community: THE HARVEST NEEDS YOU . . . CHANGE DEFEAT INTO VICTORY . . . In the capitalist world they always urge egotism, personal interest, individual enjoyment: ENJOY EAGLE BEER, IT'S BETTER THAN EVER.

»»»

Before the Revolution only sixty per cent of those of working age had regular full-time employment.

In the rural population, only eleven per cent drank milk, only four per cent ate meat, only two per cent ate eggs.

Forty-four per cent had never gone to school.

Eighty per cent of the inhabitants of Havana did not have enough to eat.

The People's Courts

I thought they no longer existed, if they ever had. We were eating in the dining room of the National Hotel, when I heard some of the South American judges and their wives say that that night they were going to go to a People's Court, while others said that they were going to the movies. In my mind I saw a mass of people in a park judging a counter-revolutionary and all shouting in chorus: Shoot him! Shoot him! I was surprised that they existed and that no one had talked about them, and even more, that now there was a completely natural discussion about whether to go to them or to some other spectacle. I asked if it was certain that there were People's Courts, and one of the Cubans told me that there were lots of them, in many parts of the city. He added: "Don't miss seeing them. They are one of the finest things about our Revolution." I said to myself: I've got to see that, for my book; and I shall put down, honestly, everything that happens there, even though it's something horrible.

We went in a bus, after supper. The Court was out to-ward Miramar, I think. A big building with a little garden in front, and a big outside porch that was used as a waiting room. Almost all the seats were occupied, a big attendance, some children, little blacks who listened with great attention and giggled. On a platform the judges: a black lady with gray-ing hair, a mulatto also with gray hair, a fat and very white lady. A young doctor, dressed in white, and an old mulatto militiaman were being questioned. The white lady was inter-rogating the doctor in a rather merciless way: "You're a doc-tor, aren't you?" "Yes, comrade." "And you are aware of the law that prohibits taking children on visits to hospitals?" "I was more or less aware of it." "And you heard the comrade militiaman tell you to stop your car because you couldn't take that girl to the hospital?" "He shouted at me very crudely, and I preferred not to argue with him and to keep going, because I had no intention of taking my daughter into the hospital. I was going to leave her outside in the car." "As we have made clear, from the guard post to the hospital it is scarcely three hundred yards. Couldn't you have left your daughter in the car at the guard post and gone to the hospital on foot?" "It didn't occur to me. I only thought that I wasn't intending to take her into the hospital but to leave her in the car, and that the comrade militiaman had no reason to stop me."

And the questions went on: Didn't he know that a child was more apt to catch a virus than an adult since its tender organism has fewer defenses? Was it not evident that he, as the father of the child (and as a doctor besides), was more obliged than anyone else to protect the health of his child? And didn't he believe that in exposing a child to the danger of contracting an illness he was endangering the health of many other children in school who might come in contact with his daughter? And didn't he believe that a doctor should be the first person to respect a health law? And didn't the comrade militiaman order him to halt, reminding him that it was forbidden to take children visiting in hospitals? Doesn't every citizen have the obligation to obey a militiaman who is performing his duty?

The black gray-haired lady afterward questioned the militiaman: Did he speak to the doctor in an angry voice? The militiaman said he didn't, that he spoke politely, that perhaps he did raise his voice when he saw that he wasn't being obeyed . . . Does he admit, then, that he got angry? He said yes, maybe he could have got angry. And doesn't he believe that it is wrong for a militiaman to speak to a civilian in a rude and ill-mannered way? He admitted that it was, and that on that count he might have acted badly, why should he deny it? (The doctor intervened to say that the man spoke to him very coarsely, or really that he was like a wild beast.) The white lady asked the militiaman if it was true that he had threatened. He said no: he had never told the doctor that he was going to shoot him, but that "he might have shot him." The lady said: "Well, I call that threatening. When a person says that with a weapon in his hand, that's threatening to kill. Or it could be understood that way."

The judges retired to deliberate. The Argentine Walsh said "That doctor is done for." There is a little sign: NO SMOKING. This surprises me because it's an open area, practically a porch in front of a little courtyard. But it's even more surprising that the sign should be obeyed in a Latin country. In order to smoke we had to go into the courtyard. The jury came back in a half hour, and everyone stood up. There was an intensely expectant silence, and the black lady began to read the sentence. She began by saying that the jury had made the necessary investigations beforehand, as it always has to, and had established the fact that the doctor came from a poor family, and that he pursued his studies with great sacrifices before the Revolution, working at night and supporting his widowed mother, and that from the beginning of the Revolution he had shown himself a revolutionary, being at Girón Beach and volunteering medical aid in Algeria, where he won high distinction, for which the jury congratulated him. Applause from the public. Afterward, it had established the fact that the militiaman was equally revolutionary, he had also fought at Girón Beach, he had been a Model Worker (porter in a plant), took part in many harvests, and that in spite of his sixty-five years of age and his infirmities, he continued to give voluntary services, taking his turn in military duty, etc., etc., and the jury congratulated him, too. More applause. The jury regretted deeply that two authentic revolutionaries had had a conflict of this kind, in which both were at fault (the one for not having obeyed as he should have, the other for having issued an order in an angry tone), even though the jury found in each one reasons that explained those faults and considered them extenuating circumstances: the doctor was driving fast and did not hear the order distinctly, the order was given angrily and even threateningly. On the other hand, the militiaman was tired after many hours on guard duty, he suffered from rheumatism and it had been raining all afternoon, and the fact that he was disobeyed exasperated him and he lost his self-control. The judges advised them, as good revolutionaries, to forget their differences and not to get involved again in painful incidents like this one, which had brought them here instead of letting them enjoy these hours in the relaxation of their respective homes. And finally they were urged to continue lending their valuable services to society and to the Revolution as they had done up to then. Enthusiastic applause.

The next case was that of a blonde girl, plump, coarse, accused of having occupied an empty room in a building without any right to it. "Did you know that you were committing an illegal act when you occupied that room without having any authorization?" "I knew that it was illegal." "And can

you tell us why you did it?" "Because I had no place to live."
"What? You had no place to live? And where did you used to
live?" "I lived in the street, I had no home." "You say that
you lived in the street. Give us more details. For example,
where did you sleep?" "Wherever night overtook me." "That's
not very helpful. We want to know explicitly in what places
you slept when night overtook you. The night before you
illegally occupied that room, where had you slept?" "I slept
in a car parked in the street. I already told you I slept wherever night overtook me."

More questions followed. Did she work? No, she was not
working then; her husband worked. She had a husband? Yes,
but they were separated, she thought he didn't love her any
more. They had recently come to Havana. They were from
Las Villas. She lived with her family, in the country, etc., etc.
The jury went out to deliberate. I thought: They won't con-
gratulate this one like the others; I don't want them to find
her guilty, but if I were a judge I would have to do so.

They returned. Everyone stood up. They read the sentence.
Not guilty. The jury did not find it a crime that she had
entered a room that was not hers, because it was discovered
that the room was not locked. "The accused did not break
any lock on entering that room and consequently did not violate any law, although obviously she is obliged to vacate it
now that the authorities have instructed her to do so." Although it absolved the accused, the jury nevertheless wished
to make the following recommendation: that she return to
her parents' house in Las Villas, in the country, which might
be a modest house with possibly a palm-tree roof, but after all
it was home, and there they lived happily, and there they had
an assurance of work, productive farm work, which is what
is most needed now in Cuba, instead of being needlessly here
in Havana, helping to aggravate the housing problem, which
was already acute. . . But this was only a simple recommendation and not an order, and meanwhile, whatever decision she
made, the jury would give her an urgent reference to the
Institute of Urban Reform and the Housing Center so that
this painful situation might be solved, etc., etc. Applause.
Marta Lynch beside me applauded enthusiastically and said:
"What learned people! I would not know how to judge that
case!"

The next case made the children laugh. It was the suit

of two women who continued to quarrel right in front of the Court. A married woman was accusing another woman, divorced, of taking her husband away from her. The divorced woman was a sensual brunette with straight hair hanging down over half her face. A lie—she said—the wife had found them kissing. The husband had tried to kiss her against her will, and she was fighting him off when the wife appeared. The divorced woman was in their house because she had come to borrow half a bottle of olive oil, and the husband had shown her into the kitchen pretending that the wife was there and had tried to attack her there, and she was struggling to break away from him. No, said the wife, she was letting herself be kissed, and she broke away from him only when the wife surprised them. The wife was very jealous of her husband, said the divorced woman, because he didn't love his wife and was unfaithful to her and made love to every woman including the divorced woman, but she had never let him in, as the whole neighborhood knew. And then there was the quarrel that they had had right in the building, at the door of a neighbor's apartment, where the wife had called the other a whore and they had pulled each other's hair and the neighbors had had to separate them. She was talking peacefully with this neighbor—said the divorced woman—when the other one called her a whore from the stairwell. I didn't call her a whore until we were pulling hair, said the wife. She had shouted at her from the stairs because these women were making fun of her. . . Several neighbors gave their testimony, but it was contradictory, and the quarrel at the apartment door got more and more embroiled, and tempers were getting hot again, and "whore" was being hurled back and forth in front of the judges—which made the kids and the grown-ups laugh out loud: "Whore was what she called me. . ." "I didn't call her whore, she rushed at me. . ." (And the judges had to ring the bell several times because the women were about to come to blows again.)

When they went out to deliberate it was late at night, and we still had to wait at least half an hour to hear the verdict, but none of us wanted to leave. We were much interested in learning how they were going to solve that very complicated case. "Now surely we will have a verdict of guilty," said Marta Lynch. "That woman is a bitch [referring to the divorced one]." I thought to myself: That's the way it ought to be. But, suppose she is innocent and the wife is a jealous woman, as she says? If I had been a judge in this case I wouldn't have been able to solve anything: I give up as a judge.

Everyone standing. The fat white lady read the sentence this time. Not guilty for the married woman, guilty for the divorced woman. The penalty imposed on the latter is, in the first place, a warning. The lady stopped reading from the paper, took off her glasses and then, in a gentle voice, gave her the warning. She said that the jury did not judge her with respect to her private life, which according to the testimony of neighbors had always been respectable and spotless, and that it did not wish to cast the slightest doubt upon her honor, but that it considered her guilty of *imprudence,* because when a woman goes to borrow something from a neighbor and discovers that she isn't home, but that only the husband is at home, she should refrain from going in, to avoid the gossip of the neighbors and the suspicions of the wife. . . And even more in the case of a divorced woman, she ought to be especially wary of this gossip, etc., etc. And the second request of the jury is to go back to school, for it had learned that she had completed only the third grade, so she was asked to report her monthly marks to the Court. Applause. And Marta Lynch said: "Incredible: they punish her by sending her to school."

They told us that the People's Courts tried minor crimes that, in the police code before the Revolution, were called police crimes and were settled if guilty by a fine or up to six months in jail. The major crimes were judged in the Criminal Courts, and the political crimes (or "crimes against the Revolution") were also judged in a separate court. The penalties that the People's Courts impose are usually, we were told, a public warning or, in certain cases, "removal" (work on a farm), and, only in very extreme cases, prison. The judges of the People's Courts are elected by the people in assemblies in each neighborhood, and after election they are given a thirty-day law course. A minimum sixth-grade education is required, and they must do their judging in the place where they live. Their work is unpaid, they do it in their free hours, and it is completely voluntary. Many other Courts like this one, we were told, are held in many parts of Havana every Thursday night. Some Courts are held right in the street. These People's Courts, besides resolving the minor conflicts

44

in the community, are very educational for the people, and the people attend them with pleasure, like a movie.

I told the poet Pablo Armando Fernández that I had gone to a People's Court, and he said: "They are marvelous. They are something Greek and Biblical: they seem to be the people of Athens gathered in the agora. And the judges have the wisdom of Solomon." Back in Nicaragua I read in *The Press* a news item from the A.P.: "President Allende has been harshly criticized by the opposition for having spoken of instituting People's Courts in Chile, and the press and the radio have said that this is the first step toward the beginning of a reign of terror like that of Red China or Castro's Cuba. It was especially recalled that in Cuba the function of these People's Courts was to send political enemies before the firing squad. . ."

»»»

"And what happens then? What happens if the Party organization sinks into that bureaucratic drowsiness? What happens is that over the administration and management of the State, and over the political management, there forms a special mantle with pretenses of perpetuity, a mantle that moves farther and farther from the masses, divorces itself from fruitful and productive work and from those who achieve it, and that changes into a privileged body incapable of advancing the people. . . There also exists the danger that in the heart of political organization and in the Party itself there is gradually built up, through the professional staffs, a special category of citizen differentiated from the rest of the population." Editorial from *Granma*, official organ of the Communist Party

»»»

I asked Cintio Vitier if it was true that Nicolás Guillén had a car with a chauffeur at his door, as those young poets told me. He answered: "What those young poets say is non-

45

sense. I don't know whether Guillén has a car with a chauffeur at his door, but if he doesn't he ought to. Guillén is President of the Writers' Union, and he is not like other people who just go from home to office and from office to home. He has to attend a lot of receptions and official and cultural ceremonies of all kinds, and there aren't any taxis now in Cuba, and to go from one place to another by bus takes two or three hours, and to have an automobile he has to have a chauffeur, because Guillén was always poor and never had a car and doesn't know how to drive, and he's old now and he's not going to start to learn how to drive at his age, and besides Guillén driving a car would be a danger in the streets of Havana. And as for his traveling about, he is our most famous writer, an international glory of Cuba, and the one who can best represent Cuba in foreign affairs, and he has to travel because they tell him to, whether he likes it or not, and I imagine that many of those trips, at his age, are not very attractive."

»»»

A very young poet (seventeen, although his beard made him look older) came to show me his poems, and wanted me to have a meeting with others of his generation. He said: "We want you to know this as it is and not to believe that all this is perfect. That it's paradise. No, this is hell. But we are creating an eternal paradise inside this hell. And I believe that socialism within a thousand years will be seen as something very savage and barbarous, just as we now see feudalism. I was expelled from the Writers' Union because I looked like a hippie, not because I *was* a hippie, because I'm not one, but because I *looked* like one. The Revolution is something that's always going on and that can always be improved. But the opportunists prefer their security to the risks of bettering the Revolution."

»»»

The first impression that the newcomer gets (because of the signs, announcements, posters, etc.) is that of a highly militarized country: AS IN VIETNAM. . . CHANGE DEFEAT INTO VICTORY. . . FATHERLAND OR DEATH

46

. . . WE SHALL CONQUER. Warlike words everywhere: columns, brigades, attack, campaign, assault, detachment, squadrons, battalions. But one notices very soon that the battle is against nature and underdevelopment, not against men. The "Mechanized Offensive Brigade" was the one that eradicated the weeds. The "First Frank País Western Front," the "Second Frank País Western Front," were youths working in the fields. The "Fatherland or Death Brigade" were workers working on literacy campaigns. "Fighters for Learning" were young men studying to be teachers. The "Piccolino Woman's Brigade of Tractor Drivers" is made up of women who were working at cultivating the green belt of Havana. The "Juvenile Column of the Centenary" is composed of more than sixty thousand young people who study and work in the fields.

In a newspaper story about the "Fighters for Learning" I saw a picture of a young Nicaraguan boy of about twelve: Augusto César Castillo Sandino, grandson of the guerrilla fighter Augusto César Sandino. The young man is a fighter for learning, the paper said. He was photographed at a desk turning the pages of a book. And none of this is done with a militaristic air, although some Europeans have so interpreted it. What they have in Cuba is something quite different from militarism and even opposed to it: it is an atmosphere of partisan (guerrilla) fighters.

»»»

SOME CUSTOMS OF THE SOLDIER ON DUTY

—Rogelio Fabio Hurtado

The soldier
has no girls on his lap.
At night he is buried up to the shoulders in a trench,
his face far from smooth yawns under his tilted helmet,
while you fornicate and fall asleep
the soldier does not sleep.

The soldier
doesn't sponge or wear medals,
he says many bad words, singing and working,
the sun burns him.

The soldier
is entering campaign mess halls
        —"up in the valley we had a camp and we ate
        in the open, sitting on a palm tree trunk"—
carrying a tray never fully filled
and when it was, the soup got scorched—"it was
the first time we made soup and we put the Sterno in it"—
And, even so, the soldier puts on weight.

The soldier
is not George the pilot in a silver plane,
nor a stout and somber telegraph clerk,
nor a cadet
nor a "Stick out your chest and pull in your belly" sergeant
the soldier almost never parades through the square.
He is sitting on his bunk putting on his boots
at one o'clock, three o'clock, five o'clock in the morning—
        somebody dead with sleep comes running
        with a match to tell you "get up, it's time"—
slipping his arms into the clammy cold shirt
he comes out of his barracks and a sudden chill engulfs
        him
he marches along with his rifle slung and his helmet in
        one hand
talking to himself to keep himself company.

The soldier is
a baker who no longer makes bread
a student who no longer studies
a young man who no longer visits his girl.

The soldier
when war is declared
jumps up in his underdrawers
grabs his rifle, his helmet, his gas mask,
goes flying across country
and two minutes later—or less—
that shirtless soldier, with anxious breath,
is then a well-oiled wild beast.

That soldier whose name is Robert and whose name
        is Lazarus.

A Conversation in My Room

"Don't you know that it is forbidden to read Althusser at the University? Because he is a Marxist. And I have just learned that the film Z was held up for nine months before they decided to show it. I ask myself: Why? When you go to the Writers' Union you'll see them with their long tongues sticking out. Ready to lick. . . We believe that the Revolution is not incompatible with our long hair, with tight pants, with jazz. What kind of a Revolution would depend on the way you dress or cut your hair? The police picked up everyone that had long hair in the parks, in the food lines, and they shaved their heads, and some fighters from the Sierra Maestra got shaved. The other day Fidel told the young men that if they wanted to wear long hair and a beard, they should earn the right as they did in the Sierra Maestra. That if they went into the cane fields they would have that right. The young men got all excited. Some of them who hadn't gone to cut cane before held meetings and said: Let's go, so we can have long hair. And they went. And they came back with their little beards and their long hair. And the teachers told them they could stay like that for two weeks, and then they had to shave or be expelled. Fidel had promised them, but he hadn't said for how long. . .

"They judge whether you're a revolutionary or not. But they themselves have not been made to pass through a fumigating bath that would have disinfected them of every counter-revolutionary virus. Who can tell whether they, who judge us new ones, do not have germs from the past? Another thing: the news. Is it right for the directors to receive a daily bulletin with all the wire stories, and for the people not to? And everybody in Cuba knows about the UMAP concentration camps—even though they were abolished—and yet they are never mentioned in the press. Do they want us to write science fiction instead of realism?

"And about Escambray: a young writer wrote a book about the horrors that went on there—I knew them because I was political commissioner of Escambray—and they wouldn't publish his book, and now he has been without work for two

49

years. Mythology and not history is what we're going to produce, then. They say that it is inopportune. So they want us to wait twenty years until everything has passed away and there'll be no need to criticize it any more? No, we must speak out now, when things can be corrected. If you criticize anything anywhere, it is taken very badly: you're a destructive critic. Suddenly Fidel comes along and sees these defects and criticizes them, and everyone admits that they were bad, and they praise Fidel who corrected them. But they give no credit to the fellow who said the same thing beforehand, that one was a destructive critic. Why is Fidel the only one who can criticize? Shouldn't every Cuban be another Fidel, get ahead of Fidel so that Fidel won't have to be always coming along to correct everything? . . It seems to me that there's a great deal of thought control.

"Fidel does think. The other directors, you hear them, and they're phonograph records, you think you're listening to records. Cuba has fought three times against the Soviet Union. When we're fighting no one can say any good about the Soviet Union, the Soviet Union is evil. The conflict ends, and no one can say any evil about the Soviet Union; it is noble. I was in Pinar del Río as a translator for some Belgian technicians at the time of the invasion of Czechoslovakia. All of Cuba was on the side of the Czechs, and everyone said so freely. Then came Fidel's speech defending the invasion. Immediately the invasion was a good thing. The Belgians made fun of us. They said to me: 'But don't you do any thinking by yourselves? Yesterday you said one thing and now just the opposite.' I had no answer. I realized that they were right. I asked for a transfer and left the camp after two days—because I didn't dare to face the Belgians. . .

"We live on slogans and overexcitement. This creates an atmosphere of insecurity in many, and in some a persecution mania. . . There are half a million people under twenty-seven, and half of them under twenty, all at forced labor. These figures are exact: they are from February of this year. Young men who fled from military service or school, or who have been brought there for other reasons, hippies, long-haired ones, malcontents, and they are in rehabilitation farms or camps. Many of them are furious.

"There is a division between us and the leaders. Pupi and I were artillerymen in the same unit. You don't know who

Pupi was? Pupi, the one they killed at Girón. He is a hero
and his picture is everywhere, his face is in huge portraits.
Well, Pupi was with me and we were artillerymen in the same
artillery unit. . . We roomed together. We had alternating
watches, four hours for him and four for me. And when they
killed him they could just as easily have killed me. And I
would now be Pupi the hero, my portrait would be everywhere, an example for youth—and he would be the long-
haired one, the rebel. Pupi was fourteen, like me. And Ascunce, Manuel Ascunce, the Literacy Drive hero, who was
assassinated by the counterrevolutionaries in Escambray because he was teaching people to read: he was fifteen and I was
almost fifteen, and I was teaching reading like him, and there
were a hundred thousand of us teaching reading. And now
he is the model revolutionary youth in meetings, in schoolbooks, everywhere. And if he were alive he'd be like us, long-
haired, with tight pants, crazy about jazz, not because he
would now be less of a revolutionary but because he'd be one
of us.

"They deny the evolution of man. Our leaders say that
we are rebels, but it was rebels who made the Revolution, not
submissive ones. And isn't our army still called the Rebel
Army? What was Moncada, what was the Sierra? Was it a
lesson in submission that they gave us? Who is Fidel Castro?
He was a humble citizen who, at the time of Batista's coup,
brought an accusation against him for violating the Constitution. They paid no attention to him, of course, and he as-
saulted the Moncada Barracks. And when they brought him
to trial he said in his speech: 'Your Honors, I am that humble
citizen who, when Batista made his coup, brought an accusation against him.' And then he said: 'You may condemn me,
but history will absolve me.' When they landed in the *Granma*
—what they really did was run aground—and somebody explained to Fidel that it was a bog, what Fidel said was: 'Fuck,
go ahead!' And what Camilo said—Che says that he didn't
know Camilo well; Che was wounded at the time of the first
defeat, and someone said in a low voice: 'We're lost, we've
got to surrender,' and Che heard this—he didn't know it was
Camilo—'Nobody surrenders here, fuck it!' What can you
expect, we were brought up in this. . . The poem that I showed
you is dedicated to Pupi and to Eduardo. Eduardo is Eduardo
García Delgado, who died in the bombardment of Liberty

City, and before he died he wrote with his blood on the wing
of a plane, in big letters, the word *Fidel*. The Party leaders
think we are less revolutionary because we are different from
them, but it's not that we're less revolutionary, it's that we're
of another generation. I can be arrested for what I'm saying,
but I am on the side of the Revolution. When I leave here
I can also be arrested because of my long hair, but I swear
to you: I'd give my life for this Revolution."

»»»

MY GENERATION

—A Song of Protest by Noel Nicola

I: BIRTH

When the bearded giants came
we were beginning to stop being children
We were then the youngest
of the hundred thousand
who sowed our fields with letters,
of the many who at Girón, dying,
defied the airplanes,
of those whose tracks
the rains erased five times from Turquino
We were beginning to stop being children
when the bearded giants came.

II: FIRST GROWTH

We got used to saying good-by
and to looking at each other with eyes that said "No"
We learned a hundred things and that song
of that great October of '62
(You remember well,
so do I)
We tried to dream an exotic dream
sitting with our backs to reality
Afterward we got married: you, I, and truth
searching always for how we could do more

(You remember well,
so do I)
We were students then
but that was not enough
We went with the artillery
to come back sure of ourselves
with tougher hides
and another vision of life.

At the Former Country Club

The former Country Club of Havana is now the National Art School. I spent the afternoon there and had supper with the boys. I had arrived unannounced and did not see the Director or the teachers. To the luxurious club building they have added other great buildings: Plastic Arts, Dramatic Art, Music, Ballet, Dance. I visited them all. In Plastic Arts, the ceramic classes were canceled. They had very good ovens and the clay was moist, ready to be shaped, and there were many students anxious to learn, but they told me that they had not found a single person in Cuba who could teach them.

Some young men showed me the luxurious dining room, which is just the way it was when it was the Country Club. The tables with crystal and flowers and a place setting for each plate. The students take turns here eating elegant meals served by uniformed waiters, to learn how to eat properly; for they will have to go abroad on artistic trips or for their exhibits. The turns last a week, and each male student must bring his girl so as to learn to be attentive to a lady. The young men introduced me to the person who was teaching them how to eat, and he told me that before the Revolution he had been a hotel manager and owner of a restaurant. He also worked for a time in this Country Club. He is very happy here, more than with the bourgeoisie, he told me—and his broad smile showed that he was not lying. One had to teach them to eat at banquets, with wine and everything, these future artists who came largely from the provinces, from the country, from the mountains. The study of music and ballet is begun very early but even the little boys come to this dining room with their girls. The four styles of eating are taught here. "What are they?" I asked. "The individual plate service, the English, semi-Russian, and Russian; Russian is for very formal meals."

The boys told me about their lodgings. They lived in houses that used to belong to the rich, in an elegant neighborhood built in the vicinity of the Country Club. The dining rooms and living rooms are kept up just as they used to be, they told me, and they are used for meetings. The bedrooms are their dormitories, and they sleep on cots, several to a room. They eat at school. What's their life like, I asked. "We live in harmony. We love one another." I asked them what social class they came from. "We're all proletarians," one of them said. And several repeated smiling: "Proletarians."

The artists were simple, modest. I saw in them no poses or pretensions, although some of them had already exhibited abroad. I saw that they did not feel themselves members of a special caste but simply common people. Their concern, one of them said, was that poets and artists should be part of the people, should not live in isolation, and should be happy to write an ode to a shoemaker. One of the most mature, a painter, said to me: "Here there are no problems with the young people, no thefts or quarrels or sexual things, except occasionally." (Several of them, men and women, agreed.)

I ate with them in the big dining room—not where they learn to dine in Russian style—standing in line like them with a tin tray. The employee who put food on our trays said: "These are Russian sardines." They took the smoked sardines out of little metal kegs. Supper was rice, Russian sardines, chocolate dessert, and bread. Delicious. It was not excessive but not scanty either. A dance student put aside part of his meal for the cat in his lodgings. He explained that it was hard to keep a cat in lodgings because there was no food there. Besides which it was forbidden. He will take the cat home.

The Director of the school, they told me, is a man whose interest is not in art but in sports. He says that sports bring medals to Cuba but art does not. He is the director because he was one of those who landed in the *Granma*, but there is no explanation of why he is the Director of the National School of Arts and not of a sports school. A teacher wrote to President Dorticós asking him to remove the Director. The President passed the letter on to the Secretary of Education, surely without realizing that the Secretary was a close friend of the Director (and also another one who valued sports above education), and as a result the teacher was fired and left Cuba. They snickered that the Director had a jeep and a car. Some-one pointed out that the car belonged to him and the jeep to the school. I said that I saw nothing evil in the fact that the Director of the National Art School had a car. What was evil was that he didn't like art.

We chatted after supper, in the warm dusk, under some

tall bushy trees in front of the building that had belonged to the former Country Club, while the lights of Havana came on, and a girl said: "It's hard to believe: here where we are they used to have their big parties; who would have predicted it? I've seen old photographs of this club, that they have in the secretary's office, and there are the young gentlemen in their tuxedos and the society girls in their long dresses at these same little iron tables where we are chatting now." Another girl gave me some poems that she took out of her handbag. (I read them later in the hotel; one of the poems was about God, and it was an atheistic poem.)

A young painter, who was also a poet: "My father was a stevedore on the wharfs of Santiago. My mother worked in a textile mill. I'm speaking of capitalist times. The money that came in allowed us to live with few worries. But my father was always sympathetic to popular movements. He had communist ideas—he still has them today—and he took part in underground meetings. Which ones, I can't say. He doesn't talk much about that."

What's your life like here? He told me as we walked along an avenue past what used to be golf links: "Our lodgings, these mansions, are spacious. Our life there is mostly an evening one because we leave at six in the morning for a ceremony at which I read the announcements and we salute the flag. We have breakfast and come to art classes. In the afternoon we have our academic classes: philosophy, history of philosophy, literature, French, art history. We have these assignments now only because of a lack of teachers. We can leave on week ends, unless they hold up our passes because of some breach of regulations. On Tuesdays we have study groups, where we discuss texts: speeches by Fidel, writings of Che, Martí, Lenin. We had planned to study Hausser but our level is very uneven. So we couldn't. The 'politician' of the lodging is the one who directs these studies. The materials are chosen by the JC!"

The Director went by in his automobile, on his way home. The young painter continued: "I know that formerly this was a club where the old bourgeoisie had its big orgies. But I don't know a great deal. Some of the cooks tell things that amaze us, like this one: that there were women, prostitutes, who to spend the night with one of those magnates charged ten cents. They walked around the swimming pool half-naked. Sometimes walking around here and looking at the mansions of the rich, which are now our lodgings, I try to imagine those things. But I can't. That decadence and moral degradation are in oblivion. It's like Pompeii. Eleven years of Revolution, that's a long time for us."

» » »

Notes:

A young artist: they asked him, when he did his military service, if he belonged to any "religious sect." He refused to answer, saying that the question was an affront against his freedom of conscience. (It annoyed him that all religions, including the Roman Catholic, were called "sects.") After an indictment and consultations with superior authorities, they agreed that he need not answer the question. When the case ended he freely revealed his religious convictions: "I am an atheist."

Cintio told me that his nephew, at a school assembly, was criticized by a companion for having "a reactionary smile."

(A young Catholic): "Here one can embrace all religions—and they can do this elsewhere—and besides the religions can embrace Marxism; and that would be an example for America."

The books and magazines that come for Cuba are frequently destroyed in Mexico.

One cannot eat whatever he chooses in the streets. Or buy cigarettes, etc.

A young Protestant (Evangelical): his church had less conflict with the Revolution than the Catholic Church. The reason: it was composed of lower-class people rather than of the middle-class, like the Catholic Church. It was a poor church. They had no privileges to lose. Nor had they been identified with the Batista regime. Batista's wife had offered them donations, which they had rejected.

Dr. Julio Domínguez of the Orthodox Greek Church of Cuba invited me to his priestly ordination, which would be in a few days. "Are there many Orthodox in Cuba?" "Formerly there were about five hundred; now there are seven hundred." "Their attitude before the Revolution?" "Their Christian testimony was as bad as that of the Catholics. They left Cuba."

Supper at the National

I am having supper at the National Hotel with two drivers. Luis is a bus driver, and Manuel drives a car. They both belong to the Drivers' Union. The dessert was, according to the menu, chocolate ice cream, Russian pudding, or French pastry. The waiter came up to us and said: "Comrades, if you will allow me to advise you, French pastry. I have just had some and it is very tasty. The best we have today."

"The best pastry in Cuba," said Luis, "is that of the Grand Hotel in Camagüey." The waiter said he could not have any opinion about the French pastry of the Grand Hotel in Camagüey because he had not been there. But at any rate that of the National was very tasty. "It's the pastry that we had at the time of the Yankees." I asked the waiter if he had been working in the hotel since the time of the Yankees. "Yes, comrade, I have been working in this hotel since 1940. What was my job like then? Well, I'll tell you, things were tough. If you got sick for a month, they didn't pay you anything. Now if I'm sick for a month, they pay me for the whole month." A waitress came up, the one who filled the water glasses, and said to the waiter: "And if you'd been ill for a month and came back to your job, you found that you didn't have a job, they had replaced you with somebody else. Because there were a lot of people looking for work, there were about three hundred guys trying to get your job, and so if you got sick they put someone else in your place."

"And also," said the waiter, "you had to give part of your wages to other people. To the union leader, remember? Or to the guy who got you the job, or to the boss himself. Other times you had to give part of your tips. Yes, because there was tipping then, and you had to live on the tips because the wages were very low, and this too was unfair, because a rich diner would give you maybe a two dollar tip, and then you gave him better service than the others got who didn't have enough money to give two-dollar tips."

The girl, holding her pitcher of ice water, said: "The Revolution raised our wages so that we had no need of tips, and tips were abolished, and now there are no tips in Cuba.

Tipping was evil, don't you agree? because it was like buying a worker." "The work was hard," the waiter went on, "and it was humiliating, because the people were very vain. For example, they wouldn't let blacks into this hotel, no black man could sit at any of these tables, they'd stop him right at the door and wouldn't let him in. And not just as a guest, they wouldn't even let a black work here. Well, maybe a mulatto might get a job, but he had to be a very light-colored mulatto. You remember? Josephine Baker, that famous singer known all over the world, was thrown out of this place the day after she registered because she was black."

Luis spoke: "And a guy who was a driver like us, he couldn't sit at this table the way Manuel and I are sitting here. Here we are with Ernesto Cardenal, who is an internationally famous poet, and we are eating at the same table with him, and I'm a bus driver and Manuel is a car driver. But at that time, and with that system, they wouldn't even have let us through the door, even though we said we were friends of yours and wanted to talk with you. No, they wouldn't have let us in this hotel because we were drivers."

I told them that they would not have been able to say that they wanted to see me, because a poet like me would not have been able to stay at a hotel like this in those times. After coffee the waiter offered us, as usual, on a tray: cigars, two kinds of cigarettes (strong and stronger), and matches. And he was right: the Yankees' French pastry was very tasty.

»»»

I HAVE

—*Nicolás Guillén*

When I look at myself and everything
I, Juan Without Anything only yesterday,
and now Juan with everything
and today with everything,
I look around, I look,
I see myself and everything
and I ask myself how it happened.

I have, let's see
I have the pleasure of walking around in my country,

master of all that's in it
peering closely at what before
I didn't have and couldn't have.

Sugar harvest   I can say,
country   I can say,
city   I can say,
army   say,
now mine forever and yours, ours,
and a broad splendor
of sunbeam, star, flower.

I have, let's see,
I have the pleasure of going
I, a farmer, a laborer, a simple person,
I have the pleasure of going
(as an example)
to a bank and talking with the manager,
not in English
not in Yessir,
but to say to him Comrade as we say in Spanish.

I have, let's see,
that I, just because I'm black,
can't be stopped by anyone
at the door of a cabaret or a bar.
I have. . .

Or else at the hotel desk
to shout at me that there are no rooms,
just a little room, not a big one,
a tiny little room where I can rest.

I have, let's see,
that there are no police
to grab me and lock me up in a barracks,
or to uproot me and throw me off my land
in the middle of the highway.

I have that since I have land I have sea,
not country club,
not high life,
not tennis and not yacht

but from beach to beach and wave to wave,
gigantic blue open democratic:
in short: the sea.

I have, let's see,
that I've learned to read, to count,
I have that I've learned to write
and to think
and to laugh.

I have that I now have
a place to work
and to earn
what I have to have to eat.

I have, let's see,
I have what I had to have.

»»»

My friend, the Nicaraguan painter Rosi López, has been living in Cuba for several years, and she has told me what the rehabilitation of the prostitutes was like. She worked on this rehabilitation. "Ernestito: there were twenty-five thousand brothels. The first thing we did was to set up centers where they could be taught to work. We took over a Matanzas cabaret as one of those rehabilitation centers. When they went in they were given medical examinations for forty days. Their clothes were exchanged for new clothes that were 'uniforms'; they were called the 'pupils.' We taught them a new kind of make-up. We taught them a different kind of manners. And there were psychiatrists working with us. The girls were given group therapy. One of my cases was Marta, who had been raped by her stepfather and afterward slept with her brother: she was a peasant girl and was in trauma; she was eighteen. We talked to them about the honor of being mothers; because the children were not loved by their mothers, and they were also traumatized. And then we got jobs for them, in beauty parlors, in factories, in hotels; and the children were put in day-care centers. We were instructed that those women must be treated with boundless affection; they must be pampered by the Revolution. They were not delinquents; they were more of the victims of capitalism. The Revolution had happened to them, too. These women were, in the great majority, peasants."

»»»

I said to Paz Espejo: "If Fidel had wanted to, he could have falsified the harvest figures." "Yes, he could have falsified the harvest figures, making the people believe that we had reached the ten million. And no one would have found out. It was so easy to do it. And he didn't do it! Here all figures are exact. That happens only here." Paz Espejo told us that she saw Fidel in the Sierra Maestra. "No, not when they were fighting," she said, laughing. "I haven't been in Cuba that long. In the Sierra Maestra of today, all filled with schools and street lights and very pretty little houses. I went to get acquainted. And Fidel was returning to the Sierra, and I saw him. How moved he was when he went back! And it was very amusing to see the informality with which the farmers treated him. Some old, toothless men hung upon him. 'Horse, you're always breaking promises.' Because that's what they call him: Horse. 'You said that the school was going to be here, and look they put it over there. Horse, you promise and you don't perform. You're always breaking promises, Horse.' He thought it was very funny."

She also said she once visited Fidel at his home, at one of his homes. "A house smaller than this one, and you see how small this one is." And in fact, it was tiny. "Simple, rustic furniture. But not elegant rustic, just simple rustic, and quite worn. His little bedroom quite attractive: a well-arranged bachelor's bedroom, that was clearly his, with some flowers in a vase. And I got the impression that it was not a house in which he lived permanently, above all because there were few books. He came here to my house, too. Not once, several times. Do you remember when he broke the tape recorder?" she asked a friend. "He sat down right here where you are and put his feet on this table." Paz Espejo brought us coffee in what she called her "revolutionary cups," which were little condensed-milk cans. She put them on the little round table where Fidel had put his feet.

»»»

Rice   Meat   Bread   Dessert (Menu in a work center).
    Price: fifty cents.

Ernesto

I had not understood the poem well, and he said to me: "I have given it the title "For the People's Best Tailor" because Camilo Cienfuegos was a tailor, and this poem is about Camilo." Afterward he said: "I have written it with a great deal of love. Camilo Cienfuegos had a lot to do with my life. I was a bootblack in the Havana International Airport when the Revolution triumphed, and there I met Camilo. I was then twelve years old. Now I am twenty-three, and I am a philosophy teacher at the University of Havana. As a bootblack I had a lot of customers; the Yankees especially liked me because I am rather blond and because my mother always sent me out well groomed and with clean clothes (even though I was as poor as the others), and also because I had learned a few English phrases, and when the Yankees got off the plane I would use these phrases, and that pleased them and so they preferred me—and once Camilo Cienfuegos passed through the airport, the Revolution had triumphed shortly before; with his guerrilla fighter uniform, his smile that, as I say in the poem, stroked his beard, his big hat, his curly hair down to his shoulders, the great hero—and he came up to me and put his hand on my shoulder and stood looking at me. And he asked me if I knew what the Revolution was going to do for us, and I was scared and shook my head, and he asked again if I knew what the Revolution was going to do for us, and I said: 'No, sir' (because in fact I had no idea), and then he said: 'Well, the Revolution happened so that you boys won't have to be shining shoes, and you are going to go to school and be useful to your country.' And he said angrily: 'And that shoeshine box, I want to see it burned very soon, because that's why we had this Revolution!' And in fact very soon after they sent us to school, and I stopped shining shoes."

Ernesto went on emotionally: "He was greatly loved by the people. The greatest man after the leader of this Revolution. There were three of them—because the other was also a mythological figure. The other one was Che. And they came down from the Sierra Maestra, the two of them, Camilo and Che, heading two columns, sent by Fidel to invade the rest of Cuba, and they swept along. Camilo, in thirty-one days, went through Camagüey Province without resting a single night, eating only eleven times, taking only three rests. Che had taken Santa Clara, and he was about to enter Havana, but Che joined Camilo to enter the city because Che had never been in Havana. They entered Havana together in triumph, and Camilo kissed his mother. Che said that he was the best guerrilla leader that this Revolution had produced, and also that he was the people's image. Camilo was the people, and he put a seal that was very much his own, the people's seal, on this Revolution. And of him Fidel has said that he didn't have book culture but he had the natural intelligence of the people. And that's why it was that after his death Fidel said: 'There will be many Camilos.' And there's that phrase of Fidel's that I'll never forget and that still moves me, when he stopped a moment in his speech on the Columbia campus to ask: 'Am I on the right track, Camilo?' "

All this was during our first talk. Ernesto talked with me many times, and he always spoke with much love about "his" Revolution. He said: "For Fidel the guerrilla warfare of the Sierra Maestra has not ended. He says he still wears a beard and a uniform because he is still waging war. He has told the people that he will cut off his beard and take off his uniform the day that all the promises of the Revolution are fulfilled." He also said: "I don't understand a writer who talks of going down to the people. If he says he's going down, it's because he considers himself above the people. And if he talks about identifying himself with the people it's because he doesn't consider himself part of the people. For us, those of my generation, the writer is simply one of the people. He has no need to go down to the people or to identify with the people, because he *is* the people."

I was once very much surprised because he had said: "Lots of young people are being seen now walking around in the street with books of poetry under their arms." And I asked: "What's the reason for so much reading in Cuba? This is incredible, unheard of in Latin America." He explained: "There's been a lot of propaganda in favor of books. And Fidel has often told the people that they must read. He has told them: 'Read, don't take things on faith.' " He told me that at the airport there used to be ten children who were bootblacks (with as many more who were adults). Of the ten children, four are now in professions, four died for the Revolution (I think at Girón Beach), and two left Cuba.

Ernesto is not a Catholic (he never had any religious training). I asked him once what opinion he had of the Church in Cuba, and he said: "I know some seminary students, and they're not interested in the Revolution. It's not that they're against it, they're just not interested." One day when we were walking along he street he told me that once on TV Che showed a bottle of Coca-Cola, a Revolutionary bottle. He smelled it and said: "It's shitty. It smells of cockroaches." He criticized the workers who could not reproduce the flavor of Coca-Cola. He showed a toothpaste that you couldn't squeeze out of the tube. Matches that wouldn't light. But then they stopped criticizing faulty goods on the television, Ernesto said. (Cuban Coca-Cola is now quite acceptable. The matches still don't light.)

He told me that now there are very few quarrels in the street. When two people start a fight, it's the people and not the police who separate them and reconcile them. The police say: "Comrades, revolutionaries should not fight." There are no sneak thieves in Cuba. Havana used to be famous for its pickpockets. The sneak thieves were retrained on farms. They were given political training, the meaning of the Revolution was explained to them, they were taught skills and given jobs. Now nobody ever lifts your wallet on a bus. The cab drivers were also retrained. They were "the worst kind of people," said Ernesto. "They were at the airport and around the hotels ready to swindle the tourists. They were crazy about dollars. You could see their thirst for money in their eyes. They were ready for any dirty business. Some were even criminals. They were one of the hardest groups to retrain, but they got retrained. You don't see a single example of that kind of person."

I asked him about political prisoners. "There are seven thousand political prisoners in the Havana jail. They are well treated; their quarters are sanitary; their food is good. I know all about it." "How do you know all about it?" "I know because I was in jail with them. I was jailed because I went to have a drink, in uniform, with some Soviet officers. It wasn't a serious error, but it was an error. And I was in jail for two weeks, and they put me with the political prisoners."

Che used to say—Ernesto told me—that this Revolution was the "skeleton of total liberty." This skeleton had to be fleshed out. According to Che the main qualification for a Marxist—and Ernesto is a Marxist—is that he be human. The

Marxist should be filled with love. In the farewell letter that Che left for his little children he told them that they should always be capable of regretting as deeply as possible any injustice against any human being; that was the loveliest quality in a revolutionary. Also according to Che, the Revolution meant giving yourself to others. There is a lot of sacrifice in Cuba, and sacrifice has been idealized. Almost all the slogans are to encourage you to sacrifice. It used to be that cutting sugar cane was the most humiliating work in Cuba; now one is proud of cutting cane and of any other heavy work; this is *making* the Revolution. And Ernesto told me also that in the Sierra Maestra, when there were wounded soldiers and they were being pursued by the enemy, Che was always the last man in the rear guard, behind the last wounded man. When they had wounded prisoners what little medicine they had was divided equally between their own wounded and those from Batista's army. After the attack on the Beach Barracks (Che said), since there was little medicine for the troops, Fidel ordered that they be left for the wounded enemy soldiers. From the time they first reached the Sierra Madre all the provisions were always bought from the farmers, never taken by force.

Back to Camilo: Commander Hebert Mattos had revolted in Camagüey. Camilo flew there to put down the uprising. He reached the barracks with only his escort; the soldiers who were guarding the entrance, on recognizing Camilo Cienfuegos, made way for him in fear and trembling. He went to Mattos's office, pointed his pistol at him, and took him prisoner. Camilo returned to Havana in an old plane that disappeared into the sea. Camilo had had a presentiment of death. A week earlier he was with Fidel and others on a farm, and Fidel was telling tales about the Sierra Maestra, and Camilo said: "Well, years from now you'll be seeing Fidel still telling stories, and he'll be an old man, and he'll say . . . 'Do you remember, Camilo?' " Camilo died soon after. Che, remembering Camilo, had said, with his Argentine way of talking: "A lovely guy, the little tailor." Once Che was hospitalized with an attack of asthma, and he had a vision, and Camilo appeared and told him to "extend the Revolution." That's why Che decided to go and fight in other "Sierras"; he had gone secretly first to the Congo, afterward to Bolivia.

Behind the hotel gardens, between the hotel and the sea,

there were some trenches and a sign that said: "Military Zone
—Keep Out." Even so, Ernesto took me there so that I could
see where he had been defending his Revolution during the
October crisis. He said: "There I was deployed in an artillery
battery of sixty men, in '62." A militiaman who was on watch
some distance away signaled to us to go away, and I was afraid
he would shoot us or capture us, but Ernesto laughed at my
fear and said: "Nothing will happen to us."

Another time near the University he showed me a bronze
plaque in the street, at the place where José Antonio died. He
said: "For me this is very important. . . I never forget these
things. This is my Revolution." He explained, his voice filled
with emotion, where the police patrol found Antonio, which
way he ran, where they shot at him, where he died. He explained to me what had been the plan for the attack on
Batista's palace to bring him to justice and to seize the government right there, because the palace was the seat of the
government. José Antonio spoke over the radio, during the
attack, calling to the people to go to the University, where
they would be given arms as soon as Batista was dead. The
attackers reached the second floor and entered Batista's office,
but Batista had taken refuge on the roof. Ernesto was at that
time a bootblack at the airport, and he remembers the emotion there when a radio announcement said that they had
killed Batista. "I was terrified, it seemed to me terrible that
they had dared to kill the President." At the University stairway he said: "This is the way all the student demonstrators
against Batista used to go down. They used to gather up
above, come down these stairs with their banners, and go out
into the street."

Once Ernesto said to me in my hotel: "There is always
the danger that they'll steal this Revolution from us. For me
the Revolution is something very delicate that we must watch
over. I'm going to show you a corner in my house. It is my
revolutionary archive. I save all those things with enormous
love. I go back to those photographs, those books, those clippings, because it is my Revolution. I say to myself: This nobody can take away from me. Because if some time some people
want to betray it, we'll have to do it all over again, the attack
on the palace, the Moncada assault, the uprising in the Sierra."

Ernesto once took me to his house and introduced me to
his young wife. A modest apartment filled with books, most

67

of them on the floor—it is very hard, almost impossible, to get boards with which to make bookcases, Ernesto tells me, because there are other priorities: the wood is needed for houses.

How had he obtained so many books? Because it seemed to me that in those great piles on the floor was all the best that had been published in Latin America and Spain since my student days. He said that they were either bought in bookstores or received through State institutions. But most of them were gifts. And a great number of them were from the libraries of bookworms who had left Cuba—the State confiscates their houses when they leave, and he said: "I'm going to show you now what I spoke about." A little room in the small apartment was the sacred corner: his revolutionary archive. He showed me albums of clippings, books, pamphlets, collections of photographs, old newspaper pages, magazines, broadsides, phonograph records, copies of letters, speeches of Fidel, poems, songs. And he said, patting the backs of some of the albums and books: "I have all this here to take care of it, to defend it."

I saw in the photographs: The entrance into Havana. Che in the middle of the street surrounded by a crowd of people acclaiming him. Camilo Cienfuegos kissing a little boy. Fidel and Che with big cigars examining a map of the Sierra, Fidel leaning on his gun. A shirtless Che reading Goethe in camp. Student demonstrators (with the University in the background) carrying banners. The sinister Moncada Barracks, faces of assassins and torturers. A photocopy: SECRETARY OF THE INTERIOR. . . Document relative to . . . accused Fidel Castro Ruz. . . Trial number such-and-such. A newspaper clipping: "My son died at six o'clock in the morning from a bullet in the head. He was in the first car in the caravan. They ran into the third post and went so far as the armory. Fidel was behind his machine." Another clipping: "From there we returned home. Abel sat down opposite me in that armchair in which you are now sitting. . ." Anecdotes of the Sierra. When they were newly arrived, a farmer was somewhat fearful. Fidel said: "No, don't be afraid, Cabrera, for we have come to triumph." And a farmer's question: "Crescencio, tell me one thing: 'What do you think Fidel's mission is, what can his ideals be?' " And another farmer remembers: ". . . . And they went around with long beards and hair that looked like women." More snapshots: Fidel and Camilo greeting the crowds in Havana. Batista with his pig's face next to the

American Ambassador. Che, open-shirted, before a microphone (Ernesto said: "In the Commerce Department he would sit down on the rug to talk. . . With his shirt off if the air-conditioner wasn't working. He drove his own car, and people in the street would shout to him: 'Che! Che!' Or they would touch his arm.") A letter from Camilo to Fidel: "Fidel, a big hug to you all. . ." (And he said that they marched for forty days without resting a single night, often with water or mud up to their knees. Every night avoiding ambushes. From Oriente Province to Las Villas, with only three men lost. Signed: Camilo Cienfuegos.) An old newspaper clipping: CLASSES SUSPENDED IN THE UNIVERSITY. Fidel's letter to the politicians when he left Cuba ("From travels like this one you either don't come back or you come back with tyranny beheaded at your feet") and his famous defense in the trial that followed the assault on Moncada ("Condemn me, it doesn't matter, history will absolve me") and his speech when he entered Havana ("This war was won by the people"). Ernesto gave me many of these items from his collection because he had duplicates and he wanted me to have them. He gave me some recordings of interviews with some farmers from the Sierra: ". . . and I took his pack and I hefted it a little and I said to him: 'Go on, Argentine, shit, son of a bitch, walk, walk.' And he: 'No, leave me here, leave me here, leave me.' He had a mortal attack of asthma and there I was up on that hill with him in tow, because he was so ill that he was dragging his feet, dragging his feet uphill. . ." And another one: "We bought our provisions in the store, and if we had four hundred pesos and the merchandise cost four hundred, we paid four hundred to the store. We never failed to pay for every kilo, we never charged a kilo. We paid cash." He gave me also an interview with Haydée Santamaría with the story of the events at Moncada: "Events which I have tried to forget in vain. Which I remember as surrounded by blood and smoke. Which I shared with Melba. Which Fidel tells about in *History Will Absolve Me*. The deaths of Boris and Abel. Death cutting down the men whom we loved so much." And another review (published in *Bohemia*): "Well, at night we would sit down to talk, and there was conversation on many topics: of the men that Fidel would have when we got together with him again, of what we'd do at the end of the war. We talked of visiting one another when the Revolution triumphed, and we all took down one another's addresses." He gave me also a recent clipping from the *Granma:* a school-teacher remembers days of terror in Santiago: "During that week trucks with corpses passed before my house." And another, also recent, from *Rebellious Youth,* where a young man said: "Those who were born fifteen years ago won't believe it: country boys had parasites coming out of their noses; when the girls began to mature they were taken to Havana to be placed as prostitutes; many times meal time came and all you got on your plate was a piece of banana; you had to begin work with your old man when you were ten years old— by that time you were already too old to go to school; the Rural Guard took anything it wanted from the huts; the sergeants raped the country girls; the police could tear out the eyes or the testicles of a boy or stub out cigarette butts on the buttocks of a normal school student; the sugar that you bought in the store was an American brand; if a boy was named Juan they called him Johnny; the young blacks on the block could not use the beach, etc." He showed me photo-copies of the mimeographed newspaper that they printed in the Sierra: THE FREE CUBAN / AGAIN IN REDEEMING MANAGUA / ORGAN OF THE REVOLUTIONARY ARMY / SIERRA MAESTRA, NEW ERA I. Another clipping: Batista at two in the morning leaves Cuba. On the stairway he took out a handkerchief and wiped his face. At the airplane door he saluted. "I have already told you why I keep all this. It seems to me that I am a custodian of it all. And I tell myself: No one will take it away from me." It was Ernesto who said to me on one occasion: "They can throw me into jail for being long-haired, but even if they did, I say: I'll give my life for all this!"

The Casino Boy

In the House of the Americas I met Ramón, who is the "expert" on my poetry, as they told me. To find an expert on my poetry was another of my surprises in Cuba. Ramón was a young boy with an honest look and a constant smile who worked for gangsters before the Revolution. He told me, smiling, that he worked in the Sans Souci, one of the most corrupt casinos. His job was to play cards with the customers: to play "for the house." He also worked in the Kennel Club, the dog-racing club, for other gangsters. His job was to inject morphine into the dog that was not supposed to win, or else to keep him thirsty and, just before the race, give him lots of water to drink. He was practically a child then and had never been to school. But besides working for the gangsters, Ramón was a messenger of the "July 26" boys. When he was sixteen the Revolution triumphed. Ramón stopped working for the gangsters, left the casinos, and began to study literature. He said: "Because that was what really interested me."

Once when we were going to the Varadero beach resort on an excursion given by the House of the Americas, we went by the former Biltmore, which had been the district of the most elegant mansions in Cuba and which is now called Siboney and is the district of the scholarship students—where some fifty thousand farm boys live in the mansions of the rich. Ramón, smiling, pointed out a huge building in the distance and said: "That is the Kennel Club, where I used to inject the dogs." The Kennel Club, I was told, is now the stadium of the country scholarship students. It was very moving to see the children of farmers and laborers in the houses of millionaires. I thought: here is where the song of Mary in the Magnificat has been fulfilled: "He hath filled the hungry with good things; and the rich he hath sent empty away."

Farther along, where the Havana slums had been: beautiful pine groves and ten-story apartment buildings behind those pine groves. Ramón told me: "These are the families that used to live in the slums. Those ghettos that used to exist around the cities no longer exist. The dirty water drains used to go right through the middle of the houses. The houses were made of cardboard and tin cans. People lived in the midst of filth. One of the first tasks of the Revolution was to get rid of all that. It was done very soon; the first houses built were for those people." Later what they call the "green belt" of Havana began: coffee fields, truck gardens, citrus groves, etc.

Ramón also told me that in parts of the countryside that were totally abandoned now there are new buildings or cities, polyclinics, boarding schools, kindergartens, playgrounds, laundries. The huts of palm and sugar cane are disappearing. In some places they were preserving them as museum pieces, next to the new apartment buildings being built for the peasants. If I wanted, I could see one. I said: "I don't need to, those are the huts of the peasants in Solentiname."

Marilú, of The House of the Americas, said: "One thing is certain: this people will never again accept capitalism. To work so that someone else gets the added value, even the most ignorant know that that is to be exploited. That the people should go back to working for individuals, that is no longer possible." Ramón told me that together with the literacy campaign they were also educating the people in cleanliness. He said that now practically no child in Cuba has not had some education.

Ramón was very much interested in my new poetry but said he hadn't studied it very deeply and that later he would want to ask me questions about it. I quoted a song of the Zuñi Indians that had been brought to mind by what I was then seeing:

All, come all, come up all, come in all, sit down all
We were poor, poor, poor, poor, poor.

"Do you really think that Fidel is a Marxist?" "He read Martí a lot. I think he probably has had more Martían than Marxist influence."

»»»

Comrade Carlos Franqui,
Editor of the Newspaper Revolution
Havana

Comrade Franqui:

I saw in Carteles, *in the "Behind the News" section, written by Antonio Llano Montes, a note that has interested me because it insinuates something about my revolutionary attitude by means of the following apparently inoffensive sentence: "Commander Guevara has established his residence in Tarará."*

I shall not analyze here who this journalist is, nor shall I mention what he has confided to my custody in the archives; it is not my intention to make accusations or counteraccusations; I owe myself to public opinion and to those who have had faith in me as a revolutionary.

I inform the readers of Revolution *that I am ill, that my illness was not contracted in gambling dens or staying up all night in cabarets but in working more than my constitution could take for the Revolution.*

The doctors recommended a house in a place removed from daily visits, and the Rehousing Agency lent me this one, which I shall occupy on this beach until the colleagues who are taking care of me give me a medical discharge; I had to occupy a house belonging to a delegate of the old regime because my wages of one hundred and twenty-five dollars as an officer of the Rebel Army do not permit me to rent a house big enough to accommodate the people who accompany me.

The fact that this is a house belonging to an old Batista follower makes it luxurious; I chose the simplest one I could, but even so it is an insult to the people's sensibility. I promise Mr. Llano Montes and especially the people of Cuba that I shall abandon it as soon as I am recovered.

I shall be grateful to you for the publication of these lines for the better enlightenment of our people about the behavior of those of us who have undertaken a responsibility toward them.

Che

An Excursion

The House of the Americas offered the members of the poetry jury a picnic in a luxurious country house that had belonged to a doctor who had left Cuba. The bus passed by plantations of sugar cane and citrus fruits. The girls from the House of the Americas recognized some lemon trees that they themselves had planted. They were excited to see that the trees were now quite well along.

They had planted citrus fruits and coffee this year, we were told. They lived out in the country, in tents. Nine hours work a day. Said one, Trini: "I just couldn't believe that we could plant so much." They also went into the cane fields. They talked about the "Liberator," the machine that Fidel announced and that was still being invented. Another, Marilú, said: "Mechanization is essential. The work that we have done in the fields is very hard." Everybody is waiting eagerly for that machine. Its name, the "Liberator," is most expressive. Work in the cane fields is very hard, and someone told about a boy who had cut his own foot with a machete so as not to have to go on cutting cane.

We passed by long stretches of young pine trees, mangos, citrus fruits, miles and miles. Cintio, who was with us, said: "There is a massive reforestation throughout Cuba. They are planting millions of cedar, eucalyptus, and other trees. Within a few years Cuba will be covered with trees. And they have planted fabulous numbers of citrus trees. Millions."

They also told me, to my amazement, that in Cuba they had abolished polio, intestinal parasites, malaria, and tetanus. Polio was abolished with a little tablet from Russia that you ate like candy. "This is not propaganda, it's the truth."

Margaret Randall spoke of the sugar cane camp where she was this year (peeling potatoes because she had recently had an operation and couldn't cut cane), and she said that at night the women listened to the Voice of America and laughed at the lies that they were telling about Cuba. Cintio also said: "Now people aren't leaving Cuba for ideological reasons, but rather for economic reasons. Those who were against the Revolution left long ago. Those who are leaving now are people who were in favor of the Revolution, but they can't stand the shortages, the standing in line, the hard life of these revolutionary years."

More fruit trees. More green fields filled with palm trees. Someone said: "The struggle is against two thousand years of individualism." Silvio Rodríguez was with us, a troubadour. One of the young composers of protest songs. And he sang for us *"Playa Girón." Playa Girón* is a fishing motorboat on which he lived four months, fishing near the coast of Africa and singing for the fishermen.

»»»

PLAYA GIRÓN

—A Song of Protest by Silvio Rodríguez

Comrade poets:
taking into account the latest events in poetry
I'd like to ask—it is urgent—
what kind of adjectives should be used to make
the poem of a boat without its getting sentimental,
apart from the vanguard or obvious propaganda
if I should use words
like the Cuban Fishing Flotilla and *Playa Girón.*
Comrade musicians:
taking into account those polytonal and audacious songs
I'd like to ask—it is urgent—
what kind of harmony should be used to make
the song of this boat with men no longer children
men and only men on deck
men black and red and blue
the men who man the *Playa Girón.*
Comrade historians:
taking into account how implacable truth must be
I'd like to ask—it is so urgent—
what I should say, what limits I must respect
if someone steals food and afterward sacrifices his life
        what must we do
how far must we practice the truths:
How far do we know.
Let them write—then—the story, their story
the men of the *Playa Girón.*

Books

The edition of ten thousand copies of an anthology of my work published by the House of the Americas was sold out in a week. Benedetti told me that the edition of his *Latin American Poetry of Love* was of fifty thousand copies and is sold out. *A Hundred Years of Solitude* had a first printing of ten thousand copies, and an immediate second printing of eighty thousand, and you can't find a copy in any bookstore. That's a lot, even if you keep in mind that in the rest of Latin America and Spain this book of García Márquez has reached a record figure of five hundred thousand copies.

A poet from Santiago told me that the University of Oriente was going to bring out a literary journal with a printing of five thousand copies. And he said: "In Cuba, compared with other printings, this means almost a clandestine edition." Rosi López told me that in a bookstore she had seen people standing in line for my volume of poetry. At the Book Institute they told me that before the Revolution they used to publish only a million and a half copies a year of all books in Cuba. In 1969 they printed fifteen million. And seventy-five per cent of those books, they told me, were schoolbooks. "And the basic needs are not met. The bookstores are empty." (This was true.)

Because of the demand for books swap stores have been set up where you can exchange a book already read for a new one. (There are sixty such stores in Cuba.) They have also set up reading rooms in bookstores where you can read a book without buying it. There are libraries in the sugar cane camps, the Youth Column camps, etc., where you can get books without a card. (As they told me also at the Book Institute: "In Cuba the book has ceased to be an article of trade.") There are bookstores even in the mountains, where the books are carried on muleback. There are libraries on the collective farms, in factories, barracks, jails. Few foreign books get in, because of the blockade, but there are Foreign Book Exhibit Centers (one in each province).

Books in Cuba have a standard price, and a very cheap one: each book costs seventy-five cents or a dollar. At the National Library you can also withdraw pictures on loan—originals and reproductions. In the children's section there is a circulating (traveling) art gallery where children can borrow appropriate books and take them home.

Children's libraries are everywhere, and they serve thousands of children. The children have also suffered because of the blockade, because children's books with good illustrations are hard to publish in Cuba, and it is very difficult to get them from abroad. In the children's section of the National Library they have had to remove from circulation Jules Verne and Salgari because the copies were worn out through use. Now they are kept in showcases. One of the librarians said sadly: "Many children want to read them and they can't." Children's books—I was told—are published in editions of fifty thousand copies and are sold out at once.

And before the Revolution Cuban writers had no publishers. There were very few literary journals, and they had tiny circulations. Poets could not live.

»»»

The Literacy Teachers in 1961	
People's instructors (simple citizens)	120,632
Fatherland or Death Brigade (workers)	13,016
Conrado Benítez Brigade (students)	100,000
Schoolteachers	34,772
	268,420

The Archbishop

At the door of the Archbishop's palace I met a priest, he was introduced, and he told me that he was the parish priest of Guantánamo (the Cuban Guantánamo). He was surprised that I had come to Cuba, and I was surprised by what he said: "What a coincidence. Not long ago the workers in a Guantánamo factory had in their study circle a week-long seminar on your poetry. Yes, of course. They have their study circle, right in the factory"—he was amused at my surprise. "They invited me to attend this seminar on you, and I went to the last days of it. You must come to Guantánamo, even though we are in the farthest corner of Cuba. The workers will be delighted to see you."

And since in the rest of Latin America my poetry is known only among certain literary circles, I said to myself while climbing the ancient stairs in the big old house of the Archbishop: "Cuba is incredible!" The Archbishop of Havana, Monsignor Francisco Oves, is a cheerful young man, with neither the costume nor the manners of a bishop—he wears a sport shirt. He told me that he was very glad that the episcopal "palace" was this big old tumbledown house with almost no furniture, which they were now repairing so that it wouldn't tumble all the way down. He also told me: "The leaders of the Revolution live austerely; it would be absurd if the leaders of the Church lived in any other way."

"Food? It's the ration card food, like that of everyone. And it is meager. You can't invite anyone to a meal, because there isn't enough." Oves is on the side of the Revolution. He told me that the conflicts between the Revolution and the Church had ended. He added: "We have another way of thinking." He was named Bishop a short while ago. And he was recently from Rome, with a post-Council frame of mind. There have to be conflicts at times. There is always intransigence on both sides. For example, now that I was going to the Isle of Pines, I could try to see some seminarists who are there in a Social Disgrace Unit, with marijuana smokers and homosexuals and other delinquents, working in the marble quarries. . ."

78

"Forced labor?" "Practically. Under very harsh conditions. It's very annoying for them to be with homosexuals, sneak thieves, and other antisocial types. It would be great if you could encourage them, tell them to cheer up and work with good spirits and keep up their social studies circles and not to stop being revolutionaries even though they are treated that way. I have encouraged them, too. I don't want them to have a martyr complex."

Oves thinks that the new revolutions in Latin America are not going to bring conflicts with the Church. There wouldn't have been conflicts in Cuba, either, if the Council had taken place a little sooner or the Revolution a little later. The Revolution occurred just on the eve of the renovation of the Church. This renovation, for Cuba, came too late. We were in a huge, almost empty room which I supposed to be the Bishop's office. Several priests in shirt sleeves came up and sat down to talk while we had small cups of thick black coffee and smoked Cuban cigarettes made of strong black tobacco.

"Is there persecution?" One priest laughed: "There is a persecution mania among many Catholics." The Rector of the Seminary, Father Carlos Manuel Céspedes—a descendant of General Carlos Manuel de Céspedes, leader of Cuban independence—thought that the Revolution would not have been possible if it had not become Marxist. And that the differences between Christianity and Marxism were less and less important. And that the People of God must support this Revolution. He was a young man, about the age of the Bishop. His family did not think as he did. His mother was in exile. An uncle of his was serving a twenty-year jail sentence. A girl cousin was sentenced to six years.

Father Angel Gaztelu, an important Cuban poet who belonged to the *Orígenes* group, told me that he used to go to say Mass for Fidel and the other Moncada prisoners in the Isle of Pines jail. He was certain that they were Catholics and not Marxists. And some of them took communion. And he told me also that not long ago he had celebrated Mass in the street in memory of José Antonio Echeverría, the Catholic student leader who was a martyr of the Revolution. A Mass in the open air, in front of the monument to José Antonio, attended by many Catholic students. Nobody interfered with it.

As far as I can tell, Cuba is the only place in the world

where Catholicism is not going through a crisis of vocation. The Archbishop told me that in the Major Seminary there were nearly seventy seminarists, more or less the same number as before the Revolution. And there was no crisis of celibacy among the priests, or of authority, or of faith—none of the crises through which the post-Council Church is struggling throughout the world. I said to them: "There is no post-Council crisis not because the Church is very good but because it is very bad: because here the Council hasn't even entered." Oves laughed, and I think he agreed with me.

Oves also told me: Before the Revolution there were twenty-three hundred religious; about two thousand left (mostly through their own decision, not because they were expelled). There used to be about a thousand priests; now there are about two hundred and fifty. Those who get baptised are twenty-five or thirty per cent of the population. Those who get married in the Church are about five per cent. The Sunday school attendance is about half of what it used to be. The Archbishop is happy that Catholicism should be a minority and not a mass phenomenon. Let people enter the Church because of personal convictions and not because of atmospheric pressures. I observed: Christ wanted his Church to be a ferment in the dough, and here it was just the opposite: Catholicism was the dough, and the ferment was the non-Catholics: the revolutionary vanguard. . .

They told me that the Argentine priest Aldo Buntig, who was here not long ago, said that the earliest Christians celebrated their liturgy clandestinely in the catacombs but lived their lives immersed in the world. Here the Christians do the opposite: they celebrate their liturgy in public and live their lives in the catacombs. They told me that Sergio Arce, Professor of Theology at Matanzas Evangelical Seminary, said that the Christians here were like the Apostles before the Pentecost: "The Church shut itself in upon itself, and when the Church closes its doors the Lord is left outside the doors. The Church must serve the world, and in Cuba that means serve the new society, not sabotage it. And he saw a special point of contact between Christianity and Marxism where others saw an insoluble conflict: the question of atheism. The true Christian, from a philosophical point of view, is also an atheist—in this he is like a Marxist. His God is That One Whom "no one knows" and Who is adored not in temples but "in spirit and in truth": in man's love for man.

Father Céspedes said: "They did what we Christians should have done, and we didn't do it." He also thought that the Revolution was irreversible. "Fortunately." A humble little man arrived, a Frenchman, and the Archbishop introduced him to me. He was a monk from the Protestant monastery of Taizé. He said his name was Brother Roberto. He was a doctor, and in his community he worked as a doctor and as a laborer. He wanted to talk with me and he had planned to come to Solentiname. His community wanted to become familiar with the social problems of Latin America and had sent him on a visit. He had seen the misery, the underdevelopment, everything. Now he wanted to round out his vision of Latin America with the Cuban Revolution. He didn't go to Solentiname because he had to come to Cuba. He came here with a tourist visa. The ICAP (Cuban Institute of Friendship with Peoples) got him a room at the Presidente, a luxury hotel intended for foreigners. But he didn't want to stay there. That had nothing to do with Cuba. He wanted to live the hard life of Cubans, as a Christian and as a revolutionary. He asked the ICAP for permission to go and live in the Seminary, and they granted it. Soon, before saying good-by to me, Archbishop Oves said again: "No, I don't want them to have a martyr complex."

A story that Cintio told me: A young man, sixteen, a Catholic student leader, was condemned to twenty years in jail. He had been in prison about nine years. His crime: putting bombs in a bus or something like that. During the years in which there was a confrontation between the Revolution and the Faith. During all this time he refused "rehabilitation," like his friends. But now they are not asked to be rehabilitated (in the sense of retracting their principles) but simply to work on a farm. He has accepted this, and his mother has recently said: "My son has told me that he no longer has anything to oppose. He has gone on studying to be an engineer and now he lives on a farm."

»»»

81

Havana, 28 October 1963
"Year of Organization"

Comrade Pablo Díaz González, Administrator
Majagua, Camagüey

Pablo:

I read your article. I must thank you for how well you treated me: too well, I think. It seems to me that you treat yourself rather well.

The first thing that a revolutionary who is writing history must do is to stick to the truth like a finger in a glove. You did this, but the glove was a boxing glove, so it's no good.

My advice: reread the article take out of it all that you know is not true, and be wary of all that you are not sure is true.

Revolutionary greetings from
FATHERLAND OR DEATH
WE SHALL OVERCOME

Commander Ernesto Che Guevara

Pablo Armando

The poet Pablo Armando Fernández was talking with me in my hotel room. Looking out the window, from where we could see the white skyscrapers of Havana lit by the last afternoon light, he said: "This was an ocean of ads and lights, you can't imagine. Down below the city was full of prostitutes."

I know the life of Pablo Armando Fernández because I have read it in the book that Warren Miller wrote about Cuba. He was born in a sugar cane plantation which belonged to some Yankees, and his father and his brothers were workers on that plantation. His older brothers worked so that he could have the education that they hadn't had. At the age of eighteen he decided to be a poet, and he left the plantation. Afterward he went to the United States, where he washed dishes. Later he had an import-export business in New York, and he was getting rich (he was earning two thousand dollars a month) when the Cuban Revolution triumphed. Two months after the triumph he sold his business and came back to Cuba. He had said that the three most important events in his life were his discovery of God, the death of his mother, and the Cuban Revolution. I had also read that Pablo Armando Fernández was a religious and a mystic.

Pablo Armando Fernández said: "From the middle of '59 the Catholic bourgeoisie began to oppose the Revolution because it considered it to be communist (that is, to be revolution). In '60 was the great flight, the Catholics were terribly pro-United States, and they still are. Nixon is their real Pope, and Fidel quite rightly has called them the Church of Washington." As a sample of bourgeois mentality: some aunts of his wife (otherwise excellent ladies) when the Revolution began to nationalize the private clubs, came home telling about the countless indignities that they had had to endure in the club and that it was *full of workers:* and they said *workers* with horror, with a tone that implied *wild beasts.*

"One form of protest was to join the Church. Many who were not Catholics now are. Not because of religious motives but because of anticommunism. They go to all the services, they sit in the first pews, and they sing defiantly. Because

they know that there nobody will come and shut them up. . .
When Cuba became officially communist, many antirevolutionaries went through the streets ostentatiously wearing cruci-
fixes and medals: it was a way of protest against the regime,
and one that nobody could prevent. If anyone tried to stop
them, they said that they were undergoing religious persecution. And many of those who became militant Catholics were
people who had never set foot in a church, many perhaps had
carried on all kinds of dirty business under Batista, casinos
and the like.

The priests console the people who want to leave Cuba
and can't get away. They tell them to have patience, to offer
up their sufferings to God. They don't tell them to be revolutionaries! The priests no longer attack the Revolution directly
in the pulpit, but they can do so indirectly, with allusions
that the faithful understand perfectly well. The Nuncio told
me, quite disgustedly, about a priest who in a sermon referred
to the Revolution scornfully, speaking of *those people*."

Pablo Armando told me that at first the counterrevolutionaries spread the rumor that they were going to abolish
parental authority and they would take children away from
their parents—which was a lie. Many parents sent their children abroad so as not to lose them, and now they are sorry
they did because they really did lose them. I was told about
children in Italy who are homesick for Cuba and who reproach
their parents for having sent them away. And there are so
many children of exiled Cubans in the United States, who like
their fellow students from the United States, are revolutionaries with Castro, and they do not forgive their fathers for
having sent them out of Cuba. In the "We Shall Overcome
Brigade" of young Americans who came to cut sugar cane,
there were two Cuban sons of exiles.

Pablo Armando told me that it was true that you could
talk against Castro in a public park without anything happening to you. If anyone made a public commotion, it would be
hard for a policeman to arrest him (if he did not submit)
because policemen are not allowed to strike anyone. They have
to use persuasion and beg you to become a prisoner. Besides,
the militiamen are students, professionals, ordinary people
who are doing their public duty service. And they all remember Batista's police, and that memory inhibits them in using
force.

Standing in line people complain freely, about the Revo-

lution, about Fidel, about everything. Once Pablo Armando
was standing in the food line, and a black woman was complaining that the Revolution was starving them to death. He
said to her: "I bet that you didn't used to eat meat once a
week." She asked him if he was on the side of the Revolution,
and when he said he was, she shouted at him: "AND AREN'T
YOU ASHAMED?"

"A curious thing about this Revolution is that there is
no privileged class. A minister stops being a minister today,
and he changes into an ordinary guy, an absolutely ordinary
guy." He admits that the repression in Cuba against homosexuals is very severe. They are not allowed to study. And he
said: "It is terrible to think what would have happened to a
Whitman or a Lorca in Cuba: they would not have been able
to study."

I offered the poet Pablo Armando some Caney rum in a
bottle that the hotel had put in my room together with a box
of Havana cigars. He said, as he served himself: "I have not
had a bottle like this in my house in a long time, in years."

To eat in a good restaurant one stands in line four, five,
and even six hours (depending on the quality of the restaurant). A short while ago Pablo Armando wanted to take his
family to eat in a good restaurant to celebrate his son's birthday, and he had to stand in line six hours just to get the
reservation. This is a luxury that one permits oneself—he said
—about once a year. The restaurant prices are all alike, although there are differences in quality: what makes some less
accessible than others is the length of the line. There are other
popular restaurants where the line is only a half hour. There
are in addition the dining rooms in the labor centers, where
meals are very cheap, and there are others where it is free. He
said also that a plate of food would never be denied to anyone
anywhere, if for whatever reason he couldn't pay for it. One
can eat free anywhere.

"There is a tendency to suppress money. People no longer
appreciate money. It is only an instrument of exchange with
which to obtain things. Now what is important is things, not
money." Many people have free housing. Those who pay rent
pay ten per cent of their wages. There are no evacuations or
evictions. Nobody can be thrown out of his home because he
hasn't paid his rent. People used to live in constant fear of
that. Now the home is a sacred thing.

And Pablo Armando said, looking at the window, through

which we could see many apartments with lights on: "It's very pleasant to be able to sleep in one's home and to know that in all of Cuba tonight there will not be a single soul who does not have a roof over him, not one person sleeping on the sidewalk or in a doorway or out in the field under a tree." He pointed out, in a building opposite us, a balcony with an awning: "There live the two best painters in Cuba."

»»»

There are no bootblacks, which gladdens me. People shine their own shoes at home. But once near my hotel, next to a bus stop, I saw a shoeshine stand, with some old men on duty. I happened to be with Ernesto, the ex-bootblack of the airport, now a teacher of philosophy. I asked him: "And what about that stand?" He explained that it was for the hotel. For travelers or foreigners who can't shine their own shoes at home. It's the only shoeshine stand in Havana, as far as he knows. He said, with a certain emotion in his voice: "At least they are not children on duty. Now there are no child laborers. Children study and play."

Conversation in a School

(Recorded by some young poets and published in the student paper *Alma Mater*.)

Student: It's true, it's true, that's the problem of all young people. My parents tell me: Your hair's too long, they'll put you in jail, don't let your hair grow . . . and so I don't have a single friend who doesn't have very long hair, because none of them do any studying or do any work. . .

Student: A waste of time. . .

Student: . . . and everyone comes to my house, and every two or three days there's a riot in the house, you know? And the old folks don't say anything, they don't care, because they know that's the way young people have fun; but they think: "In my time, young gentlemen. . ."

Student: I think that up to now this is the most interesting topic that we've discussed here, because there's no question, it's a problem we face every day, not the contradictions or the problems with our parents, because those definitely are the easiest to solve; but it's clear that there *is* a contradiction between our way of thinking and our parents' way of thinking, the old men in the street, the young old men in the street, the way of thinking of our teachers, the diagrams they have in their heads. It's a problem that we've got to attack quickly. We definitely have to impose our ideas, but that depends a little on our starting to think, on our creating for ourselves a certain prestige in our own eyes, on our facing problems with a little more responsibility. That is, to create the bases for making demands on the old people—and when I say old I mean people who have old ideas—because there's no question that there are thousands of young people who aren't young, they are much influenced by the ideas of the past. We have to create the bases to be able to face up to that and eliminate the problem. Of course the problem will go on existing, right? Because whenever there's an older generation and a newer one springs up there's bound to be contradiction, but. . .

Student: I really . . . would not know how that problem could be solved, because that is a problem that we've always faced. . . Then I'd like you to tell me how you plan to solve that.

Student: I . . . the solution, it's hard to find it; so hard that I can't be precise; but you have to try to get young people to be a little more responsible in order to make demands and so that the old people will have to accept us. Whether or not they understand us, because we've got to be a little drastic. We have to impose ourselves, and they've got to accept that we wear our hair long, and that we're a little freer in our love affairs, and that we have our new form of marriage; let them understand all those things, and if they don't understand them, well, we've got to be able to force them in a responsible way.

Student: The problem, look . . . of course they think that they are in the right, and that's why we shouldn't attack them straight on, because the poor things think they are right, and we think we are. Then we'd have to talk putting the cards on the table. Give a reason why we're right. The reason they always give is "tradition"—"such a thing has never been seen"; well, it's never been seen, but now it's going to be seen. Let them give us one reason why we can't do that. You see how it is? Let them give reasons for their reasons.

Girl Student: Well, look, at home they understand me pretty well, I don't have any problem. Now, I know that they're not all like that, because at times they get, you know, impertinent, so to speak. You tell them one thing, and they come back with this and the other, because people, if they say. . .

Student: Here's the problem of old and young, and it's not just the parents. It's twenty things, sometimes the people in charge, the educators, who have twenty old things in their heads, and at times, guys, we don't realize it because we live a little . . . and we don't think; but the truth is that they're not training us very well, and we've got to face up to it and not limit ourselves to the problem of whether my mother won't let me go out because she thinks that way. This definitely can be solved more or less, or you can manage . . . but there are things that are affecting our education, and we have to begin to think about that, begin to think.

Student: I think free love is a very good thing.

Student: Free love is an advance. After all, marriage, what is it? Signing a piece of paper and nothing more. The other's just the same, but you don't have to sign anything. The moment that two people stop liking each other, well, you go your way and I'll go mine, without any fuss or any of those shackles. In my opinion that's better than marriage.

Girl Student: It seems to me that if youth were a little more responsible for its actions, perhaps we could apply that new formula; but it seems to me that it's not sufficiently qualified to . . . there's a lot of irresponsibility. . .

Student: The man has always had the bigger share in free love. . .

Girl Student: Yes, but why? Because of the same oppression, because of the very system that he has had. You can't put an end to that in one moment, like from night to day. There has to be a process, right? Maybe our children's children will understand this.

Student: He says that the woman loses. I want him to tell me that. . .

Student: I didn't say anything about losing or winning. I say that the man is more in favor of free love than the woman.

Student: But why?

Student: Because of the way our parents have taught us: the man in the street and the woman in the house; because if from the beginning there had been equality between men and women, that way of thinking would not exist.

Student: In marriage the basis must be equality between man and woman, equality in every sense. Just now you were talking about eliminating the problem of signatures and all that. Of course the signature and the ceremony and all that stuff have no reason for being, it's simply a tradition. Now to eliminate that in a moment can't be done. But neither can we resign ourselves to what she was saying just now, that that's the way the children of the children's children will be. I think that in many things we're accustomed to the idea that we can't do it now, that we have to wait until time passes. I think we ought to be a little more, I don't know . . . and break with all that, right? All about let's wait until time passes. What for? They were talking, too, I didn't hear well, about whether the woman loses or the man loses. I think that nobody loses; because the woman, what's she got to lose? Her virginity? It doesn't matter if she does. There was a lot of stuff about that. Maybe in the eyes of society, at this moment, she loses. Now what we've got to do is forget all about that, right? That stuff about what will people say. Sure, you live with people, and at times you have to keep in mind . . . because, logically, we live in a society and with public opinion, but we don't live *on* public opinion. Here's what we must do, guys, to impose ourselves. Let people think what they want. I don't have to be governed by what people say, because then we are limiting our lives. Why do we live, then? To live a limited life? If on top of being short, life has to be limited, no thanks.

Student: Everybody doesn't think alike. It's really not important whether or not a woman loses her virginity but it *is* important that some people think so.

Student: Do you think it's important?

Student: Not at all.

Student: You? . . . no; you? . . . no; you . . . no.

Girl Student: Notice, what I see is that within the school we have one of the greatest existing contradictions, right? The one that thinks that this is nothing important and that it's normal and logical and the one that thinks it isn't. That exists among young people in this school and all the schools, because they are very retarded in this sense.

Student: Of course we're retarded. I think that the fundamental problem is that people are afraid of free love, because they think it's love. . .

Girl Student: That it's an aberration.

Student: Aha! And when it's practiced around here, the coach is going to be in charge, because it's going to be a sport. And free love is not a sport, gentlemen. People are mistaken, and that's why young people, many young people, are afraid of free love. And old people too. It is simply love, gentlemen.

Girl Student: Yes, but there are also the stories that one has heard.

Student: We are facing a problem in education, right? Of course we can't really practice a lot of free love because we don't get any sexual education. Besides, what can you do if you plan to discuss this in a school and the superintendent says this can't be discussed in the school? Well, if they educate us that way they're not giving us any sexual education.

Student: All study plans ought to include sexual education. I've heard that in France the boys get sexual education from elementary school on. . .

Student: If they don't begin in elementary school they'll

be just as bad off as we are. It has to be from the beginning.

Girl Student: I think that right here in Cuba a whole series of abnormal things are happening: men who are mentally ill raping boys and girls. That's part of all that, you know, we don't have. . .

Student: Maturity.

Girl Student: Aha, maturity in that sense. Well in primary school they have found boys together with boys, girls with girls, gosh, things they do without knowing why. Then that is part of why we don't have that development in sex.

Girl Student: Look, I agree, in part, with the definition of free love. Now I don't agree that people should practice it just like that. Because well, first everyone would have to agree and say: They're going to practice it or not. And then, as I believe. . .

Student: Look, the question is: If you agree, practice it, and if you don't agree, then. . .

Girl Student: Well, look I personally don't like it. If I'm going to join a man it doesn't make any difference to me if it's with a paper or not. Now, if it's not, if a certain moment arrives . . . that also is why there exists what you call a sport, you understand?

Student: Notice, that depends on the nature of the person. One of the things that one should preserve is fidelity, and you're not faithful just getting married through the Church, through the notary, or wherever. For example, a woman marries a man or a man marries a woman. . .

Student: Of course, we're not in England.

Student: No, that's not what I meant . . . on both sides, that there's no fidelity. A man may marry a woman and not be faithful to her, and one can practice free love and have fidelity, because free love isn't what people think—lewdness—understand?

Student: You get married, go to Nuptial Palace, sign, whatever, and you decide a week later to get divorced and you get divorced, you sign another paper and there you are. It's all the same. Although it's true, in the eyes of society you're more proper because you got divorced, but it's all the same.

Girl Student: Look, look . . . in ten years, in twenty, it doesn't matter to me. Now, would you view as equals a girl, your fiancée, or another girl who has lived with a man without being married to him or anything, for a year, two years, five, as long as she liked, and then afterward takes you for a bridegroom and marries you or whatever?

Student: That has nothing to do with it because, look, there are men who marry divorced women. This is part of our complexes. That's something you have to be sensible about: "No, but she was married." "Ah, she lived with a man." What's wrong with that? It's the most natural thing that a woman be with a man. That's what I believe.

Girl Student: But most men aren't like that.

Student: Well, most men . . . because. . .

Girl Student: Most of them, most.

Girl Student: If all young people thought as you're talking here. . . Because there are people who say: No, because I believe that this is a very good thing, and at bottom what they think is completely opposite. On the street corner they say that free love can exist, and when they go to choose a wife they choose just the opposite of what he said. Besides, if we're living in a society, why should we go against that society? If society here accepts the indispensable requirement to have . . . let's suppose, a sense of duty, that is, good morals, why should one go against that?

Student: Then you think that women who aren't virgins are immoral?

Girl Student: No, they're not immoral, but society doesn't accept them. Because you have to have good social relations to be, for example, a member of the Party, because if you're a loose one, and you try to get to be a Party member, you're crazy.

Girl Student: Yes, they all agree that if a girl has been with a man and afterward, well, if he likes her, he stays with her. If one of them has a sister in that situation, I'd like to know if they accept it as logical, as a normal thing. Do they really accept it? Well, I've heard opinions of boys who when they talk about a girl from here, who without practicing free love, may be a little loose, let's say, right? And they talk about her. . .

Student: But don't confuse looseness with free love.

Girl Student: If free love was that a woman lives with the man she loves until she stops loving him, right? I consider that a very logical and normal thing. Do you accept this? All right, if in our society, for example, what she said, you're going to be a Party militant, right? You have to be an example in everything, before the laws of society, and, o.k., moral laws, right? What is considered moral?

Student: Then you consider that a woman, because she liked a man and she failed, she failed in her love and afterward went with another man, you don't consider that she's moral?

Girl Student: I didn't say that.

Student: Then, that's what we're discussing. Of course, you're not going to confuse free love with a . . . with, with . . . what do you call that? With a prostitute, right? Those are distinct and different things. Of course, such a person is not allowed in the Party; but that's not practicing free love. That's not what we're discussing.

Student: There was talk that with free love it could be that the family would disappear. There is nothing falser than that. The family is not going to be made by any piece of paper. What is going to make a family is definitely love that is born between two people even though they practice free love. They were also talking about society; but this society that we have now is not the one we want. We are working to transform society, right? From all points of view. We are moving toward a better society, and if we don't impose our wills on it, when are we going to have a better one if we let it go on being like this one?

Student: I agree with what many of the girls are saying, that society is what is confusing those ideas that we have of free love. The comrade spoke of socialist society; if at this moment this is not the society that is wanted, toward which society are we moving? If he says that a better society is wanted, what can we do here to bring it about?

Student: Logically we cannot desire this society. This society is still almost more the other one, the former one. Because the society still in our thoughts is the one that disappeared twelve years ago. We cannot desire this society where we are all full of prejudices, where man still is not free. I can't give you a broader meaning to the question of the word "liberty." I don't believe that anybody can feel himself free, you understand how things are? Then let's make a society where man will feel himself fuller, freer, I don't know, maybe build the famous new man. When we have built him and when we have overcome a heap of things, then we will have the society that we want. Don't misunderstand me, because we don't want. . . Well, the fact is that we cannot desire this society, my friend, because really we have to improve it. And that we'll accomplish as we gradually acquire more economic development.

Student: Yes, I'm understanding you; and it's true: this society could be an intermediate step toward one that will come farther on.

»»»

INTRANSCENDENTAL BIOGRAPHY

—Domingo Alfonso

When she died she left her clothes,
her schoolbooks, her intimate diary,
a childish, fifth-grade love,
idolatry for Fidel and Che.
The young woman dead at fifteen with whom I used to talk
of trivial things watching her breasts quiver;
she left other things that I don't remember,
those dreams of being a mother,
of having a room with shiny copper pots,
a bunch of flowers from time to time,
a little air to breathe.

»»»

I was in a car with Ernesto, and we passed by the University, and groups of students were coming out on the street with books under their arms. Ernesto told me that as we passed, a girl said: "There goes Ernesto Cardenal."
I think again that Cuba is unbelievable.

»»»

Oliva told me: when Fidel was dedicating the Camilo Torres School, with Camilo's mother there, he declared that in the Latin American revolution Marxists would fight side by side with Christians. Fidel also has said: "Every Christian ought to be by definition a revolutionary."

»»»

94

A sign with psychedelic colors: THE BEST ONES TO
THE PARTY.

»»»

New notes:

I was telling Pablo Armando Fernández that the fishing boats have libraries. And he said: "Yes. And in Venezuela when they confiscated the *Harlequin,* a fishing boat,
they didn't believe they were fishermen, they thought they
were spies, because they were decently dressed, decently
behaved, and they had books."

Roque Dalton: "The Communist parties in Latin
America are more corrupt than you can imagine. I speak
to you on good authority because I am a militant member
of the Communist party in my country. But I joined the
Communist party of El Salvador because I believe that
decent people ought to join these parties and not leave
them entirely to the bastards."

"That is one of the great tragedies of revolutions:
you have to suppress man in order to save him." *Fidel*

Bars: they are open only Saturday and Sunday nights.
And you can get in only if you line up ahead of time to
get a reservation. They won't sell liquor to anyone who
is drunk. They close at 2:00 A.M.

Three or four months ago was the last time that anyone could buy a bottle of rum with his ration card. From
time to time you can get beer (which is very good).

Monsignor Pérez Serantes, the Archbishop of Santiago, who had hidden Fidel, and who afterward made a
bitter attack on the communism of the Revolution, said
on his deathbed: "All that is happening to us is provi-
dential. We had more faith in our schools than Jesus
Christ." Formerly he had said: "With communism, nothing." And also that the struggle was between Rome and
Moscow.

"Young fellow. . ." "Idiot. . ." "Comrade. . ." "And
what do you think?"

They ask me: "Can you be a communist and a Christian?" I answer: "The first Christians were communists,
and they were the best Christians of all time." "Can you

be a Marxist and a Christian?" "According to you, no, because you think that Marxists can't believe in God. But I think that a Christian can be a Marxist and still believe in God."

I also said to them: "There are sanctimonious ones among Marxists as among Catholics. Those who are shocked by any criticisms of the Revolution. Like the Catholics who are shocked at the criticisms we make of the Church. I have seen Marxists who remind me of those who preside over Marian congregations, very servile toward the superiors in the college, very well behaved and sneaky gossipers."

Fidel works eighteen or twenty hours a day, they tell me. Celia Sánchez, a guerrilla fighter from the Sierra Maestra, is the one who takes care of him and goes with him on his jeep trips, and is also his secretary.

The chamberman in the hotel: "There are never any empty rooms. The minute one guest goes another one occupies his room. Because there is a scarcity of housing in Cuba. In this hotel all the rooms are filled."

When the Cuban bishops reached Medellín in Colombia they learned that many of the things recommended were being done by the Cuban Revolution.

Saturdays and Sundays a cabaret is open in this hotel.

With Catholics

In the sacristy of a church, a college student: "I am with the Revolution, but Fidel betrayed the Revolution." I asked him why he felt that way. "Well, Father, he emerged from one imperialism to fall into another." Then he told me that he was a revolutionary but that he wanted another kind of revolution. "What kind?" "Christian Democracy, for example. We don't know much about Peru, but we are very optimistic about that revolution."

"Do they accept Catholics in the University?" "No, nor in any approved projects, if they know that they are Catholics. They have to conceal it." "Most of the University students are Marxists?" "About thirty per cent are sincere Marxists. About thirty per cent are false Marxists. The rest are not Marxists."

Several young men were in that same church the next Sunday, and I asked them about the Revolution. Some of them supported it. Others only halfway. Others were opposed. Some wanted "a third way." A girl said: "We have our eyes set on the revolutionaries of Latin America. . ." I said: "Well, set your eyes on Cuba because most of those revolutionaries have their eyes set on this Revolution."

A young man who acts as sacristan says that thanks to God the Cuban Church was purified. . . It doesn't meddle in politics —before maybe it did meddle—and in his opinion, it is the best Church in Latin America. Don't I agree? I told him to pardon my frankness, but that it seemed to me that this was the most reactionary Church in Latin America. That it was not a question of *not* getting involved in politics but of getting involved in politics and being revolutionary. And that I did not have the impression that this Church had been persecuted, or that it was purified.

A young Catholic in front of my hotel: "They could put out a Catholic publication if they wanted to. The State would give them the paper and the press, as it does with the Protestants. But they don't want to, because they would have to make some allusion to social matters, to cite at least some encyclical. And this would irritate the faithful—unless they cite an encyclical to attack the Revolution . . . which they can't do. So they prefer not to publish. All they publish is a parish leaflet that is purely liturgical, and the State pays for it."

Another young Catholic (who supports the Revolution): "They accept few Catholics into the University. Just a few, I think, so that people can't say there aren't any." "In the Communist Youth?" "In the Communist Youth they ask about religion. They accept you depending on your answer to the question about religion."

"And if a Catholic wanted to attend the University or join the Communist Junta and said that he is Catholic but at the same time totally revolutionary, that he is a hundred per cent with the Revolution, and that he is as revolutionary as Camilo Torres, and that he feels that the duty of the Christian is to make the Revolution, and that he would give his life for this Revolution. . . Would they refuse him admission because he was a Catholic?" "If he talks to them as you have talked, I don't think so." "And wouldn't it be better if they didn't accept Catholics, not because they are Catholics but because they don't consider them revolutionaries?" He thinks for a while, and answers: "Of course. . ."

I was riding on a bus with Cintio. We saw the sea deep blue, some boats with their wakes of white foam, and on the other side of the bay the great white lighthouse and the fortress of La Cabaña where the political prisoners are kept. Cintio said to me: "Many idealistic young men died there against the wall. They died shouting: 'LONG LIVE CHRIST THE KING.' They thought they were dying for Christ, and they didn't know that they were being used by the agents of the CIA and the Batistans. That is what is so sad."

》》》

Havana, 31 May 1963
"Year of Organization"

Comrades of the Factory
Motorcycle Assembly
Automotive Unit 0–1 E.C.
Lorraine No. 102
Santiago de Cuba

Comrades:

There is an error in your planning. The workers who are responsible for the production of any article do not have any rights over these plans. Bakers do not have a right to more bread nor do cement workers to more bags of cement; you don't have a right to more motorcycles.

The day when I visited you I observed that you were using one of the tricycles as a kind of little bus, a thing that I criticized right then; a member of the Communist Youth went off on organization duties on a motorcycle, a thing that I doubly criticized, given the unwarranted use of the vehicle and the incorrect attitude of using time paid for by society and for tasks that one supposes are an additional delivery of time to society, in an absolutely voluntary way. In the course of the conversation I made it clear that I was going to concern myself with seeing about the conditions of payment; and if it were possible, to supply machines to some workers and technicians.

On turning over to the Minister of Transportation the whole task of distribution and merchandising of the machines, it is hard to see how this can come about.

With revolutionary greetings from
FATHERLAND OR DEATH WE SHALL OVERCOME

Commander Ernesto Che Guevara

»»»

The poet Heberto Padilla told me about the letter that he wrote to Fidel, because nobody would give him work after the magazine *Olive Green* (of the Armed Forces) attacked him severely for his book *Out of the Game*. The book had won the Writers' Union Prize. The Union expressed its disagreement

99

with the jury, because it felt that the book was against the Revolution, although it did not fail to award the prize and to publish the book. *Olive Green* then attacked it, saying, among other things, that Padilla had misappropriated funds of the Revolution in a foreign diplomatic post, which was counter-revolutionary, and that he was even an agent of the CIA. "This was ridiculous," Padilla said, "because a CIA agent in Cuba gets shot; he is not denounced in an article on literary criticism in the magazine of the Armed Forces." Because of those attacks he lost his job on *Granma* and couldn't find work anywhere else. Many friends also shunned him, he said. He had to live on his wife's earnings: After a year of being in this state he decided to write to Fidel.

Fidel answered him within twenty-four hours, sending him to the Rector of the University of Havana so that Padilla could tell him what he wanted to work at. Whatever job he chose he would be given. "I think that Fidel was impressed by a paragraph of my letter, in which I said that whatever the opinion of me and my book, I ought not to be denied work in my country, socialist Cuba. And the fact is that in Cuba work is sacred, it is not taken away even from a bad worker; this is one of the great principles of the Revolution."

»»»

THE OLD BARDS SAY

—Heberto Padilla

Don't forget it, poet.
In whatever place and time
you make
or endure History,
there will always be lying in wait
some dangerous poem.

Interview with Ernesto Cardenal

A young woman told me that in the Humanities School of the University of Havana they gave the students the following assignment: "An Imaginary Interview with Ernesto Cardenal." (If you had the opportunity of knowing Ernesto Cardenal personally, what questions would you ask him?) I told her that I was very eager to know what questions they had wanted to ask me, and that I also wanted to answer them. She brought them to me later. She removed, she said, those that were repetitious or similar. This is what the young people asked:

—If you accept the theory of evolution ("Psalm 103"), how do you explain the concept of original sin of two persons or two peoples or two races, etc.: Adam and Eve?

—What do you think about violence (Latin American guerrilla fighting) as a way of defeating tyrants?

—What do you think of marriage for Catholic priests? Could it happen without lessening the love of God?

—What are your living conditions in Solentiname?

—Do you consider that in every underdeveloped country poetry should be denunciatory?

—Do you still subscribe to the idea that poetry can save the world?

—What do you think of the division into three periods that José M. Oviedo makes of his published work?

—Would you agree with those who say that your theological concept, rather than orthodoxically Catholic, is Spinozan?

—Do you admit having been influenced by English-language poetry, especially that of Robert Lowell, William Carlos Williams, and Thomas Merton?

—In what degree do you feel yourself an heir of Rubén Darío?

—What do you think of the poetry of William Agudelo, Coronel Utrecho, and Nicanor Parra?

—What attitude should a Latin American priest have with regard to the revolutionary struggles on the continent?

—Are you satisfied with the structures that you have achieved in your published works, or do you plan to experiment with new ways of expression?

—Do you think that there are contacts between Christian ideas and the struggle for freedom of the peoples of Latin America?

—What do you think of Camilo Torres?

—Do you think that Marxism and Christianity are two currents of thought totally opposed?

—What do you wish to express in your poem "The Lost Cities" when you ask in the last verse: "But will the past Katunes return some day?"

—Hasn't your work or your life in some way been affected by the Spanish mystics (Fray Luis de Leon, Santa Teresa, or San Juan de la Cruz), or do you feel closer to Thomas Merton?

—Do you consider yourself an ascetic or a mystic? Do you aspire to be a mystic?

—For you, in poetry or in religion, does every task have a sense of eternal search, without any thought ever of an answer or a definitive find, and therefore without there being any talk of certain error or success? Do you think there is need for a certain response that guarantees something?

—Can you explain "exteriorism"? What relation does it have with conversational poetry?

—What was your objective when you reworked in poetical paraphrases pre-Hispanic texts?

—How do you explain the relation between your poetic work, so attuned to the reality of Latin America, and your life of withdrawal?

—Do you accept the description, a compromised mystic?

—Don't you believe that an excessive interest in pre-Columbian themes brings you dangerously close to a certain nativism which, through the narrowness of its view, was a failure as a literary current in our continent only a few decades ago?

—Do you think that your poetry (for example: *Psalms;* "Gethsemani, Ky."; the poem on the death of Thomas Merton, etc.) could be considered Pop?

—Describe the current tendencies of Nicaraguan literature.

—If you had to mention a single poet among those whom you most admire, who would it be?

—If you were granted the possibility of carrying out an act—just one—of absolute power, what would you do?

—Aside from being a poet and a priest—which we think in your case are identical concepts—what would you have liked to be?

—What have you tried to say, ultimately, in your poetry?

»»»

A black poet:

—I used to sell vegetables and meat in the market before the Revolution, when I was fifteen years old, to be able to live, and I studied at night. Since the triumph of the Revolution I have devoted myself completely to cultural and artistic matters: theater, poetry, radio scripts. For four years I have been writing these poems that I bring to you. Before that I wrote poems but I tore them up. (He showed me the poems.)

A Mass

Sunday, at the church door, two beggars—two aged white men, very clean, sitting on the ground, holding out their hands to all those who were going in. "Two beggars? Unbelievable!" said the poet Pablo Armando Fernández when I told him. "Why there aren't any beggars in Cuba! Those must be the only two beggars in Cuba. If they are old men they must be retired and they certainly have pensions. And what do they want the money for? Here everyone has more money than he needs. And they must have their ration books just like every human being in Cuba. And why did they choose a church? The 'worms' must have put them there, so that they could say that we still have beggars. Or so that people, on the way to Mass, could feel that they were still in the old regime. . ."

The fact is that there were two beggars at the church door. (And I saw no others anywhere in Cuba.) In the church, very few people. Serious, sad faces. Almost everyone was old or a child. Few adolescents. No blacks.

A priest announced at the microphone that I had arrived, invited to take part in the literary contest of the House of the Americas. I went up to the altar without knowing what I was going to preach, and not even knowing whether I ought to preach. I didn't dare speak frankly about the Revolution. To preach the Gospel without alluding to any social or political reality would be false. Wasn't it better not to say anything? But was I going to celebrate Mass in Cuba without daring to give a sermon? In Managua at times I was afraid when I preached. But there it was because of the government; here it was because of the people. Here I saw myself in a strange situation; my preaching, which had always been subversive, here turned out to be too official-sounding. (I didn't want to be taken for a government agent.)

The Gospel of that day dealt with riches: "It is easier for a camel to pass through the eye of a needle. . ." I then spoke against wealth. There was no problem, it was sufficient to say what was most traditional in Catholicism to be very radical: the rich are excluded from the Kingdom of God. One can not be rich and a Christian (serving two masters). A devotion to riches makes it impossible to love God. It also makes it impossible to love one's neighbor. Money hardens the heart, etc. But here I saw myself in a strange situation: this Biblical denunciation of riches had no reality. For the first time in my life, it turned out to be superfluous. And there it was that I had to make an allusion, at least discreet, to the Revolution. I said: "But at least you can give thanks to God that here there are no longer any rich men. Elsewhere there still exists the contradiction that there are rich Christians and a rich Church." It seemed to me that some listeners showed surprise, others showed outrage or indignation.

When Mass was over, a group of faithful surrounded me in the sacristy: ladies, girls, some young students, two or three children, an elderly gentleman. It was the ladies especially who did the talking. They interrupted one another: "Father, we want to tell you the truth because you are a foreigner and perhaps they have not told you the truth about Cuba. . ." "To judge by your sermon, you can not be well informed. . . It is true that there are no longer any rich people, and that, as you said, is a good thing, although not all rich people were evil, there were good rich people too . . . but you mustn't believe there are no rich people in Cuba, the communist leaders now are the new rich." "If you could see how the communist leaders live, the privileges that they have. . . And you'll say that this is an exception? No. The rule!" "They all have new cars, and we take the bus," said another of the ladies. "And they get a bigger amount of food, while tonight I don't know if I'll have anything for supper in my house." "I have a communist next door to me, and he eats better," said another.

"There used to be a great abundance here," said another lady. "The food was very good here. Oh, you should see all those streets full of restaurants. Anybody could eat what he wanted. . ." "And the poor?" I asked. "The poor? There were restaurants for poor people, too. Where they ate very well, too. . ." I was glad when a student interrupted; I could hear a young voice (and he looked like a revolutionary): "Production is increasing more and more. They are constantly producing more milk, more tobacco, more meat. And the greater the production the greater the scarcities. Everything is for export, and we're left with nothing. . ."

"Look at this child!" interrupted a red-haired lady very angrily. "He is eight years old, and there's no milk for him.

He gets an adult ration, and he needs more for his development!" She points to a little blond boy who is holding her
hand and looking up at her with big startled eyes. It was very
hot in the sacristy, and I was soaked in sweat. The ladies were
all fanning me at the same time, affectionately. And while they
were all fanning me they all talked to me at once. The fanning
was rapid, the talking was rapid. "Poor Father, you're so
warm!" "You say that anyone can criticize Fidel in a public
park without anything happening to him? Who told you such
a thing? Nonsense! Try it and see what happens. They'll carry
you off to jail. They might even shoot you. . . Do they still
shoot people? They certainly do. Maybe tonight they'll be
shooting someone. And be careful of what you say, all the
hotel employees are spies, they are hired by the Department
of the Interior."

"That one is leaving Cuba." They pointed to a girl in a
corner. She said: "Yes, and I've been working for a year in the
country. Because those who are going to leave Cuba lose their
jobs and can't get work anywhere else, only in the country,
until they let you go. And there I have suffered horrible things.
And I have another year to go." "I'm going to send my two
sons to Spain," said a lady of about forty, "because with the
scholarships that they give here I see them only two weeks in
a year. They practically take young children away from you. I
have suffered for my children. I didn't bear them to have them
taken away from me." "My father fought in the Sierra. Now
he is in Miami. . ." "We were very happy at the fall of Batista.
Don't you think that we're defending Batista. But we don't
like all these changes." "Don't think that the people are in
favor of all this. The demonstrations are not spontaneous.
They put pressure on all us young people to go to them. And
when we get there they put banners in our hands. . . The
blood donations for Peru? Yes, that was spontaneous." "Indeed
it was. But because it was something humanitarian!" "I'm in
favor of the Revolution. . ." said one girl, and another interrupted: "Well, I'm not in favor of the Revolution!" "I'm in
favor of the Revolution," the first girl said again, "but these
people have betrayed the Revolution."

I asked them if they didn't at least believe that the great
social victories of the Revolution were fundamentally Christian. Literacy campaigns. . . "There are still people who don't
know how to read. I'm sure of it because I was a literacy

worker," said the girl who was leaving Cuba. "The situation in the country, you say? Those are the ones who are worst off. And they're the ones who complain most." "Free education? It's not free, because they make you cut sugar cane. That's a way of paying for your studies. And you can't choose the profession you want. Besides, they discriminate against Catholics."

A mulatto girl with yellow hair, slender and pretty, said that she was "almost revolutionary" and that once in a little town in Las Villas the communists threw her down and kicked her and spat on her. She and others were preparing the people for the visit of the bishop ("Of course we ought to have notified the authorities that we were going to go from house to house.") She didn't hate them, she said, because they had kicked her and spat on her, and while they were striking her on the ground, she kept telling them that she didn't hate them.

Afterward they talked about the prisoners. One girl said: "They protest about prisons in other countries, and their own are just as bad. They stripped me naked when I was going to see my brother. The cake that my mother had made with such loving care they ruined with bayonet thrusts to see if it had any message." The lady who had the scared little blond boy by the hand: "We can't stand any more! We've had *eleven years* of this. Imagine what it's like to go through this for eleven years. To have to stand *that man!*" A woman said she was against Batista and that at the beginning she was for the Revolution, but that this is worse than Batista's regime. And that now she would prefer Batista. She added: "Even though it was a horror." Others disagreed, especially the young people: "No, it's neither this nor that." "My husband was jailed by Batista, and afterward he was jailed by the Revolution. . ." "They came down from the Sierra Maestra with rosaries and scapularies. . ."

They told me that during Holy Week of the previous year they had blocked off the street where the church is to make it a play street, and they put loudspeakers with music outside the church to interfere with the services. "Father, they've got you fooled!" I took my leave, and the girl who had been spat upon by the communists walked along a few blocks with me. She said: "These people who told you all those things in the sacristy are the brightest and boldest ones, and they can talk. The other ones, who didn't say anything to you, and they're the majority, have gone muttering around in the streets, scandalized, saying that you are a procommunist priest. That's what they said up and down the street; I can still hear them." She told me that she had converted to Catholicism and that before that she had been an "integrated one." I asked her what that meant, and she said: "Integrated ones are those who are integrated with the Revolution: the communists or those who are for communism. Afterward I belonged to a secular institute, which has been dissolved because of certain problems that it had . . . not problems with the Revolution, but of another kind that I'm going to discuss here. I've gone to the sugar cane fields and all the farm work, but I'm not for them."

"Who are they?" "The communists." I told her that I thought that the Christians ought to become integrated with this Revolution. She asked surprised: "So you can be a Catholic without being anticommunist? I didn't know that . . . Pius XII forbade all collaboration with communism." I quoted to her the very different words of John XXIII on Marxism. "Where did he say that? . . . I'm going to look up that encyclical."

We said good-by. A young man was with her, walking behind us, and I thought that he too would say good-by to me, but instead he took leave of her and said to me: "I am going to walk with you a few blocks more. May I?" Dark, with a light fuzz on his lip, and a clear gaze. When she had left he began to talk: "Father, I was in the sacristy, and I heard everything that those people were saying to you, and I don't agree with them. Even though I am a Catholic, I don't agree. Don't you believe what they said. They said that in Batista's time they were revolutionaries but that they are against the present regime. I don't believe they were revolutionaries. I could indeed be unhappy with this regime because I am the son of a Batista lieutenant. And in those days we were well off. A lieutenant of Batista could have all he wanted. And a boy, the son of a lieutenant of Batista as I was, even though I was very young then, could have all he wanted. But now I'm a Christian; before, I wasn't one, and I'm the only Christian in my family, and I see that a Christian must defend this Revolution, as you told them very well in the sacristy. That way of talking is not Christian. When I became a convert I got to know what real Christianity is. Even though they call me a 'communist.' That girl who went away is a friend of mine; she says she's a revolutionary, but how can she talk that way . . . the Revolution has done marvelous things in Cuba. I'd like to talk with you later, I can tell you many things. When can I come to your hotel?"

I reached the National Hotel at lunch time and went directly to the dining room. There I found the poet Margaret Randall with her three small children, and she greeted me with a kiss as she always did. I sat at the table with them, and she told me that, because it was Sunday, she was with her children. That every week end she took them out of school (where they had boarding scholarships) so that they would not lose contact with the family. I told her about a lady who was going to send her children to Spain because with this system she saw them only two weeks a year, and she said: "There are all kinds of scholarships. The farmers whose children have city scholarships see them only once a year, but for two months, not two weeks. And this lady, who can send her children to study in Spain, is probably not from the countryside. People who live in the city can have their children on a half-boarding scholarship, as I do, bringing them home Saturdays and Sundays, besides the two months' vacation. And other scholarships are for day students, who live at home. And besides, it's not necessary to have the children on a scholarship."

I told Margaret that I had just come from saying Mass, although I didn't think she would be interested, because she was a communist. But she was keenly interested and wanted me to tell her what my Cuban Mass was like and what I preached about.

»»»

THE 1958 EXILE

—*Antón Arrufat*

The one who has to leave
takes the sheet off the bed.
He will wear his clothes again,
he will put them in the cardboard suitcase
or just in a bundle on his shoulder
like the neighborhood laundress.

He will travel once more.
His friends leave him with a smile
and flee from him.
They all are left with company
and he leaves.
Nobody will go to say good-by to him,
his parents are under the ground.
Listen, it's myself I'm talking to,
but it would be terrible otherwise.
Wake up, the plane is going to leave.

»»»

Other notes:

"Is there sexual freedom among the young?" "It's coming in, but that freedom is not Marxist."

Luis, the chauffeur: "Among the floats that they are preparing for the carnival there is one that will reproduce a discriminatory barbershop from the past; another one about unemployment, another one about evictions, and another about the political corruption of that era."

They also told me stories about Che: A plane came to bombard them, and he said: "If you're scared of it, go and hide." Everyone ran to seek shelter, and he went right on writing. Whatever cigars he got were distributed immediately. They never saw him set aside any cigars for his own use.

Once they were carrying some wounded men through the Sierra, and some of the troops wanted to surround Che to protect him; but he pushed them away and ordered them to go to the rear, and he went ahead in the lead. He also took care of the farmers. He would sometimes halt the march forward to look after a sick person.

Oliva said that last year, for the first time in a pastoral letter, the bishops condemned the blockade, which had been in force for eight years, and they condemned it in a rather gentle way. But there were priests who, even so, refused to read the letter, and there were faithful who walked out during the reading, furious because the Church was "taking the side of Communism." He also said: "The error of Catholics was to identify Christianity with anticommunism. The only thing they cared about was finding out if the Revolution was communist." "And haven't you also fallen into the error of identifying Marxism with antireligion?" "They began it first."

Many Catholics were irritated by the shift of the Christmas festivities to the 26th of July, and they thought it was a scheme to put an end to the Christian celebration of Christmas. (As if these festivities had anything to do with the Christian celebration of Christmas.)

"For the country people it was a great surprise to see city people come out into the country to help them in their work. And an even greater surprise to see soldiers arrive to build houses for them, dig wells for them, open up roads for them. They thought they were dreaming."

In a letter to León Felipe, Che spoke of "the failed poet that I have inside of me." In the Sierra Maestra, Che would read Neruda to the troops at night.

A Teacher

At Paz Espejo's house again. She told me that Fidel had just
been at a bus terminal solving a transportation problem: "He
arrived, from what I was told, to have a meeting with the
drivers. The first thing he did, as he always does, was to ask
them who were the leaders, and then he said to them: 'You
go outside, because I want to hear the complaints.' The drivers
then gave him their complaints. Ten hours a day was too
much. They also need a few minutes for a snack, for a cup of
coffee. Because otherwise they got sleepy and, being tired, they
had to go slower to avoid accidents. Fidel stayed with them
until seven in the morning. He had breakfast with them. And
when he left he had the hours, the routes, the rest periods all
planned and all problems solved. He had gone to the meeting
because a woman in the street had told him that the buses
on a certain route weren't operating right and that was why
she couldn't get to work on time."

And she added: "It's amusing how Fidel is always against
the leaders and in favor of the people. It's as if he were still
in the Sierra Maestra fighting against the authorities. I don't
think that Fidel has got used to the idea that he is now the
supreme authority. Psychologically he still feels himself in the
Sierra Maestra."

I told her what Cintio had told me: that Fidel is the head
of the opposition in Cuba. And she said: "An Italian journalist said that: that here Fidel was the head of the government
and also of the opposition. Fidel is everywhere," she said. "He
usually comes to meetings at one in the morning and stays
until seven." I asked her when he slept, and she said laughing:
"He sleeps when he's sleepy."

Fidel eats at the University with the students, and he
lines up just like them in the dining room, with his tray. He
eats in the factory dining rooms with the workers. For a long
time he used to eat at midnight in the kitchen of the Habana
Libre Hotel with the cooks and waiters.

Paz Espejo is a Chilean, a Marxist, and she teaches philosophy at the University of Havana. She is very enthusiastic
about the dialogue between Catholics and Marxists that goes

on in Europe, and she regretted that it was not going on also in Cuba. She said: "I, a Marxist teacher from Cuba, lived in a Dominican monastery in France in a room next to that of Father Congar, and we understood each other marvelously."

I took notes as she said: "Here everyone is religious, in spite of Marxism. Among the people a kind of syncretism is being created that is very curious: a mixture of Catholicism and Marxism. Both of them rather superficial. Dogmatic Catholicism was never profound; neither is the Marxism. Believe me, here in Cuba at bottom *all* (or almost all) are believers, although few say so. Scientific materialism is not deeply accepted. Only superficially. Catholicism, too, had been accepted only superficially."

And after a pause: "The opportunity that the Church lost in Cuba with this Revolution was a unique one. A Catholic revolution, which was neither communist nor Marxist, the only great world revolution made by Catholics, some of them militant Catholics, and with no communist or Marxist having fought in it in the years of struggle: and it was pushed into communism by the United States and the Catholic Church! Fortunately for us. It is unbelievable that the Catholics didn't take advantage of this Revolution!"

We talked about the Cuban Church. She told me that when her friend Father Blanquart, the worker-priest of France, was invited to come to Cuba the priests wouldn't let him celebrate Mass, and he had to celebrate it in a private chapel. The Nuncio told him: "It's better this way, because a Mass said before a congregation of that kind perhaps would not have been valid." "That's my worry," I said to her, "whether my Mass in San Juan de Letrán was valid." She had met a French priest who, on seeing what Cuban Catholicism was like, refused to preach in Catholic churches and chose instead a Protestant church.

She said that Father Blanquart told her that the Catholics of Matanzas complained about the government because it did not authorize them to import ballpoint pens to give out in Sunday school. And he had said to them: "While atheistic materialism is replacing material stimulation by moral stimulation, you are complaining that they won't allow you to teach catechism with material stimulation." "They would have called that persecution," said Oliva. And she added: "When visiting priests come they don't meet with Catholics or with other priests but with revolutionaries, in this house or in other homes like this one."

They told me about Father Sardiña, who was the chaplain in the Sierra Maestra and a Commander in the Rebel Army, and a great friend of Fidel, and who is now dead. He used to say: "Here we do not have the Church of Silence but the Silence of the Church." Paz said again: "This people is always religious, but now the religious impulse is channeled into the Revolution." She told us that she saw in a clinic a sign that some workers had made at the time of the failure to reach the sugar cane goal: "We are with You in Your grief, Fidel," the You and Your in capitals as if it were addressed to God. And Oliva, who was also a Marxist, laughed and said: "I saw in a barracks in a sugar cane camp a mystical Che, looking very much like the Heart of Jesus that used to be seen in many houses and that is still in my house."

"While we are getting less religious, you are getting more so," I said. And Paz: "I think the greatest danger of the Revolution is theocracy." I told her that I found in the Revolution the same defects as in the Church: clericalism, Phariseeism, sanctimoniousness. Also that in Cuba it's very easy to distinguish the true revolutionaries from the false ones by the way in which they talk of the Revolution: the true revolutionaries criticize it, the false revolutionaries don't dare to, all errors they deny, they find excuses, they defend them. And she said, raising her voice and looking out at the street as if she were talking for the benefit of the whole neighborhood: "Well, all the defects of the Revolution I shout from this terrace as though I had a loudspeaker here in my house, and that's what should be done! Outside of Cuba I would die for the Cuban Revolution, but here I criticize its defects. Here I belong to the opposition, like Fidel."

I said that the *Populorum*, published in *Critical Thought*, was being read in a study circle at San Juan de Letrán, and she found it a good sign for Cuba that a Papal encyclical published in a Communist journal should be studied in a parish.

Paz said: "We can give Christians more social consciousness, which is not their forte. They can give us the principal contribution that Christianity has given to the world, which is love. And we can understand one another. You believe that Jesus of Nazareth is God, magnificent! Allow us to believe that Lenin is a marvelous person. The only thing we ask of you is that your religious faith does not make you counter-revolutionaries. You will have the right to ask of us that our economic planning does not make us antireligious. With regard to transcendence we can have our differences, and we're not going to come to blows over that. But what we *do* have to agree about is private property, and that nobody should be allowed to exploit another man or rob the worker of the product of his work. The Papal encyclicals uphold the right of private property. Shall we be able to agree on this?"

I said that for the Holy Fathers property in common was more perfect than private property. That Saint Benedict in his rule speaks of "the baneful evil of private property." That the early Christians lived in a community in which there was no "thine" or "mine," no rich or poor, and that the religious orders had been established to live this ideal. And that the economic system of the Gospel is: "He who hath two cloaks, let him give one to him who hath none." As for transcendence? I remembered what the poet Coronel had told me not long before in Solentiname: "Christian faith consists in believing that the revolution does not end in this world."

»»»

Haydée Santamaría told me that they have had very great sufferings in this Revolution, so great that several times she has wanted to die: "And not only before the triumph of the Revolution. Also after the triumph. The last time was when Che died. I didn't want to go on living. And Fidel consoled me. He said: 'People have to live.' And he also said: 'People have to work to forget.' He has always given us courage in our failures."

Che's Pilot

Supper with Rosi at the home of José Luis. A modest middle-class house. José Luis is a pilot. He told me that he stopped school at eleven because he couldn't pay the tuition, and he went to work in a bakery. But he loved airplanes, and he wanted to be a pilot. Sundays he would go to the airport to see the planes up close, and to touch their wings when no one was looking. One day a pilot saw him and told him he'd pay him something if he'd wash a plane for him. He washed it trembling with emotion. Afterward he managed to get a job at the airport as a plane washer, and he was very happy with the job even though he earned less than in the bakery. Later he was a mechanic's helper, and he began to learn about planes. And finally he learned to fly. When the Revolution triumphed he was a pilot in the Cuban Airline.

José Luis was the pilot who took Che on his trip around Africa that lasted four months. I asked him to tell me about Che. He told me that when they were leaving for Africa Che had no socks because his last pair had worn out and his ration card didn't authorize him to have a new pair for some months. It never occurred to him to ask for new socks if this was not authorized, and so he went without socks and wore high boots. And that's the way he was, going to go off to Africa at the head of an official delegation, but a few moments before the take-off someone learned of this and obtained a pair of socks and insisted that Che accept them.

Che would not accept anything to which his ration card did not entitle him. And besides, the question of clothes was something of absolutely no interest to him. (José Luis laughed.) He wasn't dirty, but he always looked a mess. His olive green clothes could be faded, and the pants one kind of green and the shirt another shade. And he would show up like that at the most elegant official reception. His shirt might be tucked in on the right side where he carried his pistol, but the rest of it would be hanging out. In those four months in Africa José Luis had talked a lot with Che. In the evenings at the hotel Che would play chess with the men, read to them, or indoctrinate them politically.

"He used to tell us that socialism was above all a revolution in habits and mentality. A revolution in the spirit. In his eyes the true revolutionary was the one who acted for other people, who thought of others, who sacrificed himself for the community. To be a revolutionary was above all to have a great spirit of sacrifice. The sacrifices of the Sierra Maestra had to be repeated in daily life. He was always talking about sacrifice. The leader must sacrifice the most. To aspire to be a leader should mean to aspire to lead an uncomfortable life; not to aspire to have privileges or to live better than the rest of the people: these had been the criteria of the old society. The revolutionary ought to suffer in his own person the suffering of every other person, he ought to be sensitive to any injustice. He ought to be a rebel against any authoritarian imposition and to uphold discussion, criticism, self-criticism. Above all, the revolutionary had to be very human. And to have love. He would say: 'Who has said that Marxism has no soul?' The most important thing was the creation of the new man, the man of the twenty-first century. This new man was the man of solidarity, devoted to others. In capitalist society the people disintegrated, then scattered in all directions like fragments of a grenade. The formation of a new conscience in man was for him more important than production. A merely economic socialism, without this new conscience, did not interest him, he said. Markets, money, material interests, these were the categories of the old society. The psychological incentives for production should not be material stimuli but moral stimuli. Labor should not be sold like merchandise but offered as a gift to the community. The happiness of all men was the ideal of the revolutionary. Che was the prototype of this new man. He was very superior to other men but he did not feel himself superior. He thought that everyone was like him, and he was troubled when he saw that they were not. He did not want to have qualities that other people did not have. He had no vanity."

Carlitos, the nine-year-old son of José Luis, came up. He was in a special school for children who, even at that age, were being trained to be future swimming champions. José Luis told me that they had a school dining room where they were taught good table manners for when they would need to go abroad. I asked Carlitos what the school dining room was like. "I think it's great. They teach us how to eat, how you hold a fork, a knife, a week for each group." I asked him what they ate, and he said: "For breakfast, bread, cheese, coffee with milk. For lunch, rice, chick-peas, milk, chicken, meat, fish, chocolate ice cream." "And for supper?" "Chocolate ice cream, and they give us also rice, they give watercress salad, they give soup, yoghurt." I asked him where his school was, and he said: "We live in Miramar in a middle-class house. There were twenty-six of us, but they threw out two boys. We sleep in bunks. There are five in our room. The school is three blocks away, we have television, and those who behave well get to see it. I have to study hard because if I don't, I'm not allowed to swim. It's a swimming school. But I want to be a baseball player when I grow up."

His father asked him to tell me about the time that Che picked him up. "Che picked me up in his arms when I was two years old. It was during a speech by Fidel. Che carried me all around the platform." "You think you'd like to be like Che?" I asked him. "Yes, when I'm fifteen." Afterward Carlitos fell asleep. José Luis opened a bottle of champagne—we were in the Christmas season—which he had brought from Madrid on his last flight. We spoke about the Nicaraguan guerrilla fighters (whom he knew well) and about the Church in Latin America and in Cuba. He and his wife are Marxists and ex-Catholics. His wife teaches children, and she told me that there are teachers who try to take out of children's minds the idea of God. That when a child says "with the help of God . . ." they scold him and tell him not to say such a thing, that God does not exist. José Luis's wife doesn't do that, and she doesn't approve of it.

Afterward she said: "It seems to me very important for Catholic revolutionaries and Marxists in Latin America to come to an understanding. But how can they understand one another if education is nationalized there as it is in Cuba, and the Marxists make it an atheistic education because Marxism-Leninism is atheistic?" I thought for a while, and then I said: "To a question stated that way, I have no answer. I don't know."

»»»

CHE

—*Miguel Barnet*

Che, you know everything,
the twists and turns of the Sierra,
asthma on the cold ground
the platform
the surf in the night
and even what fruits
and yokes are made of.

It's not that I want to give you
a pen for a gun
but you are the poet.

In the Habana Libre

"When he was fifteen or sixteen my son was very religious and mystical," said Mrs. Jannette Debray in the Habana Libre. In the Yankee-ized dining room of the former Habana Hilton I was having lunch with the family of Regis Debray, a prisoner in Bolivia: his mother Jannette, his Venezuelan wife Elizabeth Burgos, his brother, his sister-in-law, and the French defense lawyer—all officially invited for the 26th of July. And Professor Paz Espejo was also with us. Lobster cocktail in a big goblet with ice and a Chilean Undurraga wine that Mrs. Jannette found as good as a good French wine. She told me that Regis, when he was a little boy, went to Mass with her every day, and that he always took communion, and that he scolded her if she didn't take communion: he would ask her why she hadn't wanted to eat the *little candy*. At sixteen he began to read Marxism. (The family was very Catholic, bourgeois— Paz Espejo informed me—and Mrs. Jannette was a Councilor of the City of Paris.) From an early age her son had great love for the poor, the humble, those who suffer, she went on. I asked her if he had joined the Communist party. "No, he didn't like them. He never joined the Party." He got his bachelor's degree with good grades, she said, and his parents wanted to give him a graduation present, and he asked for a trip to Miami. From Miami he went to Cuba. "He came to Cuba during the literacy campaign, and this was one of the finest and most emotional periods of the Revolution," said Paz Espejo, "and he went to work in the campaign in the Sierra Maestra. He was much impressed by the literacy campaign. He was also impressed by Che."

Paz said that Che's father (who was also in Cuba) had told her that his son was very religious as a child. And turning to me: "You ought to talk with the father so that he can tell you about Che's Catholicism." Paz also said that she had seen letters that Fidel had written to a girl in which he talked many times about God. And she also said that when Fidel was in prison on the Isle of Pines, after the assault on Moncada, and his little boy Fidelito came to see him in prison and asked him where were Abel, Boris, and the rest of the friends of Fidel who had died at Moncada, Fidel didn't tell the child that they were dead. He said: "They are in Heaven." Mrs. Jannette asked me which church was closest to the Habana Libre so that she could go to Mass. When we were saying good-by, Paz Espejo—who is a Marxist—told her that her son Regis was still a "mystic." And Mrs. Jannette, holding out her hand to me, asked me in a tearful voice to pray for him: *"Priez pour lui."*

»»»

"People abroad don't know that in Cuba there are Communists in jail," I said to my friend.

"Yes, for conspiring against Fidel. Three times, and each time there have been arrests. The first attempt was a very strong one. The second was less strong, the third even less. Now they no longer have any strength." He told me that the conspiracies were made public and that the judges' decisions were even broadcast on television.

"Here everything is publicized," he said laughing. "Fidel doesn't like secrecy. The public heard the conversations of the conspirators, which had been taped. Before they could defend themselves they began to hear the record of their own voices, and they had to accept the evidence. It was amusing because one of them said: "How do we know they don't have an apparatus to tape our conversations." And they did indeed have one. He was talking at the door of his house, and the mike was on a light post in front of his house. They said that they were counting on the aid of the Russian Ambassador to get free of Fidel. The Ambassador later was discreetly withdrawn by Russia. He told me I ought to read Fidel's speech against "sectarianism" (old-time communism).

»»»

"People easily manage to forget the past," said Cintio. "There are unhappy people. Common people now unhappy because they forget how awful things used to be."

Sectarianism

They brought me Fidel's speech against sectarianism. It was at the time of the fall of Aníbal Escalante and his group, who were trying to get rid of Fidel. Fidel said: "There is no question that we have great weaknesses, because it would make absolutely no sense, it makes no sense, in the conditions of the Cuban Revolution, that a worker, a member of a co-operative, a farmer should be unhappy.

"A farmer to whom we have given land, whom we have freed from the rent that he had to pay to the landowners, to whom we gave credit, workers whom we have freed from seasonal layoffs, for whom we have built schools, for whom we are building towns, how is it possible? What explanation could a malcontent have for all these groups who have been so benefited by the Revolution? What reason could there be for the slightest discontent except our own errors, our mistakes, our ill-treatment, our scorn of the people, our insolence toward the people? Because one has to be insolent toward the people to stop in any town and say: These are all counterrevolutionaries, bring the gallows, what are these manifestations but manifestations of petty-bourgeois spirit? That is the true petty-bourgeois spirit because the petty bourgeois, when the people is annoyed as a result of his errors, does not blame himself, he blames the people, and then he believes that he is the only revolutionary and that the people is antirevolutionary.

"The comrade who has stopped in a square and who has said such a thing has shown that he has the spirit and the reactions of a consummate petty bourgeois who seeks to blame the masses for his own errors and who ends up accusing the masses of counterrevolutionary acts when the masses are turning not against the revolution but against its arbitrary actions.

"The worst is that we end up depriving the masses of being counterrevolutionary, because if the masses are counterrevolutionary we are absolute idiots, because we would have set about making a revolution where there was no room for a revolution. But that's not so, because in no contemporary revolution have the masses given so many proofs of support to the Revolution and of enthusiasm as the Cuban masses have given to our Revolution. How can we now reach the conclusion that our stupidities of all kinds are not the causes of the displeasure of the people and that on the other hand we are very revolutionary while the masses are very counterrevolutionary?

"It is evident that if the Revolution has freed those classes from exploitation and if those classes were not one hundred per cent for the Revolution, it is not the masses but we who would be to blame, the weakness would be in our work with the masses, the weakness would be in our anarchy, in our tendency toward authoritarianism, toward despotism, in the lack of political tact, in the lack of skill of us who instead of trying to join together for the Revolution and win the people over to the Revolution, should turn every day against the popularity of the Revolution, treating the people with kicks and creating for ourselves ten thousand enemies.

"The weakness is in us, and we have to begin by understanding that, that we are very weak as politicians, we are very weak in our revolutionary work, and that we have to improve the quality of revolutionary work on all fronts and in every department. That is the conclusion that we must reach.

"How can we blame the enemy? The enemy takes advantage of our weaknesses, but no enemy radio, no enemy campaign will prosper where it does not have a reason for prospering, where there are not many people aggrieved, discontented, displeased, not with the injustice that has been done to them but with the injustice that they have seen done to others and that they think may tomorrow be done to them.

"And that is the mentality that has created among us Cubans an outbreak of barbarous anarchy. Not socialism, anarchism; anarchism is what we were seeing in many places, not socialism. And when a worker is unhappy about this, he has reason to be unhappy; because he does not approve of depravity, and depravity is not socialism. He does not approve of arbitrariness, and arbitrariness is not socialism. He does not approve of disorder and anarchy, and disorder and anarchy are not socialism. What nobody has a right to do is to try to smuggle depravity, disorder, anarchism, and despotism in as socialism; because then the masses react against that. Don't believe that the masses, when I spoke on the 26th, reacted only to the problem of sectarianism. The masses put together all the problems, the abuses, the arbitrariness, the excesses of authority, the jailing of people without cause. The politics of abuse, of arbitrariness, of imposition, of scorn of the people, of ignorance of the masses. The people understood in the declaration of sectarianism the compendium of a series of errors of the Revolution which we have to overcome, and that therefore this problem of Aníbal is part of the problem; it is, if you wish, the moment of switching from a path of errors to a path of successes."

The Psychiatric Hospital

One place where the tenderness of the Revolution may be seen is in the Psychiatric Hospital of Havana. The insane are in pavilions with floors as shiny as those of a luxury hotel. The rooms are attractively decorated, and each has a private bath with bathtubs of marble from the Isle of Pines. (A Cuban friend who went with me said: "You see? This is the way rich men's bathtubs used to be. Now the marble is for the crazy people. Maybe you'll say that this Revolution is crazy, right? But the Revolution was made also for the mentally ill. They all get the treatment that one would wish for his mother or sister.")

In the reception rooms, where the insane see their visitors, there are sofas and luxurious armchairs, paintings of modern art, fresh flowers. They have movies, theater, a ballroom where they dance in couples, a library, a music room, fields for all sports. I saw two madmen playing chess. Others in a class. Others were getting political instruction. There was a beauty parlor for the ladies, operated by women patients. A barbershop, also operated by men patients. In the dining room, equally clean and gleaming, they served themselves with trays in cafeteria style. There are five thousand patients, I was told, and ninety per cent of them work. They themselves do the cleaning and some of them take care of other patients. They do handicraft work, make furniture, toys, cradles. They grow flowers and supply flowers for the whole city of Havana; and they run a poultry farm with seventy thousand chickens, also for the consumption of the people of Havana. Some of them go out cutting sugar cane. There are patients who go out by the day to work in the city, and there are others who get passes to go home for the weekend. Of course, the hospital is free.

In an austere little room, which contrasted with the luxury of the hospital, was the office of the Director, a robust man with a thick black beard. He was Commander Bernabé Orgaz, one of the bearded ones of the Sierra Maestra and a Catholic. While he fought by Fidel's side during the day he would say the rosary at night with the troops. (The patient who showed me around the hospital was also a Catholic.)

When we took our leave a black singer, famous in the cabarets, sang over the loudspeakers some cabaret songs in our honor. The young man who accompanied her on the piano—we were told—was not insane: he was a musician who had once come to give a recital for the patients, and he so much enjoyed making them happy that he stayed in the hospital.

In one room there was a display of photographs that showed how this was a place of horror before the Revolution: disheveled, crazy people, in rags or naked, sitting in their own filth. (Besides they used to beat them, steal their food, and the male nurses raped the women patients.) I said to them: "I don't need to see photographs; I have seen the insane asylum in my own country."

»»»

My Nicaraguan friend Rosi López came again to see me and said: "I attended the wounded from the Playa Girón, and there was one who was dying from napalm burns: all you could see of his face was a slit where his mouth had been; and he told me through that slit that he was happy to die because he was dying in defense of the Revolution." Ernesto, the bootblack who got to know Camilo, also talked to me to-day about Playa Girón. He said: "Many, many people went there, without weapons, because they didn't have any. They heard about the invasion on the radio, and they jumped on a bus or a car, or walked along the highway. Many died there machine-gunned on the highway. They went without arms to fight against the invasion. Some of them found a gun on the way."

»»»

A newspaper reported that during vacation the seventy-five secondary schools in Oriente Province will have the following recreational programs: sixteen sports matches, seventy-one dance festivals, a hundred fifty excursions, nine hikes, twenty-seven big Sunday festivals, besides camping on the beaches for ten thousand vacationers.

»»»

The painter Portocarrero, in his apartment opposite my hotel, showed me a huge number of paintings: flowers or abstractions. He paints all day. The State supports him, and he doesn't need to do anything but paint. There are some other well-established painters who have the same privileges as he. The State acquires the paintings for offices, public buildings, embassies, or as gifts. The young painters have to work at other things besides their painting, but their other work is always related to their painting. He said: "In Cuba before the Revolution painters were starving to death."

Portocarrero showed me a photograph of his great ceramic mural in the Presidential Palace. He told me that at a reception some Russian or other communist delegates asked Fidel scornfully: "And this, what does it mean?" (Meaning: and this, what does it have to do with the Revolution?) Fidel answered: "Nothing. This doesn't mean a thing. It's just some madness stuff painted by a madman for some people who like this kind of madness, and it was sponsored by the madmen who made this Revolution."

The Isle of Youth

At the airport a huge somewhat faded sign: WELCOME TO THE ISLE OF YOUTH. The Isle of Pines, Stevenson's *Treasure Island,* is now the Isle of Youth. Here they have tried out, with young people from all over Cuba, the communist society of the future: without scarcity and without money. Here too are the seminarists of whom Monsignor Oves spoke, working in the quarries under the command of a Lieutenant Rabasa. As soon as we arrived I asked to see them. The members of the jury of the House of the Americas were staying in the Colony Hotel built by the Yankees for the superrich who didn't deign to pass through Havana on their way here. In the hotel with us were cane workers on vacation, many of them black, and workers on their honeymoon.

They took us to see the horrible jail that now is vacant and is soon to be demolished, they said, to build a school from its materials. It is an immense circle of twelve floors, with about a hundred cells on each floor. This is where Batista's political prisoners were kept, and afterward those of the Revolution. Cintio told me that he had come here to visit a relative who is now rehabilitated. Next to the circle there is another one-story jail, full of cages, where we saw the cell where Fidel had been jailed for two years after the assault on the Moncada Barracks. Batista once visited the prison and approached one cage, pleased with himself, thinking that the prisoners in it would acclaim him, but the prisoners were Fidel and the others of the "26th of July," and they insulted him.

Raquel said in Havana that after the triumph of the Revolution she worked four years in this prison (she still works in the Department of the Interior) and that it was a *horrible* job. "That murmur, Ernesto. I can still hear that murmur at six in the evening. An enormous murmur, when all the prisoners came out into the corridors of that heap of circular galleries one above the other. I couldn't stand it. I became ill. After that for a long time I had to see a psychiatrist." Her chin trembled when she spoke. She wouldn't talk about it any more.

The Martí house. Cintio wept when he saw the chain that

Martí brought from prison, then still fastened to one leg. "He was seventeen when they condemned him to work in the quarries. With one of those links he made himself a ring. It was a wedding ring . . . that of his marriage to Cuba. He was madly in love with Cuba (Cintio's voice trembled) although he was the son of a Spaniard. Since he was a little boy, his obsession was *his island*. He was the man who has loved Cuba most. My Cubans, he used to say. A sentence of his sums up his life: 'I suffered with love.' Another passion of his life was the poor. 'For them I work,' he would say. He talked of 'clutching the poor in a bundle.' "

A little old lady who was a niece of Martí showed us around the museum-house, and Cintio went on talking: "He was religious, but very anticlerical. He understood deeply the mystery of the Cross. He said: 'One must learn to die on the Cross every day.' He was convinced that there was a future life. He spoke often of eternity—according to him, eternity prevented life and tenderness from being useless. 'Death is a way and not an end.' They never called him Chief, or Leader, or gave him a military title. The titles they gave him, and still give him, are religious: the Apostle, the Master. He was an evangelical man, and his greatest tragedy was that he had to start a war; but he preached that it should be without hatred. War was to free the enemies. He spoke of joining men in patience and piety. War must be waged with 'charity, energy, and vigilance'—and charity came first. For him war was very grievous. His own father was Spanish. It was a war of love. War must be *cultured and wholesome,* he said. Not only heroic. He dreamt of an antimilitaristic republic, where one could discuss matters, with absolute respect for all the rights of the citizens, without class privileges and without discrimination, with culture and wealth divided equally. The government must be the 'supreme equity.' For him Cuba was the sacred isle of liberty. He had a premonition of what is going on now. . . That man was passing from the individual to the collective. The greatest kind of men, according to him, were those who sacrificed themselves for others. Fidel considers him the founder of this Revolution. He named his movement for Martí's birthday (July 26th), and he attacked Moncada on the centenary of that birth. And when the judges asked him who had instigated the attack, he answered: " 'José Martí.' "

Next to the sacred chain we saw a text of Martí: "The

pride with which I shake these chains will be worth more than all my future glories, for he who suffers for his country and lives for God, in this or other worlds, has true glory." The ring that was tightened around his ankle had been covered with blood and pus, Martí wrote.

The quarries of Martí brought again to my mind the seminarists who were working near here. They had told me that they hadn't been able to locate Lieutenant Rabasa. I insisted, and now they told me that they had located him and that he was going to call me. (But time passed, and he didn't call.) On the road I asked Cintio the meaning of those herds of very skinny cows, practically skeletons. He said: "It must be that the State for some reason has no interest in them. Here everything that the State loses interest in is condemned to perish." I asked him if there would be suckling pig on the 26th, because I had heard talk on the bus of the traditional Christmas suckling pig, and he said: "If there's enough for all Cubans, they'll have it. If there's not enough for everyone, they won't. Here if something doesn't go around to everyone, there's none for anyone. That's the way things are in Cuba." He smiled and puffed his cigar. (Note: There was a tiny portion of suckling pig, for everybody.)

We passed by enormous groves of citrus trees. Thousands, millions. Most of them were the same age as the lemon trees that we planted in Solentiname, that is, they were two years away from harvest. I thought that when they got harvested, the world market would be flooded with lemons.

Cintio told me that Fidel had a reckless bravery. He had often been very close to death, but he had a kind of mysterious destiny, or providence, that always saved him. When the farmers rebelled in Escambray, he often exposed himself recklessly at the head of the troops. One night he left the camp alone to inspect the surroundings. He reached a little stream and washed his face, and a rebel farmer who was aiming at him from a tree did not dare to kill him. Afterward the rebel farmer was captured, and Fidel said they would have to shoot him. "Because the Revolution was made for them, we have given them everything, and it's ridiculous that they should be fighting us now." The farmer said: "All right, but I want to tell you that last night I had your life in my hands and I refused to kill you." He told how he had seen Fidel at the stream when he was washing his face, and Fidel realized that this was true. He asked him: "And why didn't you kill me?" "Well, Fidel . . . because you were Fidel." I asked Cintio: "Did they shoot the farmer?" "Of course not."

Cintio also told me that once in the Sierra Maestra Fidel slept next to a man who was sent to kill him, and his generosity saved him. A farmer who had been a guide of theirs was bribed by the Batistans, and he came to the camp to kill Fidel. It was cold, and Fidel saw that the man beside him had no blanket, and he covered him with part of his. And so that night under the same blanket slept Fidel and the man who had come to kill him. Maybe that's why the man didn't dare to kill him. The man had a .45 pistol and two hand grenades they had given him to cover his retreat. The next day the plot was discovered, the man confessed and was shot. Before he died he entrusted his sons to the Revolution. Because he said that he saw that the Revolution was going to triumph, and he wanted his sons to be educated better than he, who through ignorance had wanted to commit that treachery. And the Revolution took care of the children, Cintio said. And Fina, who was with us, added: "That was the treachery of Eutimio. Che said that when they killed him there was a storm and that just as they fired at him, a thunderclap sounded so they didn't hear the shots."

They told me another anecdote about Fidel. After they landed from the *Granma,* while they were receiving tremendous bursts of machine-gun fire, Fidel said to the others with a perfectly calm voice: "Those men are terrified: listen to the way they are shooting." Che also told this story. And I told them the anecdote of Fidel in the lion's den in New York, which Coronel—who was there when Fidel arrived—told me: They took him to the Bronx Zoo and Fidel, to the stupefaction of everyone, suddenly jumped over the barrier into the lion's den. The diplomats and the FBI didn't dare to shout to him to get out of there for fear of startling the lions. Fidel stood there for some minutes without the lions paying any heed to him and then left calmly.

Trucks passed filled with sweaty and happy young men returning from the morning's work (no doubt in the citrus groves) on the way to lunch in their lodgings. A poster: THE WELFARE OF MANY IS PREFERABLE TO THE LUXURY OF FEW.

Cintio told more stories. When they were fighting in the

Sierra Maestra, Che went down incognito to a village house where they prepared a room and a bed for him. But he wouldn't sleep in the bed. He said that while his comrades were sleeping on the ground in the Sierra he could not sleep in a bed. And he slept on the floor. "That's the way Che was." (Fina afterward showed me a poem to Che that related this anecdote.) Also the story of the communist shot by the revolutionary government for having informed against some Catholics. Some conspirators were gathered in a building in Havana, in Batista's time, and the police arrived and assassinated them all. They were Catholics, and the only one of the conspirators to escape death was a communist who was not with the group at the moment. He rose to a position of some importance after the triumph of the Revolution. One day it was revealed in the archives of Batista's police that he had been the informer. He confessed the truth, and that he had done it because they were Catholics. And he was shot.

And the story of the Cuban writer who was living abroad and came home when the Revolution triumphed. The Revolution became the center of his life. He worked as a journalist with great enthusiasm, with great euphoria, writing propaganda for the Revolution. But they found out that he was a homosexual. They didn't want to wound him by any accusation, and they didn't fire him from his job. They just said that he could go on drawing his pay but that he must stop going to the office. He understood why they told him this and became deeply depressed. He was rejected by the Revolution that he loved so much. He left Cuba and committed suicide in Rome.

Two women went by driving a tractor. One white, the other black. With red kerchiefs on their heads. One of them dressed in yellow and green, the other in blue. They talked and laughed while the tractor bounced along the bumpy road. They bounced, too, bumped heads, and laughed. An enormous building behind some trees: an elementary boarding school. Cintio said: "One of the finest things about this Revolution is that now we all eat the same. The fellow in that hut (he pointed to one) eats exactly the same as I do in Havana. We both have the same ration book. Maybe he eats a little better than I do because he can have his hens and his eggs."

The landscape of the Colony Hotel is described in *Treasure Island:* "The island appeared in large part covered by woods whose dark tones contrasted with the yellow sand of the beaches. Tall trees of the pine family rose here and there, isolated or forming little woods. The effect was monotonous and sad. The hills that overlooked all this vegetation had strange shapes and were made of naked rocks." There were palm trees of many kinds and dwarf coconut trees around the swimming pool, and on the coast between the hotel and the sea. The sea intensely blue and always calm. We swam off the end of a very long wharf, and the transparent water—in which we could see the fish clearly—came up to our waists. You could walk out into the sea for a mile or two with the water only up to your waist.

At dawn, on the Isle of Pines, in the Colony Hotel, I said my prayers sitting on the floor of the balcony of my room that looked out upon the sea, while the sun came up out of the sea. The hotel was still in deep silence; it seemed that nobody had waked up. The only sounds came from two maids who were cleaning near the kitchen, but they must have been shouting to each other because I could hear everything they said. One told the other that she had a very beautiful poem. Or rather that she had two. And one of them she had sent to her mamma on Mother's Day. The other maid talked about her classes in the hotel and that she was taking down a dictation on the United States. They said something about their Ancient History class, and that they were taking a "History of Cuba up to '57." One of them said the arithmetic and algebra classes were the dullest ones, but the other said she liked them. I watched them go off with their pails leaving the red terrace floor shining with water. In the hotel kitchen, a notice on the wall that said:

The Best Worker of the Month
Carolino Baro

Next to the swimming pool, a young poet from the House of the Americas said: "I was a Catholic. I studied at Catholic University, governed by North American Augustinians. The Rector was Father Kelly. Although there were also some Spanish priests. The North Americans looked like liberals because they dressed like clergymen and drank beer. But basically they were conservatives. The students took no part in the struggles of the National University. They were mainly upper middle class, except for a few of us who had been expelled from the National. Those priests could not accept the Revolution. The Catholic University was closed. I stopped being a Catholic."

»»»

On a page of my notebook:

On the highway, we stopped at a Children's Circle. 287 children. This is where the children of working women spend the day. Three sections: nursing infants, infants, preschool children. A permanent doctor and nurses. A sign: "Shaping Men in Che's Image."

On another page:

Workers' Social Circle. TV. Party Room (birthday parties, dances with orchestra). Game rooms: dominoes, chess, ping-pong, piano. It is the people's social center. Coffeeshop next door. They show movies with cars in mobile units.

Also in my notebook:

Girls' camp. They are working planting citrus trees. In the afternoon classes, reading, theater, dances, chorus. Most of the girls black or mulatto. They get two weeks at home every three months. They are from various parts of Cuba. The director, a black girl of nineteen. She said, like one reciting a lesson: "We feel very proud to be on the Isle of Youth because here we are helping to build communism." I asked her how communism was being built there. She said: "By planting citrus trees."

»»»

The dining room of the Colony wasn't yet open, but the bar was, so that we could have an *apéritif* before dinner. I looked for someone with whom to talk about the Revolution, and there was Trini sitting at the bar drinking a daiquiri in a sugar-edged goblet. The seat beside her was empty, and I asked for rum on the rocks. I asked her what her family did before the Revolution. "My father was a mailman, and he still is. But between his work then and his work now there's a great difference. Before, he was often without work. And he had to keep getting votes for certain politicians. Especially when he was out of work. And besides, his children would never have been able to get a university education. Whereas now I have studied at the university. And I remember that it was hard to make both ends meet in our house. Even though I was very young then. Especially at the end of each month." "And now?" "Now the months don't have ends."

Again in the Colony bar we had rum with Cuban Coca-Cola (it no longer had that cockroach taste that Che described), and a communist leader of about twenty-five sat at our table. In her conversation she mentioned "moral taboos." "Which ones?" "All the taboos on sexual matters. For us they have disappeared. The fact that two young unmarried people copulate ought to be regarded as something quite natural. There is nothing sacred about sex. Nor is there anything mysterious. Making love is simply a physiological necessity, like defecating." (Her face was pretty but cold. She gave the impression of a dry and loveless nun.)

The ICAP people told me that Lieutenant Rabasa had finally answered. The seminarists could not be visited at this time because they were on military maneuvers. The military maneuvers were secret. Besides, they were scattered in various places for the maneuvers. They would be finished on Monday. That was a pity, because we were leaving on Sunday. To try them out I said that I was willing to stay over two days. They said it wasn't advisable because they might not be back on Monday. With military maneuvers you never knew. I might have to wait in boredom in that hotel for a whole week. It was better for them to let me know in Havana when the maneuvers were over. They would pay my plane fare, I could come and return on the same day. I said "Fine" to see if they ever let me know. (In Havana I never had word from them, and I did not insist.)

We spent a week on the Isle of Youth, but we did not see the young people with whom they were trying out the communist society of the future (except for the girls' camp where they were planting citrus trees). One of the people in the ICAP who planned our trip said it was because at that time there were almost no young people around, almost all of them were cutting cane in Camagüey. Another one said: "There is a Youth Corps, but this experiment can't be shown off as if it were a building. You would have to live with them several months." Another said: "You've already seen the communist society in formation, in that girls' camp." And I said: "But that was a boarding school!" One evening a top director of the Isle was going to come to the hotel to give us a lecture on the Youth Corps. He didn't come. Instead another man came to talk about ditch digging. In Havana a young revolutionary told me: "There is no Youth Corps any more. The experiment failed. I was there three months. The young people were unhappy because they had to work a lot and could study only a little. The experiment with free love didn't work out either. Several girls committed suicide by throwing themselves out the windows because they were pregnant."

Another young revolutionary, equally sincere, told me: "Yes, there is a Youth Corps, and it's inconceivable that you didn't see the young people. The experiment is going on—I was there three months ago—and it's stupendous. There's no need for money: movies, transportation, ice cream, fountain pens, everything is free, and you don't have to stand in line, there's plenty of everything. And the spirit of those young people (a great majority) is that of the new man, with no egotism. We had a party, and some boys didn't go to the party because they had to inseminate some cows that were in heat, and nobody was making them do this, because they were the only ones who knew that the cows were in heat. They went to get them and came back at two in the morning, tired, covered with mud and manure—because insemination is a very dirty job—but they were happy because they had inseminated all the cows that were in heat, and they had done something useful for the community, for other people." His black eyes shone with enthusiasm when he told of that experience. He wanted me to denounce those who didn't make this known.

I told the ICAP comrades and those of the House of the Americas that I was thinking of calling one chapter of my book "The Mystery of the Isle of Youth."

»»»

PRAYER FOR THE DEAD*

—Fina García Marruz

I remember his muffled and unboastful voice after the
    battle of Santa Clara
Frugal, gentle, inflexible. He provoked respect, not love.
When he came down from the Sierra for supplies and
    provisions, the owner of the store offered him his
    fluffy bed.
"I can't sleep on a mattress while my soldiers are shivering
    up there," he said.
And he divided men into two groups: those who can sleep
    on a mattress while others suffer
and those who can't do this. This was all he knew, and so
    he didn't talk much.
With a puff of ironic smoke from his inhaled cigar, his
    rural confidant, he blotted out all the watchwords of
    committed poetry.
Committed men he wanted, silent soldiers.
In the congresses, staying at luxury hotels, all kinds of
    people argued and dined,
bearded *a posteriori*, rebels in apparel, after-dinner
    guerrilla fighters,
signers of the valiant proclamation written in the country
    now freed, of course, by others.
But in the silence of the valley, only a few men. Alone,
    nameless dead, roots of the God-tree.
Words were not your forte. When you said we must become
    cold killing machines, we drew back frightened.
Respect changed to distrust; everything became even
    more confused.
I remembered you, our Sermon on the Mount, foundation
    stone, act of Montecristi,
where the answer to the brutal enemy was not the hatred
    that makes us resemble him, but love,
not dark vengeance but high justice, serenely armed,
for like the temple in the mountain, love must be on
    the heights.
I was angry with you because I could not follow your

* The dead one here is Che Guevara.—D.D.W.

137

embrace, your cause, which was the most just cause
because it was the cause of the most wretched.
The ointment poured out at His feet was the one to
give to the poor, no other.
One thing or the other, and not both at once,
either here or there, either with Him or with us, either
you deny Him or you are out of things, on the sideline of
the march,
lost among the malefactors, as He was lost among the
malefactors, and even unworthy of this,
either heads or tails: they cast lots upon his vesture,
at the foot of the Cross the soldiers' wager: one wins,
another loses,
either He or we, that barter is impossible,
that savage statement, that rending
in the name of His people, blot Him out from the living,
put upon His head
the sign of a cause which was not the one for which He
was dying on the Crossbeam.

A Lay Theologian

He is the son-in-law of Cuba's leading communist, and he is a Catholic lay theologian, perhaps the best informed on the new theology in Cuba. His wife is also a Catholic, converted by him. They told me that Carlos Rafael Rodríguez, his father-in-law, said that this Catholic was the most revolutionary of his sons-in-law. We talked at length about Catholicism in Cuba in a corner where nobody could hear us. He said: "Catechism? Once it was a nuisance. Not now."

"In my opinion education is quite tolerant."

"In certain places more than in others. In the National Art School, there it is quite tolerant. I am a teacher there even though I am a Catholic. That was clearly a factor against me, but in spite of that I am there. It is true that there was a scarcity of teachers, but the fact is that they accepted me, and they don't get in my way."

I asked him about the religious orders. The contemplative orders interested me especially. Were the Carmelites reactionary? "They have an attitude of collaborating with the Revolution. Carneado, of the Central Committee, is charged with dealing with the religious orders; when he deals with those nuns he does so with exquisite delicacy. I know this because they have told me so. He does not talk about religious matters with them, only about practical things. The Carmelites are supported by the government, like the Catalines, another contemplative order; they used to live on rents from the houses that they owned."

He told me also that the Sisters of Charity are especially favored by the government. That it isn't true that the seminarists are antirevolutionaries, that they are of all persuasions. That he knows one who is working in the quarries, in the Social Disgrace Unit on the Isle of Pines, and that this one was formerly more pro-Revolution than he now is; now he is very irritated. In his opinion, there are few young men in the Church because in Cuba there are very few priests who are attractive to young people. There are nuclei of young revolutionaries in the parishes: but there are few of them. The priests try to satisfy everyone, and therefore never take a stand on any political matter.

"Catholics as a whole? They complain of some things and collaborate in others, they take a middle position about the Revolution between the extremism of the antirevolutionaries and the enthusiasts for the Revolution. I would rather say that they are reacting against the concrete, badly and well. That is also the tonic of the general man, Catholics or not. One doesn't hear so much talk good or bad of the Revolution as a whole as of people or specific cases. At least that's the way it is in the place where I work."

"There are no private libraries, and therefore there are no Catholic libraries. No Catholic books reach Cuba. But no books of any kind reach Cuba, because of the blockade."

"The saying of the rosary?"

"Very little among young people. As for religious education, one has to keep in mind that the religious schools create many atheists. You know that Fidel was educated by the Jesuits. There is an actor, a friend of mine, who stopped believing in God because his mother had been brought up in a religious school and there she saw injustices—that is, they treated her like a servant. And the teachers ate better than the students."

"What atheists least like about Catholics is their lack of vitality. And that they don't participate, they don't share their things like revolutionaries, they are not loving."

»»»

Recently a rehabilitated prisoner was released, and the Secretary of the Interior paid his family's fare to Havana to stay a week at the National, so that they could be with him and celebrate this event in the best hotel in Havana.

The Chamberman

The chamberman who made up my room in the hotel asked me if I knew Neruda. He knew him because Neruda had stayed at this hotel. The chamberman told me—while he made the bed—that he was fond of the theater. He had played the title role in Sophocles' *Oedipus Rex*. They had added some lines with social content to the part—he said—because Greek theater had no social or political content. He had also played Hamlet.

I asked him what he was before the Revolution, and he said: "I was a servant to rich people. I'm from a little village near Santa Clara, and I came to Havana to work in the theater, because I like the theater. But this didn't work out, and then I worked in the houses of several millionaires. My idea was always to work in the theater at the same time that I held those other jobs, but you couldn't do this before the Revolution. After the Revolution I came to work in this hotel, and now I work in the theater at the same time. I am still an amateur in the theater—we perform in cabarets—but I hope to become a professional. In three months I'll take an examination, and if I pass I'll stop working in the hotel and I'll work only in the theater."

I asked him if the chamberman's work was hard, and he said it wasn't. They had offered him better jobs in the hotel, but he had refused them, because the hours conflicted with his theater work. The chamberman's work is always in the daytime. In other more important jobs in the hotel they had to take turns working days and nights, and if he asked to work only during the day, he would be asking for a privilege that the other comrades didn't have, and this wouldn't be fair. One thing that bothered him about his work was that he couldn't talk about Sophocles or Shakespeare with the comrades in the hotel because they wouldn't understand him. He lived in a boarding house where there were some students and other educated people, and with them he could talk about those things. They lent him books, and he added: "Because one of the handicaps of us workers is that we can't buy books." I was surprised to hear this (in socialist Cuba) and I asked him why. "Because all the books that are put on sale are sold out at once, and by the time we get off work there are none left in the bookstores."

He had done a quick cleanup in the bathroom. He had changed the towels. He had finished my room, but he went on talking, holding the towels and sheets: "I had always wanted to work in a hotel, instead of being a servant to a millionaire. But before, it was very hard to get work. In hotels it was almost impossible, because these jobs were much sought after on account of the tips, and certain people gave these jobs to their friends. Any job was hard to get. If you went to the telephone company you couldn't find work, because all the jobs were taken. Only with influence and with recommendations could you get a job. Now in this system anyone can work without having to go around looking for these recommendations. Nobody now is without work."

Before he left, he hesitated a little and then asked me if I read the Bible. "I used to read it a lot. And even now at times I read it. I had a Protestant education, but I sometimes went to Catholic Mass. The last man I worked for was a little old Catholic, and I had to take him to Mass every day. He told me that there was no need for me to go into the church, that I could stay outside, but I used to go in because I liked the Catholic Mass." He stood thinking for a while. "Now I am ideologically confused. Is there a God or isn't there one? Religion tells us one thing and scientific atheism tells us another." He shook his head. "I prefer not to think."

I told Pablo Armando Fernández about my conversation with the chamberman, and he said: "It's not only the workers who can't buy books. The same thing happens to poets and intellectuals. No matter at what hour one gets to the bookstores, one finds no books, they're sold out at once."

»»»

"It is true: in the School of Humanities no Catholics are accepted." (A professor of philosophy)

»»»

A news item in *Granma:*

INAUGURATION TODAY IN VARADERO
VACATION CAMPS
FOR ASTHMATIC CHILDREN

Set for today is the inauguration of the First Vacation Camp for asthmatic children, which will be on Varadero Beach.

This camp is part of the vacation plan that is being developed all over the country, and its activities will be the responsibility of the National Institute of Sports and Recreation and of the Department of Physical Education.

The first contingent, composed of about eighty asthmatic children between the ages of six and fourteen, coming from the Province of Pinar del Río, from Havana and Matanzas, will leave today for the Varadero Beach Resort. An adequate program of specialized medical attention and recreation, including swimming and respiratory exercises for asthmatics, will be given to these children.

Sports and recreational activities, showings of films for young people, bonfires, artistic and cultural performances, excursions to historic sites and centers of production form part of the program arranged to make a happy and instructive stay for the children in this camp, which also has a children's library.

The opening of other vacation camps of this type, serving the provinces of Las Villas and Oriente, is set for next August.

»»»

And more notes:

Cintio refused the royalties that a German publisher was going to pay him. He told me that Lezama Lima had also refused payments from Mexico, France, etc. Cuba does not recognize author's rights to the sale of their works. "And this is how it ought to be," said Cintio. "In a socialist society literary property cannot be private." (They refused the payments voluntarily, he made it clear.)

A young man: "We eat badly. But that's because Cuba exports her food to import tractors. The tractors are needed to free mankind."

In Batista's time it was common to tear out eyes, pull out fingernails, cut off testicles.

Fidel often comes to the University to talk with the students. When he is going to make changes in the government or in politics he usually comes to talk at length with the students and to hear their opinions.

Pablo Armando: "Everything is sold on the black market, and there are even real clandestine shops. There are also clandestine restaurants."

A Young Catholic

A young man of seventeen. They had told him at the parish house that I wanted to talk with young people to find out about the situation in Cuba, and he also wanted to ask me for advice. We sat by the edge of a pool at the National Hotel watching people swimming who looked like Yankees but who were really Russians.

"Look, Father, I am from a bourgeois or rather from a petty-bourgeois family, and I was trained to be anti-Castro, but I see that the Revolution has done many good things that we ought to support. I see above all that in the Revolution there is a great deal of love for one's fellow man. Many things that we read about in the Bible are things that they are doing. For example, going out to cut sugar cane even though you're not obliged to, or working more than they ask you to. The Gospel says that if they ask you to carry a load one mile, carry it a second mile. And that's what the revolutionaries say. My Block Committee decided to devote this past Sunday to cleaning and fixing up the street, which was in very bad shape, all full of debris. I am a member of the Block Committee, and I was in doubt whether it was my duty to go to Mass or to work with them. It seemed to me that I ought to work with them because that was helping your fellow man. So I didn't go to Mass. We didn't finish until late in the afternoon, and we left the street beautiful, just like new. Do you think I did the right thing?"

I remembered that I had read in *Time* that the CDR was an organization that kept spies on every block in Cuba. I asked him about that. He looked at me with an expression that seemed to be one of surprise. He thought for a while and said: "The Committees for the Defense of the Revolution (CDR) defend the Revolution. And they set up guards, because somebody can plant bombs, for example. They are also on hand to solve any problem, attend to any need. Now I think we can sometimes run into bad people, bad individuals. For example, a while ago we had a farewell celebration for some friends of ours who were leaving Cuba. We Cubans do a lot of shouting, and there is always a lot of noise at a celebration. The girl in

145

charge of the Block Committee came to make us stop the noise. She was angry because we were upsetting the neighbors. We tried not to make noise, but she came back later to say that we were shouting a great deal and were also talking against the Revolution and she couldn't allow that because she was a revolutionary, and that if we went on with the celebration she would prevent the departure of the family that was leaving the next day. We were not talking against the Revolution. But she knew that this was a 'worm' party, and that must have bothered her. I don't think that what she did was spying, but what she did was unfair."

Later he said: "We were surprised to see that the *Popularum Progressio* was published in a government magazine. Why was that?" I told him that the *Popularum* was an encyclical against capitalism and not against socialism. "The Cuban Church is behind the times? . . . Well, you probably know this because you come from outside. We didn't know that we were behind the times."

He said afterward: "Every night we hear the Voice of America, and the ones who always talk are those who have left Cuba, and I've noticed that they always say: 'I left because there are no nylons, because there are no good beauty parlors, because there aren't any good shoes, because you can't get any butter.' Never, really never, have I heard anyone say: 'I left because there is no freedom.' For me the most important thing in life is freedom. I say that there is freedom here if you are a revolutionary, because everything that the Revolution imposes on you is just what the revolutionary wants. And if you're not a revolutionary you can go and find some other society that pleases you."

I asked him about the prisoners. "Those who co-operate are treated well, and if they want to be rehabilitated they are sent to farms. Those who resist get bad treatment. For example, they strip them naked. An uncle of mine was treated that way." After a pause: "One thing seems unfair to me: when anyone leaves Cuba the government seals off his house and confiscates it with all its furnishings. Do you think that is fair? Why?" And finally: "I think that the young Christian's obligation is to work on all the tasks of the Revolution, because that is to serve one's fellow man, even though many Marxists make things hard for us and mistrust us. What do you think?"

»»»

A young lady: "I enrolled in the Communist Youth saying that I no longer believed in God and that I no longer went to Church—and I didn't go any more. But I needed something, I felt a great vacuum that couldn't be filled with material things; food, economic security, medical service, a house of my own, and all the rest. After several years of atheism I have returned to God and the Church. I have also gone to Mass, but I prefer to go to Church when nobody is there. The counterrevolutionary people in the Church repel me. I have sometimes taken my four-year-old daughter to Church because I want her to get used to going, and the other day I asked her if she wanted to go and she said: 'Is that the Church where Fidel is?' For her, Fidel was a Heart of Jesus with a beard that was in that Church."

»»»

A practicing Catholic, in a monastery, while we walked around the cloister, whispered to me: "The Revolution has been too tolerant of the Church. Here we have an enormous building just for three people. With the housing crisis in Cuba, I would have taken all this away from us." (No convent or monastery or religious house has been confiscated in Cuba.)

»»»

BÁRBARA

—*Victor Casáus*

You were of a world that I hated
against which I would have wanted to hurl my best
        battle-axes
or spit upon it
                but we really came together
at the Martí Monument in 1960 to talk
I to persuade you with feeble arguments not to leave
        the country
that you . . . me . . . that it's your father no, please, it's
        what's expected

I looked at you looked above all at your breasts trembling
    in the night air
your legs I think wild and I recited phrases
    from some book
I don't know whether Martí or history

There's little known about those who left some time
    before you did
Two women teachers who live suspiciously together in
    Pittsburgh
the owners of the school who of course are well off in Ohio
    I don't know
about you, we really have no news. Now
you must be like me twenty-odd years old I remember you
because we are reaching the end of the decade each in his
    own way
That thing that annoyed your father so is ten years old
We are in a long year that your father wouldn't approve
    of either
At the place where we talked in 1960 at the Martí
    Monument, Bárbara
I'd have fewer rote phrases more things to tell you now
I am singing a hymn that you would not understand
God bless your breasts wherever you may be
It's too bad they never came to tremble in History

The Son of Batista's Lieutenant

The son of Batista's lieutenant came to my hotel. I took him out into the gardens so that we could talk by ourselves. We looked out at the intensely blue sea with great white ships that may have been Russian. "Those people who talked with you are people accustomed to living very well, in big houses. Many of them still live in those fine houses. And they used to have servants, a chauffeur, a gardener. And that's why they are unhappy. The parish of San Juan de Letrán is in a district that had been very elegant, the Vedado. Many left but others go on living there in the same houses, houses that they owned or that belonged to relatives who left. They are backward people who want the Church to stay just the way it was. They were very unhappy when they stopped saying Mass in Latin, and some of them stopped going to church. They are bourgeois, behind the times, and that's why they are all counter-revolutionaries. They were also unhappy when the altar was turned around to face the public. The blood donation for the Peruvian victims, which took place all over Cuba after Fidel gave his blood, did not fill them with enthusiasm. They said: Why blood? The Christian thing to do is to offer up prayers. Christians should pray for Peru, not give blood."

"And did they pray?" "I don't think they prayed much. In church they asked for prayers, but very coldly, as if they hadn't much faith in them. What they *do* pray for with great fervor is to get out of Cuba and to go to the United States to live better. They are wounded each time they hear Nixon insulted, because they are very fond of him. For them the United States is above all the country where the living is good. That's what they say. I talk to them about what the Revolution has done. The achievement of literacy in the country in a year and a half, the education that practically everyone now has, the free medical aid for all, free housing for a great part of the population, and the fact that there is now no misery, that everyone has work, that everyone has enough food: and then they tell me that I'm a materialist. When I defend the Revolution they tell me that I'm being contaminated by communist materialism. They don't think of the people, the blacks, the men who used to have to spend their whole lives, until old age, cutting cane on starvation wages. For them Cuba is only the small bourgeois well-to-do class to which they belonged. The others, the proletariat, the farmers, they don't count, as if they didn't exist. Vietnam means nothing to them. . .

"I am the only Christian in my family. I have a colored cousin who was not accepted at the Catholic school where I studied and who had to study in the public school, because he was dark. And so he was not educated in a Catholic school like me, and he's not a Catholic. Another cousin of mine was a nun in a religious school, and there if a girl came poorly dressed or not wearing the uniform (which was very expensive) they wouldn't let her into Mass with the other girls on Sunday but made her hear Mass behind a grill where she couldn't be seen. Catholics talk a lot about communists having privileges; sometimes it's true; maybe some of the captains. When they tell me this, I say: 'And what about the bishops? And the Papal Nuncio?' They say: 'Oh, bishops are bishops. And the Nuncio is the Nuncio.' I tell them: 'Well, the leaders are the leaders.' Of course, according to communism there should not be any privileges. But also according to the Gospel. We've just had a Mass for the Pope on St. Peter and St. Paul's Day in the Cathedral, and the diplomatic corps and certain other gentlemen were in reserved seats, a single gentleman occupying perhaps a whole bench. And the rest of the people mostly standing packed together. Little old ladies, some of them ill, unable to sit down. So in the Church, too, there are privileges and preferences, so why are they talking? They criticize the communists who don't let the communist youth go around with long hair, but in the San Juan Parish Church they won't let you be an altar boy if you have long hair. . .

"The Church is in very bad straits in Cuba, of course, but those who are to blame for the conflict between the Revolution and the Church are the ones who have left Cuba. They have left instead of staying to build the Revolution: they have left because they like to live more comfortably. . . Oves is a real revolutionary; I like to see him with his wooden cross on his chest and wearing a loose shirt. He is a humble archbishop . . . I tell them in the parish: 'Look, the Revolution gives the farmers a furnished house with an electric kitchen and a refrigerator, and the refrigerator stuffed·with food, and with running water and a bathroom, television, radio, clothes in the closets, because those farmers may not have the right clothes to live in those buildings. They even leave an envelope for them with the first month's rent.' In addition, they've found regular work for the man so that he can meet other payments during the next months, and they find work for his wife, if she wants it—because this is the truth, they do all this and not in isolated cases but for whole towns—and when I tell them all this they tell me that I am a materialist."

Two Officials

Two officials of the Ministry of Foreign Affairs came to see me at the hotel. They wanted to know my opinion about the situation of the Church in Cuba. Was I satisfied with the unrestricted freedom of religion that was enjoyed in Cuba? Had I noticed that the Church was now limited to what was strictly religious, as it should always have been, and that in the area of religion it was in no way disturbed? Did I notice that all the temples were open? They were surprised when I told them that I wasn't much interested in temples and that the question of ritual was unimportant.

"Catholics here are very retrograde," I said to them. "But I see that on one thing Catholics and communists are agreed: in believing that Christianity is only a matter of ritual. Catholics believe that they practice it merely by celebrating certain rituals. And you also believe that the Church is as it should be when it is confined only to ritual." They opened their eyes wide when I said: "The Gospel is essentially political or else it is nothing. Its policy is not reactionary but revolutionary. They could just as well close the churches. For the first Christians, said St. John Chrysostom, every house was a temple. Many priests are not now interested in building churches, and the best Masses are said around a dinner table."

I also told them that the message of the prophets was that God did not want ritual. He wanted exploitation to end. God had asked the people of Israel, through the mouth of Isaiah, why they came to appear before Him, for their solemnities and feasts were repugnant to him, he could not abide their incense, and he did not hear their prayers: let them seek social justice, let them head off the oppressor, let them give justice to the orphan, let them defend the cause of the widow. And through the prophet Amos, God had said that he wanted not their songs and their harps but righteousness and justice. And the Apostle Saint James had said that the true religion was to succor orphans and widows, which is what we now call being revolutionary.

They had formerly been Catholics—they told me—and so had practically all the present Cuban Marxists. They did not know about the changes in the post-Council Church, and

they were much surprised when I told them about the trans-
formations that Catholicism had undergone in its theology,
morals, Biblical interpretation, liturgy. When I described to
them our Mass at Solentiname, in which the farmers comment
at times on the words of Che as well as the words of the Bible,
one of them said: "Well, the other liturgy, the Revolution
tolerates it. . . This one, it's not a question of tolerating it but
of imposing it, as an important factor in the creation of the
revolutionary conscience of the masses. Isn't that it?"

"Correct."

"Masses of that kind could still be allowed in Revolution
Square on the platform where Fidel speaks. . . But a revolutionary Church like the one that you describe will be interested
not in liturgies like that in Revolution Square but in listening
there to Fidel just as all the rest of Cuba does. . ."

"Correct."

»»»

"They still haven't found a way to have freedom of the
press in a socialist regime," said Cintio. "It's a problem,
because if the newspapers are official—and they cannot help
being official—they can not write a true criticism; the criticism
will also be official. I think that journalism as it is known in
the capitalist countries must come to an end. Perhaps what
we'll have will be some news bulletins. Merely informative.
Orientation and criticism will be left for the journals, above
all, the specialized journals."

Benedetti told me that he, Cortázar, and the other South
Americans told Fidel that Cuban newspapers were very boring
and very bad, and Fidel said: "I agree with you. Why don't
you stay here and help us?" On another occasion a young poet
said: "Everything in the Revolution is dangerous. There are
no divergent political channels." There are only two newspapers in Havana: *Granma* in the morning and *Juventud
Rebelde* [Rebellious Youth] in the afternoon. Four pages each.
And very little news. A writer said: "They don't give you full
information. And there's no need to hold it back, because
eleven years after the Revolution the people of Cuba can take
all the news. And they get it all, because the Voice of America
can be heard by anyone who wants it." There is a mimeographed bulletin that the leaders get every day, with complete
news of the international agencies. A young poet told me it

was easy to get copies because anyone might have a friend who was a leader and who would pass a copy on.

»»»

	1958	1970
Unemployment	686,000	75,000
Working women	194,000	600,000
Pensions	114,700,000	320,000,000
Employees in Public Health Work	8,209	87,648
Public Health Budget	22,700,000	236,100,000
School Attendance	936,723	2,289,464
Illiterates	24–30%	4%
Education Budget	77,000,000	290,600,000

»»»

A young poet wrote: "Here in Cuba things change very swiftly from one day to another. We scarcely keep any dreams to fulfill tomorrow because they all have to be fulfilled; they are all important. The world has tremendous crises, but I think that some day poetry will be the language of man. That's the way it has to be. Your island belongs to us too in some part of the heart. We love it as we love this earth. That's all for now. Your twenty-one-year-old friend, José."

»»»

An intellectual (revolutionary), on seeing me writing everything down in my notebook: "I suppose there's no need to tell you this, but I'll tell you anyway: when you write your book don't put the names of people who have said unfavorable things, because it may do them harm." (I write this, too, in my notebook.)

»»»

A SMALL HOUSING PROBLEM

—A Song of Protest by Noel Nicola

I ask you:
Have you heard the persistent miaowing of cats in heat

right there let's say on the tile roof
of the house that's been empty for more than three years
and they haven't yet assigned it to anyone.

I ask you:
have you heard the lusty sound of the pigeons
when they make love to their females right there let's say
    at the window
of the room occupied by those people with eight children
and it rains harder indoors than out?

and I ask you:
do you by chance know what happens between my legs
when the cats and the pigeons are silent
and you as if to say "give me another kiss"
tell me "I want a woods to grow up where there will
    be space
for all the lovers"?

Be patient.

>> >> >>

At the movies, a propaganda documentary of the Revolution shows the slums of South America, huts, starving faces, naked children with swollen bellies—and in the audience exclamations of amazement. The commentator says that that's what Cuba was like a few years ago. In rapid succession the words flash across the screen: MALARIA . . . GASTRO-ENTERITIS . . . POLIO . . . MALNUTRITION . . . ILLIT-ERACY . . . UNEMPLOYMENT. . . (We had all these in our recent past.)

>> >> >>

While we swam in transparent waters, of a gemlike color that I didn't know, at a beach that was formerly only for millionaires, we talked about sharks. And someone said that the bay of Havana was full of them: "But when I was a boy we swam there, because we poor kids didn't have swimming pools or bathing resorts before the Revolution. It was hot, and so we had to bathe among the sharks."

>> >> >>

The Children of the Sierra Madre Remember Che

The magazine *Cuba* published some interviews about Che, given by the children of the Sierra Maestra. Some of the children said:

Dead in the Papers

Che was a very brave patriot
He marched through the Sierra, he had a beard,
a shotgun, a revolver. He also had
a mule. He went with Camilo and with
Fidel. They killed him in Bolivia
and there he was dead in all the papers.

The Picture

I saw him in the picture and he was a man
who was laughing,
with hair on his face,
riding a donkey, pretty strong,
and with a shotgun and a pistol on him.

A Pipe in His Mouth

Once he came to my house
and he had a pipe in his mouth
He gave injections
He was a man who sat
on the footstool.

The Eyes

Che didn't have blue eyes
Che had eyes of another color

A Shotgun on His Back

He was a short man
who carried a gun on his back
He smoked tobacco, big cigars
he rode a donkey
and he fought against the tyranny of Batista

Asthma

He fought against the guards
He fought against the shootings
He was very good around here:
he pulled teeth; he took care of the wounded
My papa says Che had asthma

He Was a Doctor

My papa says he came to fight
but also he helped babies to get born,
he took out teeth and other things
In the Malverde fight
they shot him in the legs

Wall

Che was very good with children
The teacher said it in class
The teacher cut out Che in the magazine
and pasted him on the wall

A School

He was the one who fought so that we
could have a school. He and Fidel.
He was tall, he had lots of hair
and a gun with a gunsight,
a pistol, a commander's uniform

»»»

Two sorrows:

When Camilo Cienfuegos died someone saw Che cry.
He said that Che didn't say a word: just two tears ran
down his cheeks.

They say that Celia Sánchez tells that when Che died
Fidel shut himself into a room and banged against the
walls and punched and kicked the doors.

A Seminarist

The Archbishop sent his car for a brother from the community of Taizé and for me. A seminarist drove the little Alfa-Romeo. While we rode along the handsome waterfront of Havana toward the district of elegant hotels, I asked the driver about the Revolution.

"Am I happy about the Revolution? Father, to tell the truth, I'm not happy. Because it is a materialistic government. An atheistic government. This is very different from the way it was before. Here people dressed very well, ate very well. These streets were filled with automobiles, you can't imagine. Before, anyone could have an automobile, and whatever make he wanted. Now only the Communists or government leaders have new cars, Alfa-Romeos, which are the only ones we now get. This used to be a very rich country. Now everything is scarce."

"And doesn't it seem to you that everything is scarce because everything has been distributed?" "Don't you believe it," he said, shaking his head. "Everything goes to Russia." "But what goes to Russia doesn't go as a gift. It must be exports, so that Cuba can import machinery, no?" "I don't know. Everything goes to Russia." We turned toward the National Hotel, and he said: "And, you see, private initiative is forbidden. If anyone tries to set up a little business to help himself, they arrest him. You can't sell anything in the streets, it's forbidden." After I got out of the car and said good-by to him and Brother Roberto, I stopped to think that this seminarist would soon be a priest. And I remembered the words of the son of Batista's lieutenant: "They tell me that I am a materialist."

»»»

Before 1959:
23.6% of the inhabitants of Cuba were illiterate.
50% of the children did not attend primary school.
90% of the young people did not attend secondary school.
95% did not go to college.

»»»

I was in the park of a town, with some young people.
One of them (a fat young man) said he was not studying. Was
he working? He blushed: he wasn't working either. Why not?
Again he blushed: because he couldn't. Why couldn't he? He
wouldn't answer. Finally he said: it was because he was leaving
Cuba. Didn't those who were leaving Cuba have to work in
the fields? No, the comrades explained, the only work they
give them is work in the fields, but they can go without work
if they have some means of support. I asked the fat young
man how he was making out, and he said, blushing again, that
his papa was supporting him. Another of the comrades: "His
papa is rich." The fat boy said nothing.

The young men took a bus. The Marxist who was with
me said: "Of course he's rich. You understand? Just what I
told you. They are bourgeois. . ." On the other side of the
park a sign said: *Be Like Che.*

»»»

Bathing at Varadero, in water of a color that I had never
seen before and that seemed to me to come from the shores of
another planet, we were reminded of the plane of Camilo
Cienfuegos that had disappeared in the sea. Every year they
commemorated that date by throwing flowers into the sea.
One year, they told me, a Secretary of Commerce went out in
a yacht loaded with wreaths, got ahead of all the other boats
and suddenly hurled all the wreaths overboard and took off
at full speed for Miami.

»»»

Ernesto told me that the clothing sold in the stores was
not to the liking of the young men. The fashion they liked
was very tight pants, but the fashion that the State wanted
to promote was the opposite: very wide pants. The boys buy
them, take them apart, and sew them up again according to
their style. (The girls do the same with their clothes.)

Ordoqui told me: The luxurious beach resorts (once exclusively for rich people), where everyone goes, are not liked
by the young new-wave people. They have their own exclusive

beach resorts, ugly, uncomfortable beaches where the bathing is not good. A favorite place of the long-haired is the "Little Beach," a tiny, rocky, ugly beach, where only the poor people used to go.

»»»

THE GENERATION OF THE '30s

—Lisandro Otero

They were born in two-story houses
on Subirana Street or in the Lamparilla,
upstairs in a school or beside a butchershop.
They played games and they couldn't keep their eyes
off the lofty banner of a scrap of paper.
They didn't always have in their pockets
the nickel to go to the movies.
But they saw in their glory
William S. Hart, Gloria Swanson, Charlie Chaplin,
    Greta Garbo.
They preferred the bus to the streetcar
because that was progress.
And they also liked jazz, the radio and aviation.
Instead of the straw hat they favored the manly
    mop of hair
and instead of the vest the open shirt
with sleeves rolled to the elbow.
They read Salgari, Vargas Vila, Eugène Sue
and the adventures of Arsène Lupin.
They got to know one another in bookstores,
in university lecture rooms,
in civic affairs.
They then took themselves more seriously and read
    Ingenieros,
Mariátegui, Rolland, Barbusse, Rodó
and the *Communist Manifesto.*
They chatted over cups of coffee, in the parks,
at exhibits of *art nouveau.*
Everything in life was exciting.
The heroes could be Diego Rivera, Cocteau, or
    Langston Hughes.

And also Sandino or Zapata
and on occasions
Jack Dempsey
Black art and Cubism, Lenin or Renan, perhaps these
     were the topics
of a long sleepless night.
And always Martí and always Cuba.
In their breasts burst an angry and expectant force
and they wanted to "overcome mountains and knead
     stars."
They loved women who were, like themselves,
beautiful and vital.
They adored the bodies in which they reflected each other,
they engendered children and wrote poems.
Afterward came the times of definitions:
they attacked minions, they signed manifestoes
and went to jail
to endure the lice that were bequeathed to them.
They did not lose their sense of humor
even though the thing was not a joking matter.
And amid jokes, quixotic acts, and fantasies,
with turmoil and commotion as a backdrop,
blending nostalgia and courage
they surrendered to the Great Midwife of History.
They died with lungs undone by tuberculosis,
kicked to death,
shot in the streets,
murdered while they slept,
fighting in the trenches of defeated revolutions.
They tried to change life
because they loved it too much.

Letter from a Woman Guerrilla Fighter

Brother Roberto from Taizé came to see me, and we discussed the conversation with the seminarist. He said: "I am frightened." He agreed with me that this revolution is a good one. Here one is living the ideal of evangelical poverty, together with equality and fraternity, and Christians ought to be the first to defend this system.

Brother Roberto said he had a question to ask me. When he saw the injustice in Latin America, he was filled with doubts about any justification for the contemplative life in these countries. Instead should not monks devote themselves actively to the Revolution? The Benedictines in Brazil told him: "We try to instill conscience in the visitors and in the neighboring farmers. But this is insignificant. We can do almost nothing." Monsignor Illich in Mexico upset him with an answer that seemed to him very reactionary; afterward, on second thought, it seemed to him that it was quite radical: "No one can do anything. But it is important that there be some contemplatives who realize this and suffer for their impotence. And if some contemplative wants to do more for his fellow man, he can always go to Switzerland and lead a hermit's life and do penance!" This question was also asked in South America of a girl who was in hiding. She told him that she did not wish to give a hasty answer, that she would think it over and would give him a written answer. Afterward she sent him a letter, which Brother Roberto showed to me.

I told him that the monasteries had always been centers of spiritual influence and that in our time that spiritual influence must be an influence for the Revolution, and that's the way we have understood it in Solentiname. I also told him what Merton had said, in a lecture that he gave in Bangkok, on Marxism and monasticism, about two hours before his death: he quoted Garaudy, who said that a Saint Teresa of Avila was important for humanity. He said that the monk no less than the Marxist had a critical attitude toward the contemporary world and its structures. The rejection of the world, in both, was with a view to change. The monk's ideal of transforming *cupiditas* into *caritas* (cupidity into love) was the same as Marx's of passing from capitalism to communism. The Marxists seek this by means of the change in economic substructures and the monks (Christians and Buddhists), by means of the change in conscience. The Benedictine vow of *conversio morum* (change of conduct) is a vow to be the new man, said Merton.

The guerrilla fighter said in her letter: "It is to all you who are uneasy that I address myself. I do not write to you who are tranquil, convinced about your way of life, satisfied about your situation, wholly assured about your vocation, settled in a decision that you made and never changed. On the contrary, I address myself to all of you who are uneasy, doubtful about your way of life, dissatisfied with your situation because you feel yourselves appealed to by the misery and the struggle of the man of today, to all of you who are insecure in your vocation because of the urgent call to the CONVOCATION, because of the historical call for the transformation of history, in short, for all of you who are forbidden by Love to settle into a definitive decision, and forced by Love to keep on searching. I address myself to all of you, whether you are of your congregation or of your community.

"Contemplatives: in the name of all humanity, of the continents that are struggling for their deep act of freedom, in the name of the revolutionary poets, of the masses of farmers, workers, and students; in the name of the scientists, the intellectuals, the artists, I beg of you: do not be afraid to live your vocation, do not be ashamed to go on living it intensely, do not put out that light that you discovered and that the world needs.

"If you cannot live your adventure to the depths, will you not be failing to give just what you are meant to offer to men? If you become cold and do not give yourselves completely to your vocation, even though you doubt its meaning, won't you be killing something that does not belong to you but rather given to you to increase?

"Contemplatives: in the name of all fighters known and unknown, of all those who are committed to the building of a new society, I ask you; no, more; I demand of you: do not renounce your vocation, learn how to wait, completely attentive, for men, radically sharing their searches, their successes and failures, their achievements, their struggles; live in the rhythm of the sufferings and joys of men, but do not be afraid to do this from your vocation. Seek new forms. Yes, but do not reject the *fundamental* truths that you have received from the Lord. The world demands this of you, even though it does not know it, even though it does not make this explicit. The world needs this even though at times this seems obscure.

"Contemplatives: do not let yourselves be misled by false lights. Be faithful to God, to the men of today, faithful to the essence of your vocation."

Cutting Cane with Love and Grace

In the newspapers there is now coverage of the work heroes as there used to be of the aristocracy. Today in *Granma* there are front-page photographs of two model workers—Lolo Cruz and Rubén Sosa—who were chosen by their factory co-workers to represent them on the platform during Fidel's speech on the 26th of July. Lolo Cruz, a worker in the candy department, has taken part in all the agricultural and industrial drives. During the past two months, after the eight-hour work day, he worked until five in the morning "to contribute to the fulfilling and overfulfilling of the production plan—the greatest of all time—of the articles intended for the celebration of the 26th of July."

About Rubén Sosa we are told that when the Playa Girón invasion occurred he was not a part of the militia but that he rushed to fight against the invaders. "Months before the invasion he was an independent worker. He hated the owners and the bosses. Afterward he analyzed things and saw that now everything was different." The comrades who chose him pointed out the following qualities in him: he does not have a timetable, and he is always ready to perform any task; a regular cutter in several sugar cane harvests, constantly concerned about his own improvement and that of his comrades, this year he could not go to the harvest because he was seriously ill, but in addition to his daily stint of work he substituted for a comrade who was off at the harvest. All these months he has worked sixteen hours a day, and also has worked weekends on farms, and "I still have time to fulfill my mission as Aid of the DOP. You can always do something extra."

The truth is that in Cuba one works for incentives that are not economic. Not one cent is paid for extra hours of work. And it's a curious thing: almost no worker works only eight hours; most of them work extra hours.

There is a massive propaganda in favor of moral incentives throughout Cuba. The spirit of Che is alive everywhere. Photographs of Che are seen wherever you go, you can't take a step without seeing one, but his famous doctrine—moral incentive—is more widespread than his physical likeness. The battle that he waged for moral incentives was great. What he said was heresy. In Russia they were paid extra for extra hours. Workers were stimulated by increases in wages. Che said: "Wages are an ancient evil, an evil that was born with the birth of capitalism. . . It will come to an end, it will go out of print, so to speak, when money stops circulating. When we reach the ideal stage, communism." Material incentives were destined to die with socialism. How? The gradual increase in consumer goods, according to the Russians, would make material incentives superfluous. But Che did not see how the abundance of material goods would create a social consciousness: "Direct material incentives and consciousness are contradictory terms in our concept." Besides, Che was interested not in the production of consumer goods but in the production of the new man: "It's not a question of how many pounds of meat one eats or of how many times a year somebody can go for a walk on the beach, nor of how many lovely things from abroad can be bought with current salaries. The real question is whether the individual feels more fulfilled, with more inner richness, and with much more responsibility." The argument was a long one. Fidel took the side of Che. The Revolution was giving benefits to the people freely—said Fidel—it would even give free living quarters in order to give birth to a mentality that would not be like that of those who "have only money in their heads," in order to create different attitudes toward property, toward material goods, toward work.

Fidel also denounced the socialist countries of Europe for this reason. Cuban visitors and scholarship holders (he said in a speech) "have often returned filled with dissatisfaction and displeasure and have told us: 'In many places there all that people talk about is money, in many places they talk only about incentives of this or that kind, material incentives of every type, increases in wages. . .' And some of them say to us amazed: 'Why, voluntary work doesn't exist; voluntary work is paid for. Payment for voluntary work is widespread; from the Marxist point of view purely voluntary work is conceived as almost a heresy. . .' Many of our people, many of our men have been more than once traumatized by that vulgarization of material stimulation or that vulgar materialization of the conscience of man."

Wherever the portrait of Che is seen with his long wind-blown hair, his black crownlike beret with the little star in the center, his serious gaze fixed on the horizon, Cubans are living the image of "moral stimulus." Moral stimulus was something indispensable for the building of the new man and the new society, said Che. ". . . a new world from which everything decrepit will have disappeared, everything that represents the society whose bases have just been destroyed."

Material incentives were a leftover from the past that still ought to exist for a certain time but that gradually ought to lose weight in the consciousness of the people. It was a contradiction to reward the best worker with material goods, that is to say, the one who had shown the greatest conscientiousness and the greatest spirit of sacrifice. "Raise high the opposite banner," said Che, "that of moral stimulus, that of the men who struggle and sacrifice and ask nothing more than the gratitude of their comrades." Work as a gift, not as a merchandise to be sold. That was why it was so important that voluntary work be really *voluntary*. Not doing it should not be considered as having failed to do one's duty, insisted Che. "Voluntary work is voluntary work, nothing more."

Peter Maurin, the saint who founded the *Catholic Worker* in New York with Dorothy Day, could not have agreed more with Che. He said in "Little Verses":

Work is not a merchandise
to be bought and sold—
Work is a means of expression,
the worker's gift to the common good.

For Peter Maurin work must *always* be voluntary.

And Che said that each worker must be in love with his factory. "Let work cease to be a painful necessity in order to become a pleasant demand." When he was Secretary of Industry, in a hall filled with workers, Che recited these verses of León Felipe:

But man is a laborious and stupid child who has changed
    work into a sweaty day's labor, changed the drumstick
    into a hoe, and instead of playing upon the earth a
    song of jubilation, began to dig. . .
I mean that no one has been able to dig to the rhythm
    of the sun, and that no one has yet cut a stalk
    of sugar cane with love and grace.

And Che said that León Felipe should come to Cuba and see how man had re-encountered the "road of play." "Today in our Cuba work acquires a new and even greater significance, and becomes a new and even greater joy. And we could invite him to the cane fields so that he could see our women cutting cane with love and grace, so that he could see the manly strength of our workers cutting cane with love, so that he could see a new attitude toward work." With socialism, said Che, people once again face work with the old joy: the joy of fulfilling a duty, of producing useful goods that will be distributed fairly among the whole population. Work, for each Cuban, will be converted into a vital necessity, as an expression of human creation, and techniques, technology, inventions will be multiplied by the thousands.

A girl from the House of the Americas was telling me that at the time of the campaign to uproot weeds, everyone went out to pull them up. The employees of the House of the Americas also went, and as there weren't enough tools for everyone, they often pulled up weeds with their bare hands (and she said this with enthusiasm, as she opened her delicate hands). Weeds were practically eliminated from Cuba. I often remembered that bare-handed weed-pulling when from a bus window I looked out at a weed-free Cuba. (Che said on this occasion that the workers in Cuba had succeeded in "cutting cane with love and grace.")

And I also remember what was said another time by Trini, who also worked in the House of the Americas. We were in a bus going across Pinar del Río, and several people were talking to me all at once about various aspects of the Revolution: agrarian reform, urban reform, scholarships. . . And Trini, in the front seat, turned toward me and said: "The Revolution is above all a thing of love. Make it clear that the Revolution is above all love, it's about feeling a great love."

»»»

In big letters along the front of a building:

WHEN THE EXTRAORDINARY THING BECOMES
A DAILY THING A REVOLUTION EXISTS

»»»

They told me the story many times. Fidel had been cutting cane for months (ever since the harvest began). He cut cane four hours a day, several days a week. Where? They told me that he cut in several places. They took him in a helicopter to cut. It was not a symbolic act like that of the Inca who traced a furrow with a golden plough. And nowhere else in the world does a statesman work like a peon, with a machete. I remembered what Retamar had told me in Mexico about cutting cane: the first days it is horrible, your hands blister, you are bathed in sweat, baked by the sun; the hours are endless, all you have is sugar cane behind you and in front of you, you get stupefied and forget all your ideas and think only of sugar cane, all you want to do is flop down, even there right in the sun, to rest.

President Dorticós has also gone out to cut cane, they told me, and when he got blisters on his hands, he said: "There can be no true socialism in Cuba until we solve the problems of mechanizing the sugar cane harvest."

Paz, the philosophy teacher, said: "I have never cut cane. My job was just to gather up the cut cane, but with the Cuban heat, that was a hellish job." In full sunlight it is so hot that your hands burn when you touch the stalks.

Fidel cut cane with the Vietnamese youth who came to help with the harvest. Afterward he cut cane with young North Americans. The last day that the North Americans cut cane the North Vietnamese joined them, and they had a contest to see which group would cut more cane for Cuba. Fidel came that day and cut cane first with one group and then with the other. In the afternoon they had a soccer match.

I remember that *Time* once reported ironically that Fidel was considered the Cuban "champion" in cutting sugar cane. But it is really true that he has a great record and that he can compete with professionals in cutting. They tell me that he has a very good cane-cutting technique (there are many techniques) which he learned from a famous cane-cutter. And Fidel is a very strong man. "Fidel is a barbarian," said the poet Cintio Vitier, puffing his cigar. "He cuts sugar cane like an animal."

»»»

LET MY BROTHERS OF THIS HOUR HEAR ME

—Félix Contreras

These are my older brothers of this hour:
Pedro del Toro, the famous cane-cutter of Niquero;
the celebrated Reynaldo Castro; Alejandro Gómez Richard,
of the Oriente Army, and many others besides like Alarcón,
Vinajera, Vaillant, who among us
make the best sugar cane tribute gathered
without a vain word. O Older Brothers,
you, you who do not speak,
your silence is golden. And it's not just a game:
Hat, gourd, and cane-knife, and at times scant sustenance,
and stone upon stone goes piling up to raise life
and not just talk about the sugar cane.

A College Girl's Story

Trini told me that she had had many experiences in the Revolution. I asked her to tell me about one. "For example, my stay in 'Los Pinares' (The Pine Groves), in the Technological Institute for Soil Conservation. We called it just 'Los Pinares.' We hardly knew that it was in Cuba. It's a very high plateau. We didn't want to go up there. We preferred the Isle of Youth or the Camagüey camps. We, a team of students from the School of Humanities in Havana, went there three years ago to do our rural service, postgraduate social service in the country. The place assigned to us was 'Los Pinares.' The explanation given to us in Havana was slight and rather inexact.

"There were about three hundred of us students, all very young. First we had to climb and climb, and it seemed as though we were going to climb up to the sky. There had never been farmers in 'Los Pinares.' The Technological Institute was up there on a plateau called The Measure. There's nothing there but pine forests. The Technological camp consisted of many little canvas tents of all colors. There was also a dining room made of pine wood, athletic fields, a library. And the boys. They received us covered with dirt. They were organized in brigades, and they were the only ones who took care of maintaining the school. Each day a different brigade was responsible for cleaning the rooms and helping in the kitchen and dining room. They had to solve all problems. None was over thirty. Neither the Director nor the Assistant Director nor the teachers, who were mostly students of agricultural engineering. We taught history and grammar. We first met with the boys in a study group in which we discussed the Debray book. But in the afternoon we ended by reading Vallejo and verses by Martí.

"We all got up at half past five. At that hour everything was always covered with mist. The boys did setting-up exercises, had their breakfast, and at seven began their classes, which were held under awnings. Studies there mixed with work in the fields. The work was mainly to get to know the soils. They had to become technicians. People had to become technicians for the Revolution, Fidel said. The plateau was a region that had been much damaged by erosion before the Revolution because the trees had been cut down. Now they were planting trees again. We heard the news of Che's death on a Sunday. That Sunday we planted thousands of seedlings, all for Che.

"Fidel made a tour with the students and talked to them about starting a school in the mountains for the children of the farmers in the nearby villages. And so, a few months later, there was the Technological Institute. The Assistant Director had been one of the first students who offered to go when Fidel spoke of setting up this school. She reached the plateau with the first students when there was scarcely anybody there. When we arrived she said: 'The political and human development of these boys is what is most interesting. Life is hard here, but we are changing many things.'

"The boys had several fields of alfalfa, tomatoes, onions. They also had pigs, chickens, and rabbits. Between five and six the clouds came into the camp. You could see them come down from the pines bringing with them a cool drizzle, and the brigades out in the fields would return to the camp. They raised the flag, and wherever we happened to be, we would stand for a few minutes. The lights in the athletic fields would be turned on, and some boys would do exercises. The boys preferred to go off to the brook to bathe. After dinner they had two hours of study hall, or individual study with teachers. Some evenings students in the musical group played the guitar.

"Lights out was at ten, and the only noise and lights remaining were those of the Agricultural Plan tractors that went on working at night. A night guard, a woman teacher and a man student, or a man teacher and a girl student, watched over the camp until dawn. We did not carry weapons. We covered the area and made sure that the peasants did not attack the animals we were breeding. In the early morning the plateau seemed to be lit up even more than by day, with an infinity of stars above the pine trees. On the plateau one could always find new things, damp slabs where we would sit down to study, great cascades to which we would give names— Sensemayá, Ñancahuazú (the deepest one), the Angel's Leap— pine trees as tall as houses, fountains with orchids—the only pretty flower on the plateau, with which we decorated the cabins and the dining room. There was as well a very desolate height, also called The Measure. The students climbed The Measure several times. The brigade with the best record in studies and work led the climb. From the top we could see the north coast, the sea, and we thought we could see all of Cuba.

"In April there was a production crisis, and the school was moved to another region of Oriente Province, near Corinthia Beach, where a group of revolutionaries had landed during the insurrection. There we cut cane and gathered stalks for a whole month. Afterward the school did not return to Pinares but was established on the plain. Pinares also changed into other things. The boys had spent two years in the mountains, all by themselves, growing up with the woods, the books, the night watches, the coming clouds, the study groups, the dust, the soils, the sowings. We spent seven months with them. We hadn't gone to work only with them but to work in other Horticultural Plan camps, teaching Cuban history or literature to the workers in the Plan, but the school absorbed us completely. Most of the time we were there, with the boys, living with them not so much in a teacher-student relationship as in a comrade-comrade relationship, with our conflicts, our decisions, our doubts. Seeing most of them grow up healthier, more agile. This was really as if we were alone in the center of the world, creating it all. And we stripped away many useless things that we had. This is an experience of the Revolution. It is not the only one that I have lived through, or the last one."

The Mother of Camilo Torres

"My son Camilo knew that he was going to die. And I knew it. He would say to me quite naturally: 'Mamma, when they kill me. . .' And I would say to him: 'My son, when they kill you. . .' We would talk about this quite naturally in the dining room."

The mother of Camilo Torres lives in an elegant house that had probably belonged to a very rich capitalist. The floors gleamed. Beautiful gardens inside the house and around it. Modern furniture in very good taste. Ivory carvings. German porcelains. Everything as well arranged as if the capitalists were still here. But the photographs on the walls are new: they are pictures of Fidel, of Che, Camilo Cienfuegos, and a picture of Camilo, her son, wearing a cassock.

Doña Isabelita told us that she loved Fidel like a son and that he loved her like a mother. They really seemed like mother and son. Fidel was really in need of a mother's love, she said. (I saw the photograph of the priest with a cassock next to a picture of the bearded Fidel, and there came to my mind the words: "Mother, here is your son. Son, here is your mother.")

She wrote to Fidel using the salutation: "Beloved son," and he would answer, signing himself: "your beloved son." I said: "That means then that Fidel had a brother in the priesthood." She nodded. She said that Ramón called her mamma, too. He told her that if she was Fidel's mamma, she was his, too.

Fidel had eight brothers and sisters, she continued. She was very close to Ramón. He didn't have a place in politics, like Raúl. He ran a farm. His house was modern, without any luxury. Once when she went to visit him she found him in a shirt, and the shirt was patched. Another time he had acute influenza. She said: "Give him a swallow of rum." There wasn't a bottle of rum in the house. She had to speak to Fidel and say: "This is ridiculous. Ramón is gravely ill with influenza, and there is not one drink of rum in his house. Send me a bottle for him right away."

She was often seen with Angelita, another sister. Angelita

also lived modestly. She stood in line to buy food—at times for several hours—like any housewife in Cuba. Of Juanita her brothers say she was always unbalanced, and always a problem for them.

I asked her if she had seen priests in Cuba. "Don't you believe it. You are the first priest I've seen here. Not one has come to visit me." Doña Isabelita Restrepo was seventy-two years old; her hair silvery white but her face glowing. Very fragile and white.

"Here is Camilo at his first and only dance. . ." (Camilo, wearing a tuxedo, is next to a delightful-looking girl.) "Here he is on the plain, with his horse. . . Here is Camilo when he was six months old. . . Here is Camilo as a boxer. . . Here he is at his first Mass. . . Here, when he was ten, on a farm. . . Here he is with the guerrillas. . . This is a souvenir of his first Communion. . ." (He was wearing a sailor blouse and had a naughty smile, *Souvenir of My First Communion. The German School. Camilo Torres Restrepo.*)

Doña Isabelita said that she was anticlerical. And that it was a sad blow for her when Camilo entered the seminary. At first Camilo had wanted to become a Dominican. She had to get him off the train with the help of a policeman. She later agreed that he could enter the seminary, but she soon regretted it, because the boys who went off to the Dominicans came back after two months, while Camilo stayed in the seminary.

She also said that Camilo, from childhood, had had a great love for the poor. He stole medicine from his father, who was a doctor, to give to the poor. He sometimes gave poor children his movie money. He became a friend of the beggars who came to the house, and sometimes she had to scold him for that.

At the age of eight he entered the German School, and the first day of class he hit a German child older than he, because he had spoken against Colombia, and he shut him up. In high school he founded a belligerent student paper, attacking the teachers. He was always a rebel.

Doña Isabelita resented the Church, because of the attitude of the hierarchy toward her son. She said: "I am still a Christian, but not a Catholic." She also said: "The bishops killed him."

At supper she scarcely ate. She drank two glasses of wine. There was very good ham, shrimp salad, and the best Coppelia ice cream, chocolate. But she scarcely touched anything. The waiter who served us was very attentive to her and begged her to eat. She hadn't eaten anything the day before either, he complained. She almost never ate. She told him that the conversation and the glasses of wine had revived her and now she felt better and was going to sleep well. She pointed out the linen tablecloth, the goblets—which she said were of crystal, "hand made"—the silver dishes ("and all the ash trays here are of silver"), and she said that she didn't like to live in this house. She was there because Fidel put her there. But she didn't like it. When she came back from Colombia, to settle down for good in Cuba, she wouldn't live in this house. And she was going to go to work. She could do ceramics, and she could teach people how to make porcelain like the porcelain of these cups out of which we were drinking. "I don't want to live off the Revolution. I am a revolutionary."

She would bring all her son's papers to Cuba, and they would open the Camilo Torres Museum. She couldn't live in Colombia until the Revolution triumphed there, and she would not live to see that triumph, so she would live in Cuba for the rest of her life. "I love this Revolution very much. My son is much loved here, and love is paid for with love."

One day Fidel came to the hotel where she was staying. He showed her a watch and said: "Do you recognize it?" She shouted: "Camilo's watch!" He said: "They brought it to me and wanted to make sure that it was his." And Fidel wept, she said. Other times, talking with her about Camilo, tears would come to Fidel's eyes. She added: "Fidel cries easily." Doña Isabelita's voice had a slight tremor whenever she spoke of her dead son. "They called him Commander in the guerrilla fighting. But he didn't allow himself to be called Commander. He said: 'I'm just a plain soldier.'" I asked her what was known about the death of her son. "He died in combat."

Her voice no longer trembled and her face was smiling as she talked of Fidel, her surviving son. A short while before she was operated on, and Fidel sent to her in the hospital an enormous box with all the flavors of ice cream that the Coppelia had. And he filled her room with flowers. A soldier arrived with the enormous box of ice cream and he said to her: "This is sent by the Commander in Chief." She said that it was too much ice cream just for her, and he said: "It's orders from the Commander in Chief." She distributed the ice cream among the nurses and the other patients.

Whenever Fidel saw her he kissed her, and she kissed him

on the cheek. Some young girls recently said to her how lucky she was to kiss Fidel, and they asked her what it felt like to kiss Fidel. She said: "He has very soft, very fine skin."

When we said good-by and when I looked again at the photograph of the other Camilo and next to him the priest with the cassock, and beside him Fidel with his kepi and a big cigar, and a little beyond, Che with his beret, smiling, I remembered what Fidel had said in a speech at the time that Camilo Cienfuegos disappeared: "There will be other Camilos." A prophecy that Che had repeated: "Camilo, and the other Camilos, those who did not arrive and those who will come." At the door I said I was going to give her a blessing as her son used to. "Bless me, Father. I do believe in God." I blessed her, and I kissed her pale forehead. And as to Doña Isabelita's saying, "Fidel cries easily," Cintio said afterward: "The Cuban people do not know this."

»»»

VOLUNTEER'S POEM

—*Victor Casáus*

Today they are the ones who take my place in the bus
I see them from the bus stop that army
changeable as a magnificent design they wait for their
    transportation
that definitely will not go to paradise for now
before that it has other stops to make
otherwise it would never reach the environs of felicity
But that they already know they don't have to hear it from
    me again
I rather direct my gaze toward that precious faun who
    peoples our finest myth
the girl who arrives still asleep in her khaki clothes
    beautiful and gray as life
the old woman clashing with her age
the comrades of the department (they still have their desks
    on their backs)
Among that poor army of volunteers they will harvest
    some cane field
give life with their water to the fruits

178

among them will be some who will happily make love
    under a sky
where at each moment on and off goes the light of the
    penultimate orbital satellite
and there will be those who make their mark and their
    names while they efficiently field the questions
and they will go on being themselves above all
even though they add thousands and thousands in the
    statistics and the signs
Because remember that there aren't two people who get
    on the bus the same way
everybody wears his past fastened as he can to his pack
and there's nothing finer than each one dreaming a
    different dream from each car window
And after this the bus can leave when it's ready.

»»»

And more things that I have heard:

In some parts of the interior they are experimenting with some critical journals, to see what results they get.

Che refused an invitation to belong to the Writers' Union because he did not consider himself a writer.

"A tropical Marxism," Aimé Cesaire called this. And he said that Cuba had invented a third way, which could be that of the whole Third World.

And the Catholic poet Marechal said that he had found in this Revolution: "The fulfillment of charity."

In the Sierra, Che always carried a huge knapsack filled with books. Reminiscing about the Sierra, there was a lot of talk about Che's heavy book sack. One of those who served as a contact with the Rebel Army said that Che asked him to send him *Das Kapital*, because he had begun to read it in Mexico and hadn't finished it. In the Sierra, Che did not smell sweet. Someone who went to interview him said that he couldn't stand to be very close to him because of the bad odor.

»»»

I asked a foreign priest his opinion of the Revolution, and he said: "There is no respect for personal dignity. This happens when you have as one of your main goals an economic goal, and it's as true of this system as of capitalism. Please don't write that down."

I had an appointment with the Archbishop, and the chauffeur of the ICAP had no idea where the Archbishop's palace was. I said: "In Old Havana, near the Cathedral, let's ask there." We asked many people in the street, near the Cathedral, and nobody knew anything. "The Archbishop's palace?" they repeated with surprise. The blacks gave the impression that they were hearing the phrase for the first time.

»»»

A Letter

Dear Old Ones:

Here we're in great shape and we have everything we need. We are eating well and they bring us oranges, yoghurt and malt. When you come Sunday, you'll see the camp. It's great; the only thing we don't have is electric light. They say we'll have it any day now because the lines come up to the other side of the road a little farther along. With a bit of cable they can bring it to here. Dad, one day I cut 110 arrobas. That was the day I cut the most, and the day I cut the least was 45 arrobas because the cane was thin. I'm not making it up, you can ask when you come. They have formed another brigade called the Martí Brigade, with the best cutters from the other brigades, and they chose me. Yesterday we cut together for the first time.

When we get to the 28th of January, if we're doing well, we'll be the Red Brigade. Mom, don't you worry, I haven't been sick or anything, but you know that here I have to go all out and behave like the revolutionary that I am. Well, write me and if you see Chachi tell him that I've already written to him.

Love and kisses.

Paqui

It sure is cold here!

180

Millionaire Cane-Cutters

In Cuba, those who cut a million *arrobas* of cane are called "millionaires." Fidel has said that these new millionaires didn't become so because of somebody else's fortune but from their own efforts. They are millionaires not because they enriched themselves but because they enriched the people. In his speech on the 26th Fidel will be accompanied on the platform by these millionaires.

I read an interview with some of these millionaires who will be on the platform. They spoke freely among themselves. Among other things, they said: "From the age of ten I began cutting cane with my old man and a brother two years younger than I. This was back in '39, when cut sugar cane was worth thirty cents a hundredweight. Afterward we went through the hard times of capitalism. During that period we suffered all the calamities of the cane-cutting worker. In those times the daily wage was sixty cents. I don't even want to think about it!"

"And there was a work system. . . For example, the cutter could cut only two or three days a week. You, the older cutters, were the ones most affected by this because you could work at times two days, three days; each farmer had a limited number of cane-cutting trips. . . You could cut only a certain amount of cane. . ."

"All right, Mariano, but notice. You know that in those times, following the system, we worked individually. The horrible condition of the shelters! Who paid any heed to the worker in the hut! That was a mess! You know that we had to cook on two stoves, and each one had to cook his meals. Why? Because in those times we were broken up and separated."

"Nowadays I can tell you that in the Suárez Gayol Column the cane-cutter gets mosquito netting, sheets, pillows, blankets, very comfortable slippers to go to the bath, a good kitchen with adequate food. But in the old days we cut cane because we had to. You had to get money together, your wife was sick, your son had to get to Havana. . . You just had to get money. Money was what was important."

"For example, take clothing. The merchant gave you

credit for clothes and shoes, depending on what you did, because if you didn't go into the fields and didn't make a payment in the first two weeks, he wouldn't give you any more credit. He charged you for lime, gloves, clothes, shoes, meals. . ."

"I was very young then. I would see the comrades go past my house with sacks on their shoulders, and that seemed to me something awful. . . You saw them with their little packs on their shoulders, and nobody would give them work!"

"I've been in the cane fields since I was nine. And I remember: the money didn't even pay for your food. If you ate, you couldn't afford to buy clothes. You'd pass by the huts and see the hearths fireless. Kids now ask me if in the old days kids didn't study. My old man wanted me to study, but sometimes we didn't even have clothes to go to school. I didn't begin to grow up until the triumph of the Revolution."

"Look, Pedro, I'm of the opinion that in the past no cane-cutter averaged two hundred *arrobas* in the harvest, while now an average cutter cuts four hundred, and there are some who cut seven hundred. In the old days it was personal interest that was important, not consciousness. You did it because there was no help for it. We're clear about that, because it's not true that today I cut cane because I have to or need to. I have my work center, my monthly salary, my family in town, and all the conveniences of a worker in this society."

"I did my first cutting in '42, because school was far away and hard to get to. The old man said: 'Look, it's better for you to pile up a little and cut me some cane so that maybe I can pay for what I got on credit in the old days.' So we went from '42 to '48, and my father died, and I had to stay with Mamma and my two brothers. Then the struggle began, with Mamma washing and ironing and I in the cane fields whenever they gave me a chance. By '52 I got to go on whole harvests. We lived in a farm area. Papa's family was in a bad way, and Mamma's was even worse off."

"Well, at that time I was living in Las Cruces, in Holguín. There was a little school attended by some sixty children out of two thousand who lived in the area. A small school for a region of six or seven square leagues."

"When I was a boy I couldn't go to school because there wasn't one in the area. I am from Santa Clara, and I couldn't study. At the age of eight I had to go to the Keys to work with my parents and afterward in a boat called the *Victoria* that hauled coal from Caibarién, Cayo Romano, Cayo Guayaba, Cayo Coco to Havana."

A woman who was also a millionaire spoke: "First I'm going to talk about the old days, when I was a young girl, because although I had no direct part in that harvest of terror, I did live through it because in my house my father and six brothers and sisters cut cane and had a miserable time. I remember that I was very small and I suffered in my flesh like my father. Once my brothers arrived a little late, and they came back very sad—almost crazy—because when they got there late the foreman had given their jobs to other boys that he liked better. They went off to another colony and my father had to be separated from them. I was a girl of seven 'placed' in a family. Everybody in the family worked, and we didn't have enough to eat or clothes to put on. In '63 I told my mother that I was going off to cut cane for the Revolution, and she was amazed, because cutting cane in her time was a punishment, a terror. She said: 'Daughter, how can you go off cutting cane if that is such hard work?' 'Well,' I answered, 'let's give it a try!' "

And another woman: "I lived in Florida. Education was a hard thing there. I only got to the second grade and, even though I was very fond of reading, since I had to go to work I couldn't go on studying. I had to scrub the breakfast dishes and do the cleaning and then go off to school. Then when I got out of school I had to go back to work and so on and on in order to earn seven cents *(quilos)*. To earn twenty-one *quilos* I had to scrub in seven houses! That's what you earned for scrubbing. Afterward I reached a salary of a dollar and a half. But that was for cleaning, scrubbing, and washing the odds and ends. The 'odds and ends' were underclothes, hand towels, and I really had to wash almost everything. . . But I couldn't go on studying. I would see the girls with wealthy fathers carrying their notebooks, all neat and tidy, and it hurt me to go to school the way I was dressed. The camp that we're in now is extraordinary, with television and radio and cultural events. There's no question that the work is hard, but that's not to say that it will kill you. And besides, the inspiration. And I tell the little girls: 'You can't imagine how happy I feel on this harvest.' I remember my parents and my brothers and sisters. Poor things, if they could have achieved even a piece of this!"

One of them finally said: "The cane-cutters used to be worth less than a dog. 'Cane-cutter?' That's worth nothing! And even if you fell in love, you couldn't get to a priest. 'No, you're a cane-cutter, you're worthless,' and today here we are sharing with the other organizations, and what enthusiasm when we reached the hotel: they are sugar cane cutters! The greatest thing in the country!"

»»»

Cintio told me that the black porter at the National Library, over seventy, has gone out cutting cane in every harvest, and he asked him once why, at his age, he did it. He answered: "The reason is that my two sons are on scholarships, and this is the least that I can do."

»»»

LOVING THEM, NAMING THEM

—*David Chericián*

I want to speak about the heroes
who make the building, about the men
I want to speak but not to say
that they are heroes but to name them
and place them here some with others
and with me and with all
the one who plants the cane,
the one who cuts it,
the one who loads it,
the one who takes it here and there
in a truck, in a wagon, in a cart,
the one who fills the scales,
the one who nurses the conveyor,
the one who feeds the mills,
the one who greases the nuts,
the one who tends the ovens,
the one who takes care of the husks,
the one who readies the lime,
the cook,
the one who keeps guard,

the one who sifts the grain,
the one who clarifies it,
the one who governs its thickness with his fingers,
the one who spins them madly in the separators,
the one who plans the harvest goals
and all those who help these men
in one way or another—
loving them, naming them.

José Antonio's Will

According to what they tell me, it was really with the speech of March 13, 1962, that Fidel began the campaign against sectarianism. Each 13th of March, the anniversary of the attack on Batista's Palace, the schoolchildren invade and symbolically seize the Presidential Palace. On that date each year, on the stairway of the University of Havana, the will of José Antonio, the Catholic student leader who died during the 1957 attack on the palace, is read.

On that 13th of March in 1962 Fidel was present at the homage to José Antonio. The master of ceremonies read the will, but he omitted a few lines in which José Antonio talked about God. Fidel then took the microphone. He said that while the comrade who was acting as master of ceremonies was reading the "Political Testament of José Antonio Echeverría to the Cuban People," he also was reading it in a pamphlet that they had given him. The comrade, said Fidel, "read the first paragraph, read the second paragraph, began to read the third paragraph, and when he was near the end of the third paragraph we noticed that he skipped to the fourth paragraph, failing to read three lines (listen, comrades, don't make a hasty judgment, don't even blame the comrade), and it seemed to us that he had skipped, and out of curiosity we read the part, since he had skipped it, and we read that he said (I am going to read the third paragraph): 'Our commitment to the people of Cuba was fixed in the Letter of Mexico, which united the youth in a single conduct and a single role, but the circumstances necessary for the student Fatherland to perform the role assigned to it did not occur opportunely, obliging us to postpone the fulfillment of our agreement,' and there he skipped. . . 'If we fall, let our blood . . .' and I read the three lines where he said: 'We believe that the moment for fulfillment has come, we believe that the purity of our intentions will bring us the favor of God to bring about the reign of justice in our Fatherland.' Pay attention, for this is very interesting. Don't applaud. I thought 'Gosh, what a coincidence: do you suppose they have omitted these three lines intentionally?' And I was left with that doubt, and I asked him, when he finished reading, who gave him the papers, who prepared this. He said: 'No, at the entrance they gave me instructions. I said I was going to read this, and they told me to take out these three lines.' Can this be possible, comrades? Let's make an analysis. Can we, comrades, can we, comrades, be so cowardly and can we be such mental cripples that we come here to read José Antonio's will and we have the cowardice, the moral misery, to suppress three lines?" (Applause)

"The true revolutionary," said Fidel, "does not commit such stupidity." (More applause.) "Using these criteria we would have to begin by suppressing all the writings of the forerunner of independence, Carlos Manuel de Céspedes, as well as those of Maceo, Máximo Gómez, and Bolívar. We would have to suppress the writings of Martí. We would have to suppress the whole revolutionary concept from Spartacus to Martí. When he invokes religious feelings José Antonio loses nothing of his heroism and his glory." (More applause.) "With those tricks you cannot develop the moral character to stand up to your enemies," Fidel went on. "The counterrevolutionaries have used that phrase of José Antonio to fight the Revolution. With the hypocrisy and moral duplicity that characterizes them, it's easy to explain why they would do it. But it is hard to explain why revolutionaries would suppress those lines." And he said: "We know that a revolutionary can have a faith, that he *can* have one. The Revolution does not compel men, it does not invade their conscience, it does not exclude men, all men who love their Fatherland, men who wish that in their Fatherland there be justice, that there be an end to exploitation, to abuses, to the odious imperialist domination, it does not compel them nor does it disgrace them simply because they have a conscience, some religious idea.

"We know that exploiters through all history have tried to use religion against the Revolution. The Roman patricians used it to persecute Christians, and Christianity was the religion of the humble, the slaves, the poor people of Rome. The Christian religion was also used later by the exploiters during feudalism and capitalism. More recently the counterrevolutionaries who landed at Playa Girón brought four priests with them.

"We know that that attitude is the attitude of the counterrevolutionaries, and they try to drag believing people into that attitude. As they do not have any worthy banner, they have no cause that will attract the masses, they try to call on religious beliefs, superstitions, anything at all. But why should the blame for that fall on a good Catholic, a sincere Catholic, one who is a militiaman, one who is with the Revolution, one who is against imperialism, one who is against illiteracy, one who is against social injustice? Why should he be blamed?"

He remembers the recent Declaration of Havana: "Well, now, we create a revolutionary document, we publish it in several languages, all the people support it, it wins the votes of more than a million citizens who are there, it has extraordinary resonance in Latin America, and what do we say? That in the struggle for national liberation, in the struggle against imperialism, all patriotic elements should unite, and that everyone should be on that front, from the sincere Catholic, who has nothing to do with the landowners, up to the old militant Marxist." (Applause.) "We declare this to the whole world, and we come here—with a nameless cowardice—to remove from the testament of a comrade the invocation of God. While on one hand we tell them that, if they are patriots and revolutionaries, they have to unite, in order to fight against imperialism, and against exploitation, this is no reason why they should not be believers, why they should not have a religion, and let the other fellow be a Marxist, let him place his faith in Marxist philosophy, for that is no obstacle, and we come here with this cowardice to suppress a few phrases! You couldn't overlook it, because what is it? A symptom, a miserable current, cowardly, mutilated, from one who has no faith in Marxism, from one who has no faith in the Revolution, from one who has no faith in his ideas." (Applause.)

"And so that you can see right here an example of the tragedy of this situation, it happens that the comrade who received the order to blot this out is a poet, he has this little book of verse and among his verses is one: 'Prayer for the Nameless God.' Then he begins to express his belief, and afterward he tells me that he has a complex about all these things. How could he help having a complex! A comrade involved in the Revolution and because of the fact that one day he wrote verses that spoke of God has to have a complicated life. And how can it fail to be complicated if he gets to this point and they tell him: 'Take out that word'? What has the Revolution turned into? Into a yoke? That is not the Revolution! Into a school for pets? That is not the Revolution!" (Applause.)

»»»

In Cuba there is pop art, op art, abstract art, surrealism, abstract expressionism. The only thing they don't have is socialist realism.

Fidel has said: The enemy is not abstract art but imperialism.

A conversation with Benedetti, Roque Dalton, and others. They said: Socialist realism is a dirty word in Cuba. It is completely discredited. In the beginning its devotees tried to introduce it. The Stalinists. There was general repulsion. Now you don't even dare to use the words.

"Socialist realism is retrograde," said Che, "because it is a return to the past, to the realism of the nineteenth century."

In Cuba, as contrasted with Russia, there is no attempt made to create an art that can be understood by the people; the attempt is to educate the people to the point where they can understand art. I was told that this has been the official policy of the Revolution.

President Dorticós received the members of the jury of the House of the Americas in 1967, Benedetti told me, and he was much interested to learn if among the Cuban participants any tendencies toward violent or dogmatic literature had been noticed.

Fidel has said that no one has ever supposed that all writers or artists have to be revolutionaries. The Revolution must act "in such a way that all artists and intellectuals who are not genuine revolutionaries may find in the Revolution a field in which to work and create and in such a way that their creative spirit, even though they are not revolutionary writers or artists, may have the opportunity and the freedom to express themselves within the Revolution. Does this mean that here we are going to tell people what they have to write? No. Let each one write what he wants, and if what he writes is no good, that's his problem."

Fidel has also said that he was opposed to any school monopolizing art: "I am in favor of the search for all types, in music, in painting, in poetry, in the drama, in the dance."

»»»

Talking with a Catholic intellectual, I asked him about the teaching of the catechism. "Everyone is free to send his children to catechism school. Of course, most of them don't.

But the catechism that is taught in Cuban schools is bad. Although I suppose that it's probably bad everywhere. . . And besides it's unnecessary at that age." He added: "It's amusing that what used to happen in old Catholic homes now happens in atheistic homes: the moment comes when the adolescent doubts all that his parents have taught him. When he reaches a certain age, the young person educated in a completely atheistic home begins to doubt the nonexistence of God. . . He asks himself the most interesting kinds of questions. It's lovely to see God rising up in youth in the form of an uprising, isn't it?"

With Lezama Lima

"That great continent of cold . . . reptilian . . . blood . . . Latin America [Lezama is asthmatic, and he talks as though he were climbing a steep hill], where they let Che die . . . one of the most eminent political figures of this century . . . and a genius at warfare . . . without followers in the great continent that he went to free . . . a man who was fit to lead great columns . . . and who had led them and carried them on to triumph . . . and he died there with at most twenty men . . . in that ill-named Sierra Maestra of Latin America . . . that is called the Andes."

Lezama is enormously fat, and yet his figure is imposing and handsome. He lives in a little house in Old Havana (in a section with quiet colonial streets that used to be full of shops with English names). His friends were appealing to Dorticós so that he could get a car because, on account of his obesity, he could not ride on the Havana buses, which are the most people-stuffed in the world. Lezama goes out only if a friend who has a car remembers him and takes him to some lecture or exhibit. ("He is the Cuban writer with the greatest international reputation, and he is ill, and it's only fair that he should have a car," said Fina.)

"I am not a *zoön politikón* . . . Aristotle says that man is a political animal . . . I am not one of that kind of *zoön* . . . I believe that true human relations . . . do not occur at the level of masses or of a nation . . . but on the level of a tribe."

In Lezama's house there was no liquor or anything else that he and his wife could offer except cigars and lemonade. That night I went without supper. Cintio told me that Lezama must suffer a great deal with the ration book because he liked to eat well and to eat a lot, and he loved to entertain his friends in splendor.

"There was a tiny little cloud on the horizon . . . that threatened to change into a great black cloud . . . and then to become a storm . . . but a gentle zephyr blew . . . and the cloud dissolved."

I knew what he was telling me because I had heard the anecdote. A petty official, with no authority for such an action, had ordered his book *Paradiso* withdrawn from the bookstores. Lezama waited, not knowing what was going to happen. The book was off the shelves for a week. Fidel found out and was very angry and ordered the book put back on the shelves.

As authors' copyrights have been abolished in Cuba, foreign publishers print editions of *Paradiso* without consulting Lezama or informing him or even having the courtesy of sending him a few copies. He doesn't have a single copy of his book, which is out of print in Cuba. His sudden international fame surprised him greatly, and it amused him. "An unbalanced little Chilean girl . . . a poet . . . writes me passionate letters . . . calling me the flag-bearer of the erotic revolution in Latin America . . . I don't know what she means by that." (He inhales his big cigar.)

Fidel was right to defend the invasion of Czechoslovakia, Lezama said. He had sent emissaries to find out if the Czechs were ready to fight and learned that they were not. It would have been madness for Cuba to fight for them. If the Soviet Union stopped sending oil to Cuba the Cubans would starve to death in a week. In that speech defending the invasion, Fidel nevertheless also attacked the Soviet Union and Yugoslavia, which he called pseudosocialist, and the liberal regime in Czechoslovakia, and the former Stalinist regime. The only country he defended was Vietnam.

Cuba has not been able to export its Revolution to Latin America, said Lezama, but it was exporting it to the United States. "Before, we used to export our main product . . . sugar . . . now we send them also our new main product . . . it is here that those students come to learn . . . and blacks who plant bombs. . . The United States used to determine the destiny of Cuba . . . now it is Cuba which has most influence . . . on their destiny." He gave me a Mexican crucifix made of straw. ("It's a souvenir from my mother.")

»»»

In *Juventud Rebelde* I read an interview with some old fishermen. One of them said: "Well, sure, we used to go to see the manager, the guy that rented us the boat, the tackle, the ice, and the cigars. We got very little with the very low price they paid for porgy and lobster. And almost always when we came back from fishing we had no more than when we went out."

Another one said it was the same in every port. The manager decided your fate. It was the same at renting time and at discounting time, because they refused to accept the results of your catch; the manager was a manufacturer of hunger.

"The day he refused us the boat or the tackle we had to scrounge around to bring something home," said another one. "Kids never ask why there's nothing to eat. They just cry."

There were small and big middlemen. They recalled names of people now in Miami. "They paid six cents for a pound of porgy. And they robbed at weighing time, because their scales were fixed. Their *arroba* had twenty-eight pounds."

Juan León, fifty years old, said that one night, when he was coming back starving after a week of fishing, his boat crossed the yacht of some bourgeois tourists who were drinking, eating, and laughing. "That day," he said, "I realized that only the rich have a right to live."

Juan Herrero, aged sixty, spoke of the fright of having his two sons gravely ill on a solitary Key. One was proud of being an old bachelor: "With all due respect, I prefer to be like a smart fish: nibbling here and there, but trying not to fall onto any hook." Another one contradicts him: "Woman and love are like light: they are turned off and on. You turn them off, and no trace is left. But then, in the dark, you need them again. A son is the product of love. The boat hasn't tied up at the port yet, and you're already thinking of how hard it will be to cast off again."

One of the old men, one who had lived all his life on the sea, said: "On the boat everything is different. Even the sun. On the boat the sun does no harm, nor the moon. Here man lasts longer." The word "fisherman" is like the word "comrade," they said. But it didn't used to be so. Fishermen were wary of fishermen, and they fought savagely over fishing areas. "A tide washed all that away. That's why that wolf business no longer applies to us."

The difference between the past and the present is "like from night and day. We went through a time in which man was treated like an insect." And another: "Today it's a joy to know that your son is going to be a fisherman. Big boats, fishing techniques never dreamed of before, machines, a sense of responsibility, you know. Because there are some very young ones who are captains or owners of important boats. It's the light, friend, that comes to brighten forever this life that a few guys made miserable for us all."

Things that they told me about Che: When he was Minister of Commerce he used to eat in the cafeteria of the Ministry with the other employees, standing in line with his tray and his battered aluminum plate. He had no chauffeur or car of his own. His only income was the hundred and fifty dollars he earned as Commander (a very low salary), and he said that was enough for him: because all he wore was the uniforms that the army gave him, his children were on scholarships, and he had nothing to spend money on. He had no servants (he said that a revolutionary should not have servants), and his wife washed and cooked. They said that at times she complained because she had a hard life: as Che's wife she had no extra privileges, but she did have special obligations, more than most wives. Che rejected everything that was "extra" in his house. In his farewell letter to Fidel, when he was leaving Cuba, he said he was leaving his wife and children no material goods, and that he had no regrets on that score, and he asked for nothing for them, because he knew that the State would give enough to them, as it does to everyone, to live and to be educated, and that that is sufficient. And they tell me: his children are being educated without any privileges because they are Che's children. They have scholarships, and they are treated as well as any Cuban child.

Someone else said: "Che was a person who was not fond of money."

»»»

A COMMENTARY TO THE MARTYRS
OF THE REVOLUTION

—*Victor Casáus*

This man did not die so that he may now be seen
on that wall, watching over our lunch
constructed with a tempera of suspicious colors
The administrator of this unit
possibly thinks that he honors the glorious fall of this man
who now smiles from the frame
Perhaps if the meal were better cooked

and if the tablecloths reasserted their color and these
waiters swiftly offered their collaboration
to our stomachs
        But no, not that either
this man hanging on the wall
was not born (and far less died) for these matters
In no way does he belong in this restaurant

On the Highway

On the roads of Pinar del Río. Enormous dairy farms. It seemed that we would never finish passing so many barns and fields filled with cattle. Herds of F-1, a new Cuban breed which is a mixture of Jersey and Holstein crossed with zebu. Later a farm where the plants don't touch the ground: each one is in a flask with water and melted minerals. In Havana, in the middle of the city, are cow barns with air-conditioning and music piped in, but I have no intention of seeing them. Later enormous stretches of chicken farms. Cane fields, clean huts with whitewashed walls. Pine groves. The palm trees that Martí loved and which, in a speech delivered in exile, he described as "expectant brides." After Che died, said Haydée Santamaría, not even the palms gladdened her heart. A sign on the highway said: GLORY TO THE MARTYRS OF MONCADA. We passed a school for farmers. Coconut trees. A nursing school. A portrait of Che (we couldn't read what it said underneath). Banana plantations. Clinics. Another school. More allusions to Moncada. Almond trees, palm trees, coconut trees, and a flower that we call "jupiter" in Nicaragua. On a great water tank, the names of some martyrs. Red and black flags on many houses. As a Nicaraguan I am happy. That flag was the flag of Sandino. Fidel adopted the Sandino flag for the "26th of July" movement, and so it became the flag of the Cuban Revolution.

The streets of the little towns through which we passed were filled with little paper flags, red and black, and in the center of each one was the number "26." And portraits of Abel everywhere. This 26th of July will be dedicated to Abel Santamaría, Haydée's brother, whose eye was torn out. Always the same portrait of a serious young man, almost an adolescent and rather sad, or else immensely sad, a snapshot from a student's identification card, a little blurred, and always enlarged in black and white, in several sizes, on paper, on signs, and also blown up—on some buildings—to enormous size. And pictures of Che with his beret, Fidel and Che, Camilo Cienfuegos. I remembered the emotion with which Ernesto told me about passing through the airport when he was a twelve-year-old bootblack. The streets of all the towns were filled with carnival masks, colored banners, the big tobacco stores with palm-leaf roofs, the agricultural airplanes sowing seeds, or perhaps fertilizer or insecticide, another school, another polyclinic, signs saying that the agricultural battle being won was as glorious as the one won against imperialism, as glorious as the battle of Playa Girón. (And when you see those planes, and the tractors, the trucks, the combines, the jeeps, you think that a battle is really being fought.) And a sign that said—on a field ready to be sown—that along this way passed the Che Guevara Invading Mechanizing Brigade (the one that pulled up the weeds). Beyond that a poster with little Vietnamese girls and a slogan: JUST LIKE VIETNAM. . . A child-care center. As we went through a little town, there was a library on the main street, and we managed to see inside where a lot of people were reading. Other handsome pop art posters encouraging agricultural efforts. More portraits of Abel. I thought of what Haydée Santamaría must be thinking seeing that portrait everywhere. I remembered what Haydée had said about the entry into Havana: "On the first of January, with the great joy of triumph, there came to our minds so many memories of so many dead. . . It was on January first that I really understood that Abel was dead, that Enrique was dead, and that they were all dead. When I saw that parade and I looked for them and I didn't see them." And the words of Celia Sánchez: "I see in everything the reactions of Camilo. For me he is still alive. I see a picture of his, an image, the City of Learning, and I think only of how he would kid us, how he would laugh." A poster says: ON THE 26TH I SHALL BE IN THE SQUARE. We entered a big station to get gasoline for the bus. I asked the attendant how much he earned, and he said one hundred forty-five dollars a month. And the others? Some earn more than he does, and others less. The station manager? He might earn two hundred dollars. Maybe less (he didn't know). Another man came up and said that he worked seven hours a day and earned a dollar ten an hour, or seven seventy a day. He ran a tractor. In the street children were playing, almost naked because of the heat, just wearing shorts. They were playing on all the corners, and among them were some very black children, almost purple-black.

»»»

WHAT WAS MONCADA FOR?
SO THAT THE FARMER WOULD NOT
HAVE TO LIVE
UNDER THE THREAT OF EVICTION

»»»

While we were on the bus some of the people from the House of the Americas told me that the Revolution had done much to safeguard the small farm property. To the independent farmers the State gives seeds, fertilizers, insecticides, machinery, technical aid, and at the end of the harvest it buys their produce (although they can keep twenty-five per cent of the harvest for their own consumption). The farmers were a group especially exploited by the old regime, and the Revolution now gave them special protection, even though in a socialist regime they no longer had a need for individual private property as they had before. The sons of the farmers are seldom interested in keeping up that little piece of property because many of them have scholarships and are studying some trade or profession. Farmers can inherit the land, but they cannot sell it to anyone except the State. The day will come when there will be no private ownership of land; it will belong to the State. It is hoped that this ideal of the Cuban Revolution will be nearly achieved by the year 2000. Since the Revolution there have been two agricultural reforms, but Fidel has already said that there will not be a third, that he will never again distribute the land of Cuba. The huts are disappearing, and the Revolution now tends to group people in towns. The huts that still survive are clean, well thatched, with whitewashed walls and cement floors. Each man is master of his house, although many pay rent on it. It was said that in his speech of the 26th Fidel might declare that living quarters would be free for everyone, because several years ago he had said that this goal would be achieved about 1970. They are planning a new kind of university to be scattered throughout Cuba, so that students may be in permanent contact with the people and the land, instead of being concentrated in a few urban centers. There is a tendency toward decentralization, and everything new (polyclinics, schools, movie houses, child-care centers, athletic fields) is usually built in the country and not in the cities. Havana is a city that has been heavily punished by the Revolution.

I was also told that a lot of class instruction is given by television. Television used to be used mainly to sell products, but now it serves mainly for education; there are televised lessons all day long. The announcements are educational. All the artistic productions (opera, ballet, etc.) are televised, whereas in other countries, for commercial reasons, they may not be televised. Mobile libraries go from town to town in buses. Batista's barracks have all been converted into schools. Moncada is a student city, and it is very impressive to note that the office of the torturer Río Cheviano is now an elementary school classroom, and that the barracks prison is the children's dining room with Snow White and Puss-in-Boots and Pinocchio on walls that were once splattered with blood. I was also told that in Cuba there are no orphanages; children without parents are educated with the other children in Children's Homes and in Child Centers and then study with the other children in boarding schools. A basic secondary-school education is obligatory in Cuba, and children finish it at fifteen or sixteen. The tendency is for all to go on to study in universities or technical institutes. Military service is obligatory, but students can perform their service without interrupting their studies, by extending them for a year. The tendency also is for young men to do their military service in their own educational centers, avoiding a barracks existence. As everyone gets an education, it becomes difficult to find people to perform certain unattractive jobs, like collecting garbage, for example. Very few girls are willing to be just typists. In the House of the Americas, for example, the shortage of typists has created an acute problem. There are no office boys to empty wastebaskets, because all the boys are studying. They have to empty their own or one another's wastebaskets. Students become part of the agricultural force at the beginning of basic secondary school, a plan that has been called "The School in the Country." The idea is to give the student an integrated education, not just a bookish one. The farm work solves many disciplinary and family problems for the boys, creates a greater camaraderie among them and between them and their teachers, mixes them up with workers and farmers, familiarizes them with the agricultural reality of the country, makes them more comradely, more generous, more mature. Fidel has impressed upon the people Martí's phrase "Be educated to be free."

The literacy campaign was carried out like a real war. More than a hundred thousand troops, from ten to sixteen years old, went from hut to hut teaching reading. There was massive use of radio, TV, newspapers, meetings, demonstrations to persuade people to learn to read. A lot of time was spent in arguing with those who didn't want to learn to read (especially the old people). There were some who wouldn't allow the literacy people to enter their houses. They taught reading even to the oldest people, which was not very practical and rather uneconomical. One difficulty was people who didn't want to admit that they didn't know how to read. Or people who lived in unreachable places. Or people who kept moving around, like fishermen or railroadmen. The literacy teachers went as far as distant islands or Keys with a very small population. The literacy teachers (workers, students, teachers) worked for nothing. In the factories many workers worked extra hours so that the illiterate workers could study. In Havana the hotel staff, waiters, cooks, had an hour and a half every night of reading classes. Each one who knew how to read taught another one to read. It was a popular movement, a cultural revolution. It would have been more economical to teach reading by television, but Fidel did not want it taught by television, because to do it person-to-person, even though it cost more, produced a greater moral effect among the teachers and the learners. In each factory and on each farm when everyone learned to read they raised a blue flag, and the whole countryside of Cuba was gradually covered with blue flags. Each town that was completely free of illiteracy was so declared. The first "freed" town was Melena del Sur. At the end of the year, in Revolution Square, in front of the statue to Martí, Fidel declared Cuba "Territory Freed from Illiteracy." Most of the literacy-squad members received scholarships and also many of those who had learned to read. They were asked if they were happy with their jobs, if they wanted to study something. The scholarship holders received, in addition to tuition, textbooks, room, board, clothing, medical treatment, all free, plus twenty dollars a month for incidental expenses. Those not on scholarships also got free tuition, but they paid their other expenses. The Child Centers used to charge according to family income, but now they are free. There are mountain schools for children who live in remote country areas and in the mountains. There they can spend their school days each week as State scholarship students, all free. The whole Sierra Maestra is covered with schools (and when they told me this I remembered Sandino, who when he was fighting in the Segovias Mountains dreamt of having those mountains covered with schools), and in one of the steepest places in the Sierra, in Minas de Frío, where Che had his quarters in a cave, several thousand students were studying to be teachers. They recalled that there was one there in the Sierra Maestra, in charge of giving out supplies to the guerrilla fighters, who said laughing, when he saw them come in long-haired and long-bearded, "These are going to be in the First Reading Class, and these in the Second, and these in the Third." Fidel's phrase, after his forces were down to twelve, when he saw the mountains of the Sierra Maestra, was, according to Universo Sánchez: "We've won the war. Batista's screwed himself." They also told me that their inability to meet the ten million goal he had set must have been very tragic for Fidel, because it was the first time that a goal of the Revolution had not been met. Up to that time Fidel had achieved all that he had promised. They could put up with shortages because they knew they were sacrificing for the general progress. Cuba catches a lot of lobster, but the Cubans don't eat it. The lobster is exported to bring in penicillin. The Revolution has had to educate Cubans about eating habits. Traditional Cuban cooking was very delicious but not appropriate for the tropics: it was all based on fat and pork. They have waged campaigns to change the traditional diet. A people's eating habits do not change overnight, but the new generation will take pleasure in a more scientific diet. A great number of workers eat free in Cuba: all who, because of their jobs, have to work in places far from home.

Formerly there were many thing that a black could not become: for example, a diplomat. The reason there are now so many black doctors—and there are thousands of them—is that they want the satisfaction of practicing professions that were forbidden to them: a black could not practice medicine and have any expectation of having white patients. And almost all the doctors used to be in Havana. Now more than seven thousand doctors are spread among the small towns in Cuba.

Before the Revolution half the children in Cuba did not go
to school (800,000). The Moncada Barracks is now called "26th
of July School Center."

That was when Trini turned around in the front seat
and said: "The Revolution is above all a thing of love. Make
it clear that the Revolution is above all to feel a great love."
She was wearing blue jeans and a man's shirt and boots, and
her blonde hair tossed in the breeze that swept through the
bus. She is pretty and green-eyed. And a little later she said:
"The way to get to know the Revolution is to pack a knapsack
and go to the mountains. You get to know the Revolution in
Oriente, not in Havana." Comrade Lazo, riding beside me,
said: "What's left in Havana is the residue of capitalism."

»»»

SOCIAL, CULTURAL, AND SPORTS CENTERS
OF THE NATIONAL
ASSOCIATION OF INDEPENDENT FARMERS

Social Circles	982
Sports Circles	2,123
Music	1,596
Theater	306
Choirs	186
Dance	35
Sports Camps	2,140

A Farmer

I was walking with André Gunder Frank along a Cuban highway. I asked him: "André: you're a Marxist?" He answered
with his German accent and correct but slow Spanish: "I do
not know. . . In my opinion perhaps I am not . . . but in the
opinion of others I am . . . I do not know . . . because I have
not studied much . . . the Marxism."

He did not say this ironically, although in the *Curriculum
Vitae* of the judges in the House of the America's contest I
had seen that André Gunder Frank had a doctorate in Economics from the University of Chicago with a thesis on Soviet
agriculture, had been a teacher of economics and social science
at several universities in the United States and Canada, and
at Brasilia University, and at the University of Mexico, and
the University of Chile; author of *Capitalism and Underdevelopment in Latin America,* etc., etc.

Gunder Frank speaks very frankly. I heard that he told
the House of the Americas people (about some program of
theirs): "The last time I came to Cuba . . . this was . . . shit
. . . but now I find it . . . much . . . worse."

We were in a luxurious mountain inn in Pinar del Río,
on an excursion organized by the House of the Americas for
the judges. That afternoon there was a trip to see some caves,
but I did not go because I said that I hadn't come to Cuba to
be a tourist but to see the Revolution. Gunder Frank also
stayed behind, and he said to me, when the bus had left, that
we could learn more about the Revolution in the hotel pool
than on that trip. I laughed, but he was serious. "In the hotel
swimming pool?" "Why not? There'll be farmers and workers
there . . . who are staying at this hotel . . . and we can talk . . .
with them." But I preferred to look for farmers in the fields
and not in the hotel pool, and so we went for a walk along
the highway.

The two of us were alone in the open country, and we
could talk with complete freedom with no one overhearing
us. I knew that André Gunder Frank had a thorough knowledge of the Cuban Revolution, and I asked him if he was
happy with it. He said yes, if he weren't happy he wouldn't be

there. Was it the best of all the revolutions that had been made? He thought it was. I asked him if he did not find it bad that there was no freedom of the press. He said that he believed such liberty was very secondary, the fundamental freedoms of man are contained in the Revolution. If freedom of the press would prevent the fulfillment of the Revolution, it is quite proper for that secondary freedom to be suppressed. The freedom to express an opinion and to dissent is important, but that is not necessarily the same thing as freedom of the press; criticism can be voiced through other channels, as is done in Cuba—at work assemblies, for example—and not necessarily in the press or on TV. Besides, is there real freedom of the press in other Latin American countries? They allow only a limited freedom of the press, only to the extent to which it is ineffective. After all, there are more important things. . . I asked him his opinion about what the enemies of the Revolution were saying: that this was a reign of terror, that prisoners were tortured, etc. He said he was not well informed about Cuban jails because he had never been in them. He believed that there was torturing in all countries, and that there must be some in Cuba also, but he had the impression that this was one of the places where there would be the least amount of torturing, and that the reason would be accident and not design. Why did he say that? Because everyone had been given a revolutionary education and had been politicized, and everyone had a very vivid memory of Batista, and everyone knew that to torture is antirevolutionary.

We reached the first farmhouses. They were of painted wood, with curtains at the windows, zinc-roofed. I looked in through one of the windows: I saw a bed with a bedspread, and upon it a toy. Outside there were some mulatto girls. Were these their homes? They nodded. Did they build them or were they given to them? The government gave them the materials, and they built them.

Twenty minutes later there was another house, palm-thatched roof, the walls of masonry, also painted. We went in to ask for some water. The ceiling was skillfully thatched, better than was usual in the huts of Solentiname. The floor was of cement. The furniture was the kind that a city laborer would have in my country. They had a refrigerator, a Coleman lamp, some statues of saints. There were just women: the mother, the daughters, and the daughters-in-law. We thanked them and left.

Farther along there was another little cement house in the midst of a patch of sweet potatoes. At the door a farmer of about seventy. I told him that I was a priest, but from another country. That I had also planted sweet potatoes, which in my country were called *quiquisque,* but that they had not grown well. "Well, here they grow wonderfully! Look!" And he was right. In back there was a cornfield. "This land belongs to you?" "Yes, sir. . . But it didn't used to; before, it belonged to a rich man, one Ubeda. All this and that over there and that beyond it, and way over there where the hotel is, and all that on the other side, and all the way to those mountains. We used to rent it from that gentleman."

"And when the Revolution triumphed?" "Ah, when the Revolution triumphed Fidel gave the land to all of us who rented it from that gentleman. The State gives us free fertilizer, and also lends us the machinery and gives us seed for planting if we have forgotten to keep some over. It also gives us insecticides to fight pests if we need them. And it sends us workers to gather the harvest when we need them. The harvest is bought by the State, so there's no problem in selling it."

"If the State is the only buyer it can set the prices however it wants to, can't it?" "Well, no, because the prices are fixed, here and everywhere, and in this month and in any other, and they are published in books. And if sometimes they change and the change is a reduction in price, the change can't be made until the next harvest, so that they can never lower the price of what is already sown."

I asked him what he ate and I noted that he got the same food as anyone in Havana, except that here the eggs are not rationed: they can buy all they want. And besides they have hens. He said: "I have a henhouse." And because he was old he got a pound of meat a week (instead of the standard three quarters of a pound), two chickens a week, and six cans of condensed milk a month. At the age of sixty, he said, you can retire with a pension. Their houses they got from the Revolution, without having to ask. This one doesn't belong to him but to a widow.

"Did they build it for her?" "Yes, sir, because she had no house. They also paid her . . . it's the pension given to every widow. And they also give her free food, because she's a widow. . . My house is off there on that hill, and it's better than this one. They built it for me. . . No, I didn't ask them to: an inspector comes along and examines your house and writes down everything that's bad, bad wood, rotted roof, dirt floor, he writes all that down, and maybe three days later trucks come with wood and cement and whitewash and sand and zinc, and they stop in front of your property, and they begin to build your house. . . What did my house used to be like? Cement floor, nonsense! It was a dirt floor, and an awful house."

Some boys went by with books, and I asked the old man if there was a school. "Yes, there's one right there, on that side, and there's another one off in the other direction. A little bus picks up the kids and takes them to school. At school they get free food. And see, they're building a boarding school opposite us." He went on reporting: he learned to read in the literacy drive. His farm had three animals, and he worked them with his three sons. I asked him if he was a Catholic, and he said he was. He used to earn two *pesos* a day. The Revolution raised everybody's salary. Before, there was little cultivated land. And he said, pointing to the huge valley covered with tilled fields:

"This used to be nothing but scrubland and brambles and wild bushes and very little cultivation; and now look at it, a marvel: crops, pastureland on every side. And there weren't any roads. You couldn't even get through there, and now see those two highways and that road going up there, and those other roads, very good ones, that cross through, and beyond those hills there are so many highways that nobody could tell you how many there are: many highways that crisscross and go in all directions, wherever you want to go."

He also told us that he got two changes of clothing and a pair of shoes every six months. He brushed his teeth with toothpaste. He used a deodorant and perfumed soap. On the way back Gunder Frank told me that on his first trip to Cuba he made lots of contacts with the farmers. He was in a small town making a study, and his notebook mysteriously disappeared. He later discovered that the person who had taken it was the priest.

When the House of the America's people got back from seeing the caves, I read to some of them a poem of Roberto Branly's about juries. I said to them: "In the poem it's a little exaggerated, but there's truth in it." One of the girls from the House of the Americas said: "It's not at all exaggerated, it's just like that."

»»»

SPORTS REPORT

—*Roberto Branly*

The judges come from everywhere: from the winter and
    the snow,
from the tropics so full of fruits and imported machines;
they come with their books, with their magazines and
    numerous data
always preceded by pertinent *curriculum vitae;*
the judges, smiling, touch down, come down the stairs
with popping ears and for each a waiting suitcase in
    the airport;
the judges come, they are put up in first-class hotels,
they eat free meals, they engage in fine, deep dialogues
with bureaucrats devoted to the tepid need to make
    literature:
the judges are astonished to see thick lips, they are
    picked up and brought
to the Chori at Varadero when it stops raining and there
    are no jellyfish;
they are taken to visit studios and art schools,
and then the members of the jury grant interviews to
    the press,
they get their pictures taken, microphone in hand,
they are full—when not totally on the Left—of
    Marxist phrases,
and above all in the conversatories they allude to Camelot
    and New World
Plans, to alienation, to the CIA;
the judges ingest several goblets of daiquiris
in the Torre Restaurant,
they go from one cocktail party to another, all through
    rose-colored glasses,
they are surprised that there is no Stalinism and that
    pop art is in,
they converse amicably, intimately, with the young
    hopefuls
and with the old hopefuls who are by now quite hopeless;
from time to time, when they have time,

they remember, perhaps, that they are judges, and they act
    like judges,
they read a typescript, they underline this or one of the
    four copies,
with their initials, as we know, on a sealed envelope
with the address of the senders unpublished, anxious, in
    the shadow;
and finally,
the gentlemen of the jury, in a solemn act,
draw the lucky number, and out of anonymity emerges
a resounding new name, or perhaps a worn-out old one,
into the world of letters.
Then after a new round, after diverse banquets and
    tributes,
after ballets, after concerts of concrete music—
war to the death, damn it, on dogmatism—
after different performances of pure native folklore,
the gentlemen of the jury,
cheerfully snap their suitcases shut,
and return, damp with love—
without ever having really sensed
what a people in a Revolution is like—
to the aluminum and cement of the airports.

Two Party Militants

In the Jasmine Hotel. Two Party representatives met with us to answer questions that we wanted to ask. The Argentine essayist Rodolfo Walsh wanted to know: in a factory when there are abuses by the management, how can the workers correct them? "Very simple, comrade: in the work assemblies. There everything is solved by voting." "Yes, but if the management controls the masses, and that is precisely what makes the abuses possible, what mechanism do the discontented ones have for showing their dissent and fighting those abuses?" "I have already told you, comrade: the masses solve those problems." "But we have just said that the masses are controlled by the management and that they vote as they are told, through inertia or fear or. . ." "Comrade, that would be to deny the revolutionary value of the masses. I can not accept what you say!"

"But let us suppose: in a hypothetical case that might occur. . ." "We reject that hypothesis, comrade." "We do not accept that hypothesis, because of its absurdity!" interrupted the other representative with great emphasis. "That situation is hypothetical and could not occur. There cannot be a factory where things are going badly and the workers do not correct them. And even if it should happen, that's why we have the Party militants, who are the vanguard of the Revo . . ."

Another member of the jury, a Spaniard, interrupted: "It might happen that the Party militants, because of a, let's say, bureaucratic mentality, would not correct those abuses. . ." "There can be no such thing as a bureaucratic militant! Marxism and bureaucracy are incompatible! So we also reject that hypothesis!"

"Crap!" said the Spaniard. "All over the world Communist parties are suffering from that evil of bureaucracy, and you claim that there cannot be a Party militant with a bureaucratic mentality. And don't think you're talking to a counterrevolutionary. I, for example, am a member of the Spanish Communist party, and in my country I have to live in hiding. Allow me to tell you that if you deny contradictions you are not a Marxist. Because Marxism believes in contradictions and is dialectical." "Yes, I am a Marxist, comrade, but the case that you propose, in a socialist society, is hypothetical. . ."

The first official came to the aid of his comrade: "In any case one can always complain to his superiors, and if they do not heed him, he can go to higher superiors, and finally to Fidel himself. Anyone in Cuba can write to Fidel. Expressing any kind of complaint that he has! You could even suddenly see Fidel in the street, and you could stop him and say: 'Look, Fidel, so and so and this and that and the other,' and this has happened thousands of times, and thousands of things have got corrected."

Gunder Frank wanted to know who decided what should be planted in each harvest by the independent farmers. "That depends on the quality of the land, comrade. One piece of land may be good for tobacco and not for citrus trees, for example. And another piece is good for citrus and not for tobacco. . ." And he went on this way endlessly talking about things he hadn't been asked, avoiding the question. Gunder Frank, with Germanic patience, kept asking again *who* decided what was to be sown, and our informant kept answering that the decisions were made *according to the land* ("because I say to you again, you're not going to sow tobacco on land that's good for sowing rice, for example").

They were clearly afraid to give an answer that we might interpret in the sense that there was too much control or else that there was a lot of anarchy. The answer that they might have given—and which I discovered later—was a simple one: the government draws the general lines of the farm plan, and the independent farmers then make a free choice—within that plan—of what to plant and in what quantity, etc.

I wanted to know how the cooperatives worked, to describe the operation afterward to my farmers in Solentiname. We were given a long lecture on the three forms of working the land that exist in Cuba (the independent farmers, the associated farmers, and the State farmers), but at the end of the lecture I wasn't sure whether or not there were cooperatives in Cuba.

As I still insisted on finding out if there were cooperatives in Cuba, the Uruguayan Ruffinelli alleged that in the exposition it had been made clear that there were cooperatives, but the Argentine Walsh maintained that the man had given us to understand that there were not, and the Chilean Skármeta was of the opinion that there were cooperatives but they weren't so called, while the Spanish Communist assured us that there were cooperatives only in name, but that they did not function as true cooperatives, and in reality they were something else. I still hoped that our informant would say the last word in this discussion, but the most emphatic thing he managed to say was that "it all depends on what you mean by cooperatives." And he was now eager to go on to another topic and ready for the next question.

At the end of the meeting they asked us to forgive them in case they had not satisfactorily answered all our questions and said that they were not really the Party leaders that we had been expecting (who were very busy that night and hadn't been able to come). Their substitutes were just militants and journalists. One of them said, with a certain solemnity: "Our mission is to orient the people."

Before they left I wanted to ask a question that could not be interpreted as polemical: About how much did a meal cost in this hotel (as guests of the House of the Americas we paid nothing anywhere).

"Well . . . this is a de luxe hotel, for tourists, and you can't take its prices as anything representative. . ." "And besides," broke in the other one, "there's another hotel a little less good than this one, which is a little farther along the highway, and you can eat there. And then there are popular restaurants, cheaper ones, and dining rooms in all the work centers, and even places where you can eat free!" "Yes, where you can eat free!" corroborated the comrade.

"But what is the price of a dinner in this hotel?" "We can't tell you the price of a dinner in this hotel because it varies. Some people eat more than others. Some have dinner with wine, *apéritifs,* and so on, while others just maybe ask for a couple of fried eggs. . ."

"But an average price more or less. . ?" "Well, I can't tell you, comrade, because as I said that varies a lot according to what you order. There are people who eat a lot, and there are those who eat a little. And besides you're going to take as typical a price that's not average. . . Here's what I spent on lunch today at my place of work: fifty cents!" (He showed me a punched ticket with 0.50 stamped out.) "So that you can see that I'm not lying. Look where it's marked. You can read it: ZERO FIFTY CENTS!" (And he put away the ticket with an

air of triumph, satisfied that he had answered with irrefutable
proof a captious reactionary question.)

»»»

A comment from a South American Marxist: "They said
that there could not be a Marxist with a bureaucratic mentality, but they themselves are the most irrefutable proof that
such people exist."

»»»

Some young poets from Pinar del Río came to see me at
the Jasmine Hotel and had supper with us. Vermouth beforehand, beer with supper, and a very large beefsteak. "Parra and
you," they kept saying. They were sorry that Nicanor Parra's
invitation to visit Cuba, as a judge of the House of the Americas' contest, had been withdrawn when it was learned that he
had accepted an invitation to have tea with Mrs. Nixon in
the White House. They didn't like Neruda. Parra had influenced them a good deal, and so had Nicaraguan poetry. They
said Nicaraguan poetry had had an influence all over Cuba.
The socialist realism of the Russians was so much shit. Cuba,
they said, has found its true socialist realism in pop art. The
poets also have found their socialist realism in the "external-
ism" of Nicaraguan poetry. Cuban poets with this "external-
ism" can now write about Moncada, waiting in line, the harvest, beaches, films, life, death, Vietnam, Fidel's voice on the
radio. They belonged to the Literary Workshop of Pinar del
Río. In every province there is a literary workshop where they
meet to learn to write poetry, and each workshop can have
its journal financed by the State. The literary workshops are
dependent on the National Council of Culture. There are
twenty or thirty of them in all of Cuba, and each one usually
has, I am told, fifteen to twenty members (almost all poets).
Vallejo? They were glad to hear me say that he still had
influence. I said more: that perhaps in the future he would
have more influence, not so much as to form but rather as to
his revolutionary content; because he had been a communist
and a Christian—and the most authentically communist poet
and the most authentically Christian poet in Latin America—
and he was the precursor of the new Revolution. Their workshop journal still didn't have a name, and they wanted me to

give it one. We stayed talking in the hotel dining room until
late at night, and from the dining room balconies we could
see all the beautiful moon-lit valley, which had belonged to
Ubeda the landowner.

»»»

3700 ROCKETS CANIMAR YEAR '64

—*Rogelio Fabio Hurtado*

There was a camp a mile from the Vía Blanca
where more than a hundred men lived in three tents of
      dark green canvas.
There was a dawn watch every other night
Our showerbath was the blue river under the bridge
And we scarcely bathed at all in the winter months.

At night we had Soviet films without subtitles
          under the trees and the stars
          shone over the trees
There was a crafty cook named Caridad who filled up
          the milk pails with water.
There was a latrine where five could get relief at once,
          looking at the full moon
          like a teat above the hill.
There was countryside and cows and canceled passes.

There was a soldier named José Rosendo González,
          who could play basketball
          with a fractured right arm.
There was a young black, from the Portugalete Sugar Mill
      whose grandmother
          had advised him: "Always keep
          your shotgun well greased, grandson."
And the soccer player Derubín Mena Gómez, who
      happened to stop a shot of lead with his leg and
      he limps
But he's still playing for the Canchas and making goals.
There was the best officer I ever saluted, named Perdomo.
There was a skinny blond baker known as Corporal Piss
          who was no friend of sleep
          and smoked through the dawn.

There was a stink of sweat in the barracks
And in the summer there were deluges that blotted out
    the trees.

(I say all this in homage to the reserve guards—
ah, I was a most effective reserve guard in San Julián—
to the telephone switchboard soldiers sleepy and girlless
and to any other soldier like a solitary man on guard duty.)

There was a swamp and out of the swamp rose the library.
There were days of great feasts and spaghetti evenings.
There was imaginary coitus by the thousands, the
    ladies abducted
            in the Interprov bus
            naked shaking down the bunks
Oh what rumba touches those rhythms had!

We were an indelible fraternity of grass and grease,
with Junco the sleepyhead and Mayito and Abreu
    "shiny boots"
and even "Skinny Plancheta" and even Herrera.

So here it is, enormous comrades of mine, friends forever
that each one goes his own way
And other soldiers perform their duties, in another camp,
    with the same functions
And here it is that two boys perished through accidents
    at work
And here is this poem told to me by you.

Sandino City

Sandino is a city built for the farmers. On the highway a big sign—like big highway billboards—with the portrait of the Nicaraguan guerrilla leader: Sandino with his red handkerchief around his neck and his hat. And in huge letters: SANDINO CITY: A CITY BUILT BY THE REVOLUTION! Below, in three languages: Welcome—Bienvenidos—(and Russian).

The hospital is close at hand, then come the houses, new, recently painted, of cement. Little houses of one story or two (for two families) and big apartment buildings of four stories. Tiny gardens, well cared for, in front of the houses. The streets planted with young pine trees (the city was built six years ago). A modern city of eight hundred houses, five thousand inhabitants, a children's club, a workers' club, a business center, where before there was *nothing*. On a plain where nothing used to be grown. The houses were given to the farmers with no payment of rent. Water and electricity free. Furniture free.

We stopped at the children's club, called "The Little Sandinos." The little Sandinos were outside, in a little park, sitting in a circle on the lawn singing: "The earth where I was born/is shaped like a crocodile asleep." There were about fifty children, between three and four years old. White, dark, and black. Very happy. The boys just wearing shorts and the girls underpants. They did not sing well. The teacher repeated again: "The earth where I was born / is shaped like a crocodile asleep."

Inside the club are playrooms, a dormitory, a nursing room. A total of a hundred fifty infants. They spend the day here while their mothers work. They stay here until they go to elementary school. There is a small library. I picked up a book at random, and it turned out to be a kind of magazine: *The Militant Communist*. I picked up the next book, and it was *Sandino, the General of the Free Men of America*. The next book was a collection of Darío's poetry. We had to leave, so I couldn't look at any more books.

The business center was a building a block long and two

stories high. It had stores, a cobbler's shop, a barbershop, a beauty parlor—about fifteen farmers' wives were getting permanents. A shop for babies' clothes. A toiletry shop, almost bare of goods: I saw some deodorants called Desodoral, perfumes, cologne. A sign that said: CLEANLINESS IS HEALTH. Also a bookstore where they sold records, and very few books: most of them technical manuals. *A Course for Molders; Patterns of Design; A Banking Manual.* The young salesgirl told me that the books are sold as soon as they arrive, and that many books arrive.

Opposite there was a social club for parties, with a dance hall where they could also show movies. A great mural of polychromed cement that I thought rather good. Beyond it a children's park. In another part of town an open-air theater where there are free movies every night.

Many of the people in Sandino City were farmers who had been brought from the Escambray Mountains where they had been raised. And many had been in jail in Havana for a year, imprisoned in houses that had been the mansions of the rich. We went into one of the Sandino City houses, the house of a family that had been brought from Escambray. The wife said her husband and her three sons had been imprisoned for a year. Her three sons were now married. They were not counterrevolutionaries, she said. Their crime was that they wouldn't be informers, they were afraid to inform because of the threats. "My sons belonged to the militia, but they were forced to quit."

A little while before, the whole family had gone back to Escambray for their vacation, and they had returned two weeks earlier. By now they could go back and live in Escambray if they wanted to. But they didn't want to. Were they happier here? Their answer was short but expressive: "Our house was made of palm leaves and boards. We lived in the woods!"

We saw a china vase on the dining table, good furniture, pictures on the walls. In a neighboring room good clothes, freshly ironed, on the bed. On the porch, a new bicycle. In front of the house a well-cared-for little garden with a lawn, carnations, violets, and rosebushes.

When we left, our guide told us: "All those who were brought from Escambray say the same thing: that their only crime had been to refuse to be informers. But that made them mutinous. There were twenty thousand of them."

Sandino City lies in a great plain entirely cultivated. There is a whole network of highways to transport the crops. Dams and irrigation everywhere. Before, it was poor land covered with underbrush. Now it has State farms and farmers who sow with the help of the State.

Total citrus groves: 500 *caballerías* (1 *caballería* = 18 hectares or 44½ acres).

Tobacco: 600 *caballerías* (its planting and harvesting are wholly mechanized).

400,000 head of cattle.

A vast program of artificial insemination.

165 *caballerías* of six-year-old mango trees (with eight varieties of mangos).

The mangos had just been harvested. We traveled back on a road that crossed through huge groves of mango trees that extended to the horizon. Many very small planes were flying in the sky. Sprayers? They were flying too high for that. They explained that there were aviation training schools near there.

They told me that a farmer sold his land but went on living in his old hut in the middle of the State farm: he would rather have his little palm-leaf hut than a free house in Sandino City. The bus pushed ahead through the enormous plantings of mangos, mangos, mangos. At a crossroads an arrow once again recalled my country's hero: Sandino   15 kilometers.

In a Hut

Zais Brothers City. In Batista's time the army evicted some
farmers because the land belonged to "Cuban Land Co."
The farmers' huts were burned down, and for a while they
had to live under the trees. Later they built their wretched
huts here. Now the Revolution has avenged these farmers by
building, on the site of their huts, Zais Brothers City: a lovely
little town of well-painted houses, gardens, paved streets, lawns,
young trees, a business center, a children's center. The houses
very prettily laid out at different angles, not all squared away
as in Sandino City. After seeing all this, Sandino City seemed
rather ugly.

We stopped at a tobacco field near the highway. A farmer
about fifty years old was cutting leaves. He greeted us cordially,
without timidity, and asked us into his house. It was a big
shack, with wooden walls and a cement floor, a thatched roof
in good condition and very high. There were easy chairs, a
big bed, a wardrobe, a refrigerator, television. A Cuban flag.
A large Sacred Heart. His wife gave us coffee and bananas,
and another farmer, a neighbor, came in to greet us. The
owner of the house said that the land was his: he had a
caballería of tobacco and several warehouses to dry tobacco.
He got one of them from the State, without having to pay a
cent. And he added: "I'm not saying this for propaganda
purposes."

He explained that he was not "integrated" into the Revolution. And that he is just "Cuban." And also that he is
"tainted," because he was a political leader under Batista (he
had been a candidate for councilor). He worked his land with
three laborers whom he paid three dollars and sixty cents a
day, and the State gave him clothes and food. In addition sixty
students came from Havana to help him with voluntary work
on his crop. The State sent him the voluntary workers when
he needed them. He earned five thousand dollars a year. He
was saving money, and he put it in the bank.

"We save because we don't have anything to spend money
on. And besides my wife is a very thrifty person. . . What do
we expect to do with the savings? Use them when there are

more things to buy. I want to mend the roof. To get more furniture. A little tractor. To build better warehouses. Understand?"

The other farmer listened attentively, and he smiled: "Well, I find myself rich in conscience and in spirit but not in money. Before the Revolution I had a quarter of a *caballería* in tobacco that netted me two thousand dollars a year. I gave it all to the State, and I work on a State farm. I earn a hundred and thirty-eight dollars a month. My three children are on scholarships. I am the manager of the farm, and I am a Party militant."

The non-"integrated" farmer took out of the wardrobe a yellowing picture of Figueres: "This, gentlemen, is President Figueres of Costa Rica who, when he was in Cuba, passed right by this shack." Around the shack were pretty flowers and some plants with many-colored leaves that I also have in Solentiname, and that in my country are called "color leaves." A technician said that the tobacco crop in Pinar del Río depended above all on the students. Eight thousand of them came from Havana. "We are creating a new type of student, one who does more than just study."

Another fact: Since May 17, 1967, interest on credits to independent farmers has been abolished. The farmer never loses on his harvest. If it doesn't turn out well, the State gives him monthly payments to support him during the year; in addition he gets a quarter of what he planted for his own use.

On the highway we stopped in front of a large group of young men dressed in green. They told us that they were from the Centenary Youth Column. They were between sixteen and twenty years old. Very happy. They were working on this State farm, and now they were waiting for the buses that would take them home for their vacations—thirteen days. They talked about their life on the farm: work in the morning, study in the afternoon, and at night political training and lectures. I asked them what they were reading, and several answered that they were reading about Vietnam, the works of Che, Martí, Debray, the magazine *Granma*.

And always on the highways and on the streets of the little towns we went through, the red and black flag. And thousands of little banners with the number "26." And pictures of Abel, Fidel, Camilo, Che, Martí. A South American on the jury of the House of the Americas murmured to another South American: "Only Cubans. . . Only Fidel, Che, Camilo, Cuban martyrs . . . not a word about Marx, Lenin. . . Only the red and black flag of the 26th of July and the Cuban flag. No red flag. . . Only references to Moncada, the Sierra Maestra, Martí, and the 26th of July, and much harping on that number '26'. . . They say that Fidel in his speech will begin a new phase, and I believe those decorations are indicative of the changes to come. . . I believe that the leaders of the Communist party must be trembling."

»»»

Fidel's cane cutting: in the summer harvest 1,776 *arrobas* in twenty-one four-hour days. In the full harvest between October 29 and January 9, he cut 13,309 *arrobas* in fifty-three days in the field with fifty-eight days work of four hours. Total: 15,085 *arrobas* in seventy-four days in the field with seventy-nine days work of four hours.

»»»

The farmers get free houses with all this equipment:
electric or kerosene stove
pressure cooker, frying pans, dishes, cutlery
washing place and dump
refrigerator
television
radio
electric iron
food supplies for a month
bedclothes (sheets, blankets, pillow slips, mosquito
    netting)
clothes and shoes for each member of the family
toothbrushes, toothpaste, soap, combs, hair tonic, perfume,
    shaving equipment,
alarm clock

»»»

Che wrote that when he said in Russia that Cuba was lacking in certain raw materials needed to manufacture deo-

dorants the Russians said: "Deodorants? You are accustomed
to too many comforts."

»»»

WORK

   —*Cintio Vitier*

Others did this,
better ones than you,
for centuries
On them depended
your sense of freedom,
your clean shirt,
and your leisure to read and write.
On them depends
everything
that seemed to you so natural
like going to the movies
or being slightly melancholy.
Yet what is natural is mud,
sweat,
excrement.
Starting from there begins
the epic, which is not only
an affair of dazzling heroes
but also
of obscure heroes, the earth under your footsteps,
the page where words are written.
Leave words behind, try
for a little
to do what they did, what they do,
and will go on doing
so that you may be:
they,
those sunk in need
and gravity,
ground by the implacable suns
so that your bread will be ever fresh,
those tied
to the iron post of monotony

so that you can ruffle all the topics,
those mutilated
by a mechanical gesture infinitely repeated
so that you can do
what you please with your soul and your body.
Diminish yourself as they do.
Taste the oven,
how it exhausts you.
Enter for a little, even though clandestinely,
into the terrible kingdom of the sustainers
of life.

At the Central Committee

In the luxurious and silent palace (of white marble) of the Central Committee of the Communist party, I visited José Felipe Carneado, who served on that Committee as a kind of minister for religious affairs—although according to what they said he does not have that title officially because the government of the Revolution does not officially recognize the existence of religions. He received me very cordially in his ministerial office. In the course of the conversation, while we were sipping little cups of thick Cuban coffee, I expressed my desire that Cuban Catholicism become more revolutionary, more like an important sector of the Church in Latin America. He said: "In Cuba one can not be a Christian and a revolutionary, because here the Revolution defined itself as a Marxist-Leninist, and therefore, atheistic, because Marxism is atheistic." I said: "Fidel has said the opposite: that every Christian ought to be essentially revolutionary. . . His speech about the will of José Antonio. . ." "Well . . . yes . . . of course. . ." (And he went on to another topic.)

The Marxist Paz Espejo said later when I told her about it: "That's missing the point of what the Revolution is all about! The Revolution can not be atheistic or Christian, the Revolution all over the world is simply the Revolution. The Revolution is one thing everywhere. It was the State that defined itself as Marxist-Leninist in Cuba, it was not the Revolution. And to maintain that is only to strengthen the enemy, the worms in Miami who say that Christians can not take part in the Revolution because it is atheistic."

»»»

They showed us newsreels from several periods of the Revolution. In one of them, Fidel was facing the television cameras. Here were his words (and I suppose that he was talking to the Catholics, in a period of religious conflicts): "To betray the poor is to betray Christ. To serve imperialism is to betray Christ." Cut, another scene.

»»»

"How many useless things used to be sold here, and people went wild buying them," said Fina. She, Cintio, and I were standing in front of Woolworth's, and where Sears and many other big stores used to be. Woolworth's is now a people's store, and it is almost empty. There's not even a sign that the others were once stores. The avenue of the great stores is now sober, without signs, almost deserted. I said: "How lucky you are." I remembered that Socrates, when he passed through Athens and saw all the merchandise on display in the stores, said: "How many things there are that I don't need." And I said to them also: "Here has been fulfilled what was said in Psalm 68: "Let no one inhabit their tents.""

»»»

An item from *Granma:*

RETURN TO HAVANA OF
THE ADVANCE TROOPS
OF THE LENIN COLUMN

The first advance troops of the Lenin Column arrived at the Havana railroad terminal last night at 11:05, after participating for two months in the final work of the sugar harvest in the northern part of Oriente Province. The Lenin Column is composed of some 1,400 people from Havana, who when they finished the harvest in their own province moved to Oriente to give their support to the cane-harvesting operations in that region.

They also carried out a program of school construction, parallel to the sugar harvest campaign, and they built 255 classrooms.

»»»

They told me that one of the girls who goes around among the hotel guests selling cigarettes, cigars, matches, *Pravda,* and one or two other items, was now working a double shift. After her regular eight hours she did an extra eight hours of voluntary work. (As she couldn't go harvesting she was making this contribution to the Revolution.)

A Poet in the Factory

A young poet who worked in a factory came to see me. We talked in the hotel. He said there was a great deal of insecurity in the work. Even the top officials could fall at any moment. The falls in Cuba are "complete" falls. The official who is toppled, no matter how lofty his previous position, can sink to the lowliest position. There are complaints that there are still privileges and inequalities within the Revolution.

Here is the case of two barbers, who were poor and jointly ran a poor man's barbershop in Old Havana. The Revolution triumphed, and they both became revolutionaries. One of them is now Ambassador to the United Arab Republic. When he comes back to Cuba he wears elegant, foreign clothes, as is proper for an ambassador. He has a luxurious apartment. The other is still a barber in the same barbershop in Old Havana; he lives in the same house he lived in before the Revolution. They were both equally revolutionary. "Of course," the poet said, "the one who is still a barber does not complain about his luck or about the Revolution."

The poet knew a pretty country girl, from the Sierra Maestra, who was living in the penthouse of a rich man who had left Cuba. She lived there because she was related to a captain. He visited the young woman because he was in love with her. The rest of the family was still living in shacks in the Sierra.

Those who criticize errors or abuses in the work centers are in a minority. But these are the authentic revolutionaries, he said. Those who maintain a spirit of rebellion. And life is not very comfortable for them. They are considered to be "troublemakers" at work. The majority, through cowardice or through opportunism, always yield to the authorities. There are others who think as you do, but they don't dare to say so, they also yield to the majority and to the authorities. And a moment comes when even your friends betray you. When there is a conflict with the administration one can appeal to the sitting judges. But the judges are usually on the side of the administration. They will say you're a troublemaker. The judges can't be impartial, he said, because they are judges and litigants at the same time.

The young poet told me about some troubles he had had. His case was taken to a higher authority, and this official took the side of the administration. He told the poet that he was "bourgeois." "He told me that I was bourgeois, and there he was sprawled in an easy chair, in front of a brand new desk, in an air-conditioned office with an expensive rug and everything: the perfect image of a typical American capitalist that you see in the movies. I have never been a bourgeois. My father was a ticket collector for a bus line, and he worked in a neighborhood bus terminal, just one of the people, and I used to help him. On the other hand, this official must have led a different life because he had been a friend of Batista's son: he and Batista's son rode the same horse." He added: "Those are now the ones who are holier than the Pope. They try to be more revolutionary than Fidel."

The poet said afterward: "In the face of the failures of the Revolution there can be several attitudes. There are those who go to the United States. And those who don't go but are on the side of the Yankees: they rejoice in the victories of the Yankees in Vietnam, in Cambodia, not because they have any interest in the Yankees or in the causes that they defend but simply out of natural reaction. Then they read the newspapers in reverse: they attack everything that the papers defend and defend everything that the papers attack. In the conflict of Israel with the Arabs they are with Israel, and so in everything else. They are saddened by whatever news the papers print as good news, and they are delighted by the bad news. There are also those who are left stunned, confused, and don't know what ideal to embrace or what cause to defend. There are others who rationalize the situation and know that to go off and live in the United States is worse. There are others who before the weaknesses of the Revolution idealize capitalism. And finally there are those who struggle, who expose themselves, who criticize. At the risk of personal security these fight against the conformity, the inertia, the routine, and the bureaucracy that are stifling the Revolution."

I asked him how they express these criticisms. Many do so by writing to Fidel, or to Celia Sánchez, his secretary. Celia, or rather, Fidel, is receiving criticisms and complaints from all over Cuba. Many problems are solved this way. Later: "It seems to me that the farmers who were once guerrilla fighters will always be revolutionaries. They won't be content with having been revolutionaries a single time."

The young poet said that when you're absent from your job they dock your salary, unless you're absent because of illness, and this does not seem to him a good system. They didn't use to dock you and then you worked more conscientiously: you didn't dare to be away from work or to get there late because since they didn't dock your pay it was like stealing from the community. Now he can stay away or arrive late without hurting his conscience because they dock his pay. He doesn't mind buying time for four *pesos*. If he wants to stay reading poetry at home a few hours more he does so with an easy conscience, because all he loses are a few *pesos,* and in Cuba *pesos* aren't good for much. Some time ago he was in the hospital, and he could have presented a medical certificate at the factory so as not to lose his pay for those days. But to get the certificate he'd have to stand in line for several hours, and instead of wasting those hours that he could spend reading poetry he preferred to lose the pay for his days in the hospital as if he had stayed away from work for pure pleasure. "I didn't even say I'd been sick," he said, "because we have more than enough money."

I asked him if the voluntary work is really voluntary or if they force people into it. He said: "They generally don't force you. Once we were working in the country, and the comrades decided to build a little park as an extra job. I didn't want to help with it because I was tired and had already done other voluntary jobs, and was also in a bad humor. When the park was dedicated they had a party, and I stayed behind in my barracks because I didn't feel I had any right to join in the party. The comrades came to invite me to the party, and when I refused they brought cake and ice cream to my barracks without making any reproaches. That really touched me. I never again refused to take part in a voluntary job. They won me over through love."

He finally said: "Many go off to the United States unhappy with this Revolution, and there they are despised. I knew a family. . . The girls were gorgeous: mulatto, very slender and gay. Now they are in Chicago, and they are miserable. I can understand. They were mulattoes, very popular, happy, fond of dancing and of Cuban fiestas, and there they are in a strange atmosphere. . . There they are *Negresses*. They work like slaves in the United States. They are very sad."

»»»

A Methodist minister. For three or four years he was a prisoner in the UMAP. Nevertheless, he said: "I am on the side of the Revolution." He also said that life in the concentration camp was hard.

»»»

More notes:

A scholarship includes everything: education, quarters, food, clothing, shoes, books, recreation, medical care, and some money for minor expenses. A third of all university students have scholarships.

At times there are street orchestras. Traffic is closed off, and the people dance in the middle of the street.

Polio used to be very common. In 1960 there were three hundred thirty cases. In 1961 there were three hundred forty. In 1967 there were forty-five cases. In 1964 there wasn't a single one. And there hasn't been one case since.

According to a 1956 (pre-Castro) survey by the Catholic University Group, only 4 per cent of the farmers regularly ate meat. Eggs were eaten by only 2.1 per cent of agricultural workers, and milk was drunk by only 11.29 per cent.

Women now attend education centers in almost the same proportion as men.

During the campaign against weeds Fidel ordered them not to pull up the weeds of the witch doctors (out of respect for religious beliefs).

At carnival time everything is sold at cost price.

»»»

WITH THE SAME HANDS

—Roberto Fernández Retamar

With the same hands that I caressed you with I am
    building a school.
I arrived almost at dawn, with what I thought would be
    work clothes

But the men and boys waiting in their rags
Still called me "sir."
        They are in a big house half demolished,
With a few cots and poles: they now spend their nights
There, instead of sleeping under bridges or in doorways.
One of them can read and they sent for him when they
        learned that I had a library.
(He is tall, bright, and he wears a little beard on his
        insolent mulatto face.)
I went by what will be the school dining room, marked
        today only by a staging
Above which my friend traces with his finger in the air
        windowframes and doors.
Behind there were stones, and a group of boys
Were moving them in swift barrows. I asked for one
And began to learn the elementary work of
        elementary men.
Then I held my first spade and I tasted the workers'
        forest water,
And, weary, I thought of you, of that time
When you kept harvesting until your eyes clouded over
As mine do now.
        How distant we were from the true things,
My love, how distant—like one from another!
The talk and the meal
Were well earned, and the pastor's friendship.
There was even a pair of lovers
Who blushed when we pointed to them laughing,
Smoking, after coffee.
        There is not a moment
When I do not think of you.
        Today perhaps even more
While I help to build this school
With the same hands that I caressed you with.

                        » » »

    Oliva told me that not long ago the Catholic hierarchy
created a Center of Ecumenical Studies, to start a dialogue
with the other religions and also with Marxism. And she
added: "There's been a Marxist revolution in Cuba for ten

years, and only now are they getting around to starting a dialogue with it, or to studying the possibility of a dialogue."

SOME RECOMMENDATIONS FOR
CUTTING SUGAR CANE

—Use gloves reinforced on the back of the left hand.
—Practical classes on cane-cutting techniques.
—Increase precautions in case of rain or dew, because the machetes slip.
—Forbid the use of both hands in cutting cane.
—Sharpen the machete and the butt end adequately and as often as necessary.

(Taken from *Economic Bohemia*)

With the Nuncio

A luncheon at the palace of the Nuncio, which he says is in my honor. Haydée Santamaría, the Archbishop, and Father Gaztelu, Retamar, Cintio, and Fina. The Nuncio told us that President Dorticós and Foreign Secretary Raúl Roa had also planned to attend but had to excuse themselves ten minutes before the luncheon because there was a Cabinet meeting with Fidel.

When I first arrived in Cuba, Retamar told me that the Nuncio, Monsignor Zacchi, was a revolutionary. I told him that I mistrusted nuncios, and he said: "It's not just diplomacy, he's really on our side. And he is a friend of Fidel." And in the House of the Americas Raúl Roa said: "He is on the side of the Revolution. He goes beyond the demands of diplomacy. We've just had a delegation from the Italian Communist party, and they told me they get along better with him than with the Italian Democratic Christian Ambassador. At the time of Girón, he sent a telegram to Fidel congratulating him on his victory over the invaders, whom he called traitors to the Fatherland—and don't forget that there were four priests among the invaders."

In an interview Monsignor Zacchi had said: "The Cuban Catholic must become a part of the popular organizations of the society in which he lives. He must participate in voluntary work, he must join the militia; he must join athletic and cultural organizations. He must also take an active part in the student movement and in professional associations. This would naturally produce a mutual influence."

Monsignor Zacchi has also said that he saw no objection to a young Catholic's joining the Communist Youth, since there was only one political party in Cuba and the Catholic had a right to take part in the politics of this country. Also, that a Catholic could adopt Marxist economic theory in the practical sphere of a revolution.

A foreign priest had told me that the Nuncio got a loan from the Vatican to open a noodle factory in Cuba. And also that he had cut cane, or at least it was so rumored in Rome. (I forgot to ask him.) When the *Mater et Magistra* came out, the Cuban bishops refused to publish it, even though the Nuncio urged them to do so, because they said that the encyclical was going to "confuse the faithful." Finally the Nuncio himself published it, and the government distributed it, not the bishops, and for many Cuban Catholics the Nuncio, Monsignor Zacchi, is a Red.

The Nuncio told me that Fidel said to him: "We want priests to come to Cuba but we want them to be good priests." He wondered what Fidel meant: priests good for the Revolution or good for the Church? And as though he had guessed the Nuncio's thought, Fidel said: "When I say good priests, I mean priests good for you. Because if they are good for you they will be good for us." He told me also about the time that Fidel came to a reception at the Nuncio's palace. Fidel later mentioned the occasion in a speech. He said that the Yankee news agencies had said that he was conspiring with the Nuncio to foster revolution among the clergy in Latin America. "And it's true, it's true!" he said. "There is a universal conspiracy among men worthy of humanity." He also said that the revolution of the Latin American clergy was a new phenomenon that the Marxist-Leninists ought to take into account. There is nothing more anti-Marxist than the petrifaction of ideas— and there are Marxists who display ideas that are true fossils. . . "When we see sectors of the clergy becoming revolutionary forces how can we resign ourselves to seeing sectors of Marxism becoming ecclesiastical forces?"

We talked in the drawing room filled with gilt Second Empire furniture, and Haydée Santamaría said that the house had been the mansion of a rich man in capitalist times, who built it not by the sweat of his own brow but by other men's sweat. The Nuncio offered us Scotch and Italian wine. Haydée was saying: "When I was religious—because I used to believe. . ." and the Nuncio broke in: "But Haydée, you have never ceased to believe. Religion is practiced not only by going to church, you know. Some people who go regularly to Mass may be less religious than you." I told him that, as a matter of fact, when they were working on their literacy campaign (directed by her husband, Armando Hart, then Secretary of Education) or giving food, scholarships, free medical aid to the people, they had been practicing true religion, in the eyes of the Apostle Saint James. She was surprised. She opened her big bright eyes wider. I quoted Jeremiah to her. (" 'He defended the cause of the poor and the needy. Is this not to know me?' said Yahweh.") She exclaimed: "Well in that sense, we really have been religious!" (On another occasion the Nuncio said that Fidel, although not ideologically a Christian, for he has declared himself a Marxist-Leninist, is, in his opinion, "ethically a Christian.")

Speaking of Cuban Catholicism, Monsignor Zacchi told me that the liturgical reforms were accepted readily. . . There was no real problem with them. But accepting the Church's new social ideas, "that was much more difficult."

Haydée sat next to me during the luncheon. I asked her about Fidel: "When he was fighting in the Sierra Maestra, did Fidel imagine the success that he was going to have as the leader of this Revolution and his influence over the masses, the great crowds in Revolution Square . . . or is the reality greater than what he dreamed of?" She said: "Fidel was always sure of winning. That the people would respond that way and that the Revolution would have the scope that it has had, he didn't imagine that and none of us who fought with him imagined it. The reality was greater than what he had dreamed."

The Archbishop and Haydée are related, and they spoke of other relatives and friends. They mentioned a lady, and Haydée said that she had recently tried to get the lady's husband out of jail. The lady had given her a letter for Fidel, and she kept it in her purse for four months without daring to give it to him. She didn't know how Fidel would react. One day she left it on his desk and said: "They gave me this note for you. If you don't like it tear it up, or maybe you can do something." And she left. The husband was old and ill, said Haydée, and he could no longer do any harm. He had been president of the Bank of Cuba under Batista. Fidel freed him on condition that he leave Cuba at once.

When the luncheon was over we were passed silver finger bowls with a carnation floating in each. Back in the Second Empire drawing room, where Monsignor Zacchi offered his English cigarettes, Haydée was playing jokes on Retamar. There had been a rumor, she said, that her husband, Armando Hart, had fallen from power, and she made Retamar believe that the rumor was true to see how he would respond. "And he fell into the trap. Do you remember, Roberto, what it was you said?" (Retamar smiled and bowed his head.) "You said:

'If Armando has fallen, I'm on his side.' " "He answered well," I said. "He answered badly!" said Haydée with her lilting schoolgirl voice. "He should have said: 'I'm on the side of Fidel.' That's what I would have said. Because, even though Armando's my husband, if he does something wrong, they ought to punish him."

The Nuncio insisted that I stay in Cuba. He took me back to my hotel in his little car that he drove himself in his shirtsleeves.

»»»

Nuns:
They are in charge of the leper colony.
Others work as nurses in the hospitals.
Others nurse in homes.
Others take care of old people.

»»»

A witness (María Elena): Calviño, here is María Elena.* Do you know me? The first thing he did, when he knocked down my door, was to give me a tremendous wallop that caved in my breastbone. Afterward he beat all over my chest and hurt me so much that I have had a bad heart ever since. Then he tore at my clothes, for I was arrested at four in the morning, I have here—because I kept them, because I swore that some day I would find myself facing you, do you remember what I told you?—these are the largest shreds of the nightgown, and they still have blood on them. And this is from the bathrobe (she shows it) that I put on, in the front here it still has blood, because you gave me a kick in the belly and I had a hemorrhage.

That wasn't enough for him. Then, when he had me stripped naked, he delivered me to Cano, to Alfaro, to all those people so they could abuse me and outrage me. How I had to fight to stop them! They broke two of my ribs. When the boy Miguelito . . . because he and Lieutenant Sánchez,

* In this account, taken from a chronicle (*Playa Girón, Defeat of Imperialism*, IV, pp. 301–11, Havana, 1961–62), two witnesses, women who had been arrested and attacked by Batista police, confront one of them, Calviño, in court some years later.—D. D. W.

because all the others are dead, because I have accused them all, and they are dead, but you were lacking. I'm lacking Lieutenant Sánchez and I'm lacking the boy Miguelito; because they did to me the most horrible things that can be done to a woman. For the blows didn't hurt me as much as the outrages they committed on me.

Then, when I was fainting from loss of blood, you came up behind me, and you did the "telephones" to me so I almost lost my hearing.

Witness: That's what I want, I want you to tell me the name of that comrade, the one who that night, down there in the basement of Precinct Number Five, and when you gave her . . . when they went at her with clubs and you kicked her on the side and she fell flat on her face. Don't you remember that? And then you stood over her and said words that I can not repeat here. So after you murdered her you profaned her, too, because you are a vile assassin.

Witness: That's the girl of Morúa, look, he was your pal! Do you remember Pilar? Do you remember?

Calviño: Pilar I never knew. Did I once know you?

Pilar: Look! You arrested me! *(She sobs.)*

Calviño: Where, Pilar?

Pilar: You killed what I loved most in life! And then you were cynical enough to tell me about it! Coward! You outraged me! I saw you kill a man right in front of me!

Calviño: In front of you?

Pilar: I saw you, you killed him in front of me, you shot him, and then you laughed at his death agony!

Calviño: Forgive me. . .

Pilar: At Number 106 Avellaneda. October 6th, at seven in the evening! Tell me you didn't! Tell me that it wasn't true that after you killed Morúa, nine days later, you arrested me, and you sat down to tell me how you had killed him. Tell me you didn't, tell me, Calviño!

Calviño: I can't answer you. . .

In the Social Disgrace Unit

The son of Batista's lieutenant came to visit me again. We spoke of the Church in Cuba, and of the seminarists, and he said: "I'm with some seminarists on the Isle of Pines." It so happened that he was working in the quarries on the Isle of Pines with the seminarists that I had been unable to see because I was told that they were on military maneuvers. He was in Havana because they had given him permission to come to see a doctor. I asked him to talk about them.

"Our unit is Number 5,570, under the command of Lieutenant Rabasa. It is a work unit, not a military service unit. If they told you that we were on military service it was because they didn't want you to see us, because there has never been any military service in this unit. Did you visit the old jail? Well, it's near it, you passed close by. It's a social disgrace unit, although it's not called that. But when we arrived we discovered that it was, because when we began to talk with the others we found out that some were there because they were homosexuals, others for smoking marijuana, others for theft or because they refused to work; and others of us were just Catholic militants, and four were seminarists.

"Yes, we work in the quarries. We cut the marble with electric drills, we get it out in blocks, and we polish it. We also make cement walls for prefabricated houses, columns, staircases, that are later put together like jigsaw puzzles. The work is hard because it's almost always in the sun. We work eleven hours a day, from seven to seven with an hour off for lunch from twelve to one. After work you bathe, have supper, and you can go into town. At times there are marathons of voluntary work, so-called (but it's not voluntary), in order to reach a goal, and then you work from seven in the morning to eleven at night. We are in this work unit instead of doing our military service, and in this unit there are no classes, only work. I have had to interrupt my studies for three years, because you have to spend three years in the quarries." He stops talking. I felt sorry for this young man, but, after a pause, he said: "I am happy."

His voice was sincere. His face was pure, his gaze was

limpid. There was no deception or deceit in him. I asked him if the work was not too hard. "The work is excessive. They ought to improve the conditions. . . But one has to be enthusiastic about the changes that are taking place here. And that enthusiasm I do not see in the Church. Do you know why people go to the churches? They all go to ask how to get out. They are all making promises to the saints if they'll get them out of Cuba. Haven't you noticed that people's faces are sad? I say that in our churches one sees the sadness of the dead Christ and not the joy of Christ resurrected. Catholics have done little harvest work, and what little they have done has been without joy. When Fidel announced in his speech that we weren't going to reach the ten million, many people wept. I saw many sorrowful people in the street after the speech, they went home with sad faces. But not the Catholics. I had a good look at the Catholics that I knew: not one had a sad face. You won't believe it, but there are some who dress badly, athough they could dress well, merely so that people will say that Cubans are ill clad here. There's not much food here, to be sure, but in other countries there is real hunger, isn't there?"

I asked him about the seminarists, if they were revolutionaries. "The seminarists aren't interested in politics. There are some who say they prefer the system of the United States, because they say that there 'one lives better.' One even told me that he prefers Russian communism to Cuban communism because in Russia 'one lives better' than here, because there are more comforts. There are revolutionary seminarists, but they sometimes leave the seminary. There are revolutionary Catholic leaders, but they often choose to leave the Church."

I was not to see him again. His pass ran out two days later, and he had to return to the Isle of Pines. I again felt sorrow. (I said to myself: "He is going back to forced labor in the quarries.") But I looked at him: he did not speak of his trip dramatically; his voice was calm, serene. The last thing that he said: "Those Catholics go off to the United States to live better. But I know that many of them are disappointed when they get there. A lady from my neighborhood went, and now she has written to her family: 'I'd swap places with any one of you, even though I had only a crust of bread each day; this is not at all the way it was painted for me. . .' Yes, and also, even though the food was good there, I think I couldn't

237

be happy eating ham knowing that other people had nothing to eat."

»»»

Under the headline: THE SOCCER WORLD BECOMES A SHOWCASE, *Juventud Rebelde* today published in the sports section the news that the soccer player Gerd Muller wants to sell himself to an Italian club. "The Milan manager wants to sign," he said, "and my answer is affirmative. The most fascinating aspect of this exchange is the money." The paper added that the player Espárrago was being negotiated for by the National Club of Montevideo. . . The vice president of the Vasco da Gama Club declared in Rio de Janeiro that he will not sign a contract with the Peruvian world champion Mifflin because his "owners" are asking a hundred thousand dollars. The daily commented: "Money also corrupts the most universal of sports. Only the socialist countries avoid this trafficking in athletes."

»»»

Walsh's wife told me that she had just been talking in the hotel with a Swiss lady who had been a millionaire and who had lost everything in the Revolution (her husband was a mine owner) and still supported the Revolution. When she hears poor people complaining she tells them: "I really would have the right to complain, and I don't complain." Some ladies were complaining of the poor service at a health resort, and she said: "Pardon me, but I was a member of this club before the Revolution, and it was very exclusive. I don't recall that you were members. . ."

»»»

PLACARD FOR 1960

—*Heberto Padilla*

Moneylenders, bandits, pawnbrokers
farewell.
You have been wiped out by the fire
of the Revolution.

The people's hands
have cut you down so far
that you will never be reborn.
For you it is over,
for you death; and if you wish,
Amen.

Those who sweated
in front of the oven, century after century;
those who bled
blow today on the bonfires
where the tax forms burn the papers
of usury and privilege.

Look at their children
who are looking at you. You see no fury
in their eyes.
They are the reasons
for these righteous fathers.

»»»

"Not everyone can be like Che," I said to Haydée Santamaría at the Nuncio's palace. And she said: "Even Che
couldn't always be like Che. He got tired at times, he came
home exhausted, and just wanted to be alone with his
children."

»»»

"What is the function of the poet and the writer in the
Revolution?" I asked a young poet. He answered: "For us
that function must be criticism. To expose and express the
truth."

»»»

At his house, Pablo Armando was telling me about two
neighbors of his who are millionaires. One has five million
pesos, the other has fifteen million, in Cuban banks. Fidel said
that those who hadn't taken their money out of Cuban banks
had shown confidence in the Revolution, and that the Revo-

lution would never take that money away from them. They can't take it out of Cuba. And they have not left Cuba, perhaps hoping that the Revolution will collapse. They live on their incomes. They buy what anyone can buy with their ration booklets (and surely also on the black market, he said). He and his wife told me about a rich lady, also from this neighborhood, who wrote from the United States to the current owners of her house, urging them to "take good care of it," and sending them a yearly sum of money to take care of "her" flowers. A Hollywood artist had come several times to Cuba to see how they were taking care of "his" skyscraper. And he complained that they were not keeping it up.

»»»

I was waiting for a bus on a corner with the young poet Ordoqui. He suddenly said: "There goes Fidel." A small car whizzed by with several people dressed in green. I couldn't distinguish Fidel. A second car followed, and Ordoqui said Dorticós was in it. Then another car. Many people waiting for the bus also turned to look. Fidel's car was far away.

Che's Orders

"I'll fight all I can against the opportunists who want to take over the Revolution, but if I can't fight any more, I'll kill myself. I'll never leave Cuba!" The photographer was very overwrought as we walked around the gardens of the National Hotel. He had come to give me some beautiful photographs of the cane harvest that I had praised when I visited his exhibit. He had had problems with some bureaucrat because of that exhibit; and he was overwrought.

"The opportunists! Those who never speak up! They don't care about the Revolution. Let it collapse: they don't care. They never criticize, they are not revolutionaries. Within the Revolution you have to be making the Revolution all the time. You always have to be attacking Moncada. Don't you agree? You have to keep the spirit of Che alive.

"You know why I took these photographs? Che commissioned them from me. And I said: 'I can't, Commander, because I just take art photographs, and pictures of sugar cane would be for publicity only, using the same old clichés and slogans.' And Che said: 'The true artist is a revolutionary, and therefore he always smashes every cliché and every slogan.' And then I began to work on the photographs. I began five years ago. I worked on them for three years.

"You know what Che wrote? That you mustn't put a straitjacket on artistic expression, and that you musn't create salaried employees obedient to official thought, or scholarship holders who live in the shelter of the budget exercising what he called freedom in quotes. Some leaders would condemn me if I gave this as just my opinion. But they have to accept it because it was said by Che."

He gave me some very large photographs. They are purposely a little blurred. It looks as though, more than the cane, the machines, and the men, he had tried to photograph the light, and through the light to express moral force. I tried to calm him down a bit. I said: "If you killed yourself you couldn't fight for the Revolution." I kept thinking of what Ernesto had told me a few days before: "We must always keep alive the rebelliousness of the Sierra Maestra. That was not just a thing that happened once and will never occur again."

»»»

The elevator operator (a blonde) closing the door: "What heat!" The hotel employee: "I'm off to Camagüey, my black one. Who'll take care of you when I'm not here?" She: "The State." He: "The State?" "That's right: the State takes care of children." The elevator door opens. He (leaving): "Bye-bye, Blackie."

»»»

In a room in the House of the Americas, decorated with pictures of all the principal writers of Latin America, two Cuban poets, Cintio Vitier and Fernández Retamar, were talking over coffee and cigars. I went up to them: they were talking about recent developments in the language in Cuba and how there were words that had been made obsolete by the Revolution, because the realities that they described no longer existed. They mentioned some of them:
Palanca [pull] (help from somebody influential in the government).
Mordida [the bite] (a Mexican term for bribe that was very common in Batista's day).
Chiva [nanny goat] (informer, spy).

»»»

A poet came to see me from Matanzas, and he said it took him six hours to get here because he had to wait in line so long. The bus trip from Matanzas to Havana takes only an hour.

»»»

Cintio told me: "All the churches in Cuba are open, except one: San Francisco, where Merton had that mystical enlightenment at the moment when some choirboys were singing. A man who had murdered several people in an attempt to hijack a plane took refuge there. And Father Laredo, who hid him, has been in jail for several years."
He told me also the story of the church built by the Communist party. The Party wanted a piece of land on which

242

there was a church. They did not confiscate the church, as they might have done, but asked the Curia to give up this church if they built another in exchange. "They built another one much better than the former one. It was amusing: the Communist party with its best architects building a church for the Catholics and decorating it in the smallest details, in accordance with the latest liturgical regulations. Only in Cuba do such things happen."

»»»

A young Marxist revolutionary:

"A hundred boys from the Communist Youth were stripped of their identity cards and all other identification and delivered to the UMAP as prisoners, to see how they would be treated. It was a highly secret operation. Not even their families knew of this plan. Afterward the boys told what had happened. And they put an end to the UMAP."

The "Venceremos" Brigade

Several Cuban magazines published articles on the "Vencere-mos" [We Shall Overcome] Brigade (North Americans who came to cut sugar cane in Cuba).

Burke gave up his job as a radio announcer because it was unpleasant to depend directly on the system. Now he's a dishwasher in a hospital, and he is exploring ways of reconciling politics and religion. Sandy, interested in the theater, said: "I was brought up in a middle-class family. They taught me that problems do not exist and the needs of society are no concern of mine, because I was a white girl." Carol, a girl who lives four blocks from the White House: "Before coming to Cuba I was a Weatherman. I left college to work in politics. At times I worked in a cafeteria, I learned that we had to make the Revolution someway or other, even though it wasn't easy. College had nothing to do with me, the student atmosphere is too unreal and fictitious." Lory was a student in a sophisticated school for eccentric girls. She realized that something was wrong. She hitchhiked through Europe. Then she decided to come to Cuba on her own. Johnny was a member of the Peace Corps; he said: "You have to see what a school in Ecuador is like to realize the changes that have been made in Cuba." Jerry stopped studying psychology because it seemed useless, he joined "Free Radio for the People." "We feel that the means of communication—press, movies, radio, and TV— distort the information." Barry said: "One is trying to change the image of the normal North American, the average man, who thinks his country is the best in the world. This is obviously a lie. It's easier to steal, to go around dirty." Jacqueline: "I live in Detroit, the great automobile center. I am black. I work to create better living conditions in the ghettos. I used to want to be a dancer. But not now." In the camp she learned many things. "The day they served ice cream for the first time, many people got in line twice, a lot of food was wasted because they threw away full trays and ate only the ice cream." She felt disappointed and indignant at the people who had done this, and at herself for not being able to prevent it. She thought that they would never serve ice cream again. But they did. The ice cream came back, and this time only a few people got in line twice. Then she learned a lesson about having confidence in her fellow man. "We come from a place where we learn to hate one another, to be distrustful, and to treat one another as enemies. But here they trusted us, they believed in the possibility of improvement. And that makes all the difference." Balkys is slender. Evelyn is determined. They are teachers. They met on the trip from Canada to Cuba. Balkys said: "The Church teaches me to love people. Che teaches me to love people. So there are no contradictions in my religion. Capitalism imprisons the people, crushes the people." Evelyn said: "Everything is so profound, so new to me. For us life means to get food for tomorrow. To be always expecting a policeman to come up and stop us. To be beaten on the street. Cuba bewilders me. Here for the first time I have learned the need for unity." Mike, from the *Catholic Worker*, said: "I had held many kinds of jobs in the United States, from office boy to bricklayer, and I remember that whenever I thought about the meaning and the value of work and about who benefited from it, I got very depressed and wanted to quit work. Working in Cuba, that hasn't happened to me. The more I learned about the ten million goal of the harvest, about its importance for the economy, about what it meant to the people, my sweat and my exhaustion made more sense. For the first time in my life I was working for the *people*."

The Brigade had everyone from a Protestant minister to an ex-Marine: blacks, Chicanos, Puerto Ricans, former members of the Peace Corps, dropouts, people who begged for money to get to Canada, and an ex-nun. There were students who resigned from college or were expelled for their antiwar demonstrations. There were the planners of peace marches, those who took part in antiracist fights, those who burned their draft cards, those who quit their jobs and refused to be compromised by the system. They came to know Cuba. They cut cane for the Revolution (three million *arrobas* of cane in two months). In the evening they read Che Guevara. They cut cane with the Vietnamese. Carlos María Gutiérrez, who won the poetry prize of the House of the Americas, told us that he asked a young fellow of eighteen, with blister-covered hands: "What are you thinking about?" He said: "About who I am, now."

»»»

CANE-CUTTING NOTES

—Cintio Vitier

THE SUGAR CANE PLANTATION

(To Tomás, a cane-cutting comrade)

Dear Poets: the sugar cane plantation
is no longer a feature of the landscape,
a symbol, a topic, not even a word.
How often we have read it
without knowing that it was something quite different:
a fantastic ache in the bones
that casts us shattered on the bunk
beneath the stars!
Then we do have inside us,
complete (gasping jade, monster
of man and cane, in the solar lens a fierce
and festive dance) the plantation, and we understand
that the bones arm the soul and disarm it
and arm it again to go on giving birth to us
in the struggle of each day,
with a fantastic ache.
Then indeed we understand, we are, and we sing
the sugar cane plantation.

THE HAND

It contracts, it catches fire,
using the machete retrains it,
the wasp kisses it,
it is starred with blisters and callouses,
it scarcely recognizes itself. In short:
the writing hand
assumes another form.

SANTIAGO

The back of Santiago
bony, lanky,

leaning forward in the dark, drinking in
the television, why did it stir me?
What mad desire to hug him,
to kiss his old fisherman's head,
his thin curls wise in their ignorance,
always a little ailing, a gentle outcast,
a tougher worker than most men.
And say to him: brother, yes,
the Revolution that you love is beautiful,
Christ died for us,
forgive my madness!

SOMEONE SPEAKS OF YESTERDAY

"The lady, the gentleman.
The gentleman, the lady.
Gentleman Alfredo wishes to see the lady.
The lady isn't at home.
The doctor is waiting for you."
It's the black billy goat who is talking
like one speaking a language lesson.
"To think that yesterday a cane-cutter
was the last word, and today . . . to think
that yesterday: The lady, the gentleman,
the gentleman, the lady . . ."
The black billy goat laughs as though, smothered,
he were sucking up all the stars in the shelter
converted into a stage for the tales
of the scorpion and the ant, Gentleman Alfredo,
his court partner, identical and rosy,
half naked, in the eternal dawn,
is tying on his boots.

THE TRUNK

In the center of the shelter
and of the world
is the trunk of Zayas:
"the much and the little, doctor."
To look at its weight, its bolts
from my bed is

a moderate and deep security:
a solid proof.
There are the nails, the thread,
the alcohol with roots, the sacred clothing,
the remedy that the old woman put on.
Next to his night trunk
that he seems to be keeping from the sun,
brother Zayas, a black as calm as he,
sits down gravely.
He is a king. And when he lifts the simple top,
a double blinding ray dazzles us:
the Sacred Heart of Jesus in dialogue
with the face of Che.

WE GO

We go through the dark,
in trucks or on foot,
in the drizzle or the moonlight,
slipping in the mud,
still sticking to the growth of the dream,
stubborn, alone, united,
armed with the coarse jokes
or the sullen silence, or the peace
that comes only from knowing things
with a taste of root on the tongue of the soul,
the anonymous ones, the peaceful
makers of a flower that will seem unmotivated,
the transitory answerers for the future,
those who do not justify themselves by success
but by the delivery of their strength to the earth,
by their daily burial alive,
in unequal groups invading
the ambushed fields, as furtive
as thieves, while the sealed glass
of light is shattered, under the lofty stars
of the sphinx who wipes the tears from her eyes
and smiles at us: thus are the roads of the fatherland,
we go, we go through the dark.

»»»

"And don't you go thinking that Cuban jails are any paradise," said a revolutionary intellectual. He repeated: "Don't
you think they're any paradise! I've seen the scars of the bayonet wounds on the backs of the prisoners. Those aren't stories,
they're what I saw. Of course, they don't do that now. The
present Secretary of the Interior, Sergio del Valle, is a doctor
and a fine person. Those things are no longer done by the
Revolution. But they used to be done."

»»»

A Marxist said: "In Prague I used to tell Latin American
revolutionaries: You want revolution, but you don't know
what it costs. Before you begin it you must be clear whether
you are ready to pay its price. I am glad we had our Revolution, but it was expensive." (I was reminded of the words of
Christ to the children of Zebedee: "You do not know what you
ask. Are you ready to drink of my cup?")

A Sermon

Celebrating Mass in a Cuban church: the feeling of celebrating a false rite in a sect, and that true Christianity is outside. Seeing the small attendance, the mournful faces, I think: the Cuban Church is crushed, no question. But it was crushed when the bourgeoisie was crushed, because it *was* the bourgeoisie. Would God really be interested in this Church?

In the sermon I reminded them of Christ's phrase: "If the salt has lost its savor, wherewith shall it be salted? it is henceforth good for nothing, but to be cast out, and to be trodden under the foot of men." I did not want to speak directly about the Cuban Revolution. I spoke of the social injustices of the other countries in Latin America: the cities still had a ring of slums just as Havana used to have, there was still prostitution, illiteracy, malnutrition, unemployment, chronic illnesses —and side by side with all this the scandalous wealth of a few people. Father Camilo Torres had said that he should stop celebrating worship abroad as a priest in order to create conditions that would make this worship more authentic. . . While I was speaking I noticed that some of the faithful got up and left the church.

A priest said afterward in a tone of reproach: "Father Cardenal, here we confine ourselves *strictly* to preaching the Gospel." "Liturgical reforms are accepted more easily," the Nuncio had said. But the truth is that the new liturgy is still rigid and formalist, as the ancient rubrics were.

In one way Cuban Catholicism is very advanced: there is no charge for administering the sacraments, nor are there fees for Masses. This is not exactly because the Church mentality has been advanced but because it had to be that way in a society as radically socialist as that of Cuba, where even the smallest private enterprise is forbidden—like the cobbler or the sidewalk food vendor. Otherwise religious services would have been the only way to earn money through private enterprise—aside from the black market. Priests live on the voluntary contributions of the faithful—and this is sufficient, even though there are few faithful—because money is in plentiful supply.

A great part of Cuban Catholicism is no longer here but

in Miami. Many of those who have stayed behind have their eyes set on Miami: hoping to go there or hoping that liberation will come from there. "Nixon more than Paul VI," as Pablo Armando Fernández said. "The Church of Washington," as Fidel said.

Catholicism was above all the religion of the bourgeoisie. As the Revolution became more and more socialistic, these Catholics became more and more antirevolutionary, and consequently the revolutionaries became more and more antireligious. Together with the intransigence of those who believed that because they were Catholics they had to be anticommunists there was the intransigence of the others who believed that because they were revolutionaries they had to be anti-Catholic.

I had said to Cintio and to Father Gaztelu: "No one has the right to cast the first stone at Catholicism. Before John XXIII and the Council—and also before Camilo Torres and Medellín—how many of us Catholics who are now very advanced, facing a communistic and atheistic regime, would not have reacted the same way?"

We now see that the Church had always preached this. It pointed out the ideal, and it lived this ideal in the religious orders; but in the past conditions were not propitious to establish the ideal in the form of a social system. The Church said to the rich man: "Remember that you are not the owner, merely the administrator of the wealth that belongs to everyone." St. John Chrysostom: "Do not say I spend what is mine, I enjoy what is mine. In truth it is not thine but another's." And Clemente Romano: "All the things that there are in the world ought to be of common use among men; but unjustly one man calls one thing his, and another man another, and thence comes the division that there is among men." And Saint Gertrude: "The commoner property is, the holier it is."

Fidel said that the new man is "freed from all egotistical incentive, especially the incentive of money." The new man of Fidel or Che is the same as the one of the Epistle to the Colossians 3: 9–11: "Lie not one to another seeing that ye have put off the old man with his deeds, and have put on the new man . . . where there is neither Greek nor Jew, circumcision nor uncircumcision, Barbarian, Scythian, bond nor free."

The "new man" and the "new society": that is where Christianity and communism could agree most fully. The objection that communism is "Utopian" (because egotism will never disappear) is the same objection that could be applied to the Gospels.

During this Mass there were very few young people with the July 26th insignia. In this church a lady near the altar rail gave the responses to the prayers of the Mass in great shouts, with a harsh and cutting voice. She seemed to me unbalanced. But perhaps it was that each time she shouted: "And with Thy Spirit" or "Let us give thanks to God," she meant: DOWN WITH COMMUNISM! DEATH TO FIDEL!

»»»

A teacher: "I don't believe in God, but I do not impose atheism on my university students, because that does not seem to me ethical. Even though it is taken for granted that I do so, and they could dismiss me at any moment because I do not do so. I expose them to all the philosophies and I leave them at liberty to choose the one they want—even though I am a Marxist."

»»»

A sign: "What we were in our hours of mortal danger let us learn to be also in production." *Fidel*

»»»

NOT TO TALK ABOUT IT EVER
WITH MY MOTHER

—José Yanes

Old woman,
if José Martí
had never written anything
(not even to Mercado).
If he had not dragged his hunger
and his shoe soles across America.
If he had died of a cold in the head.

If Beny Moré
had never been born,
if he had never poured into the air
his *Saint Elizabeth of the Steep Places.*

If I had not learned the philosophy
of Marianao Square,
if my ears had not found out
that someone could be in the *tíbiri-tábara*.
If nobody had said to me:
"*Nague,* I am the flame."

If in this country
people were not capable of talking without words
and were as serious as a fence pole.

If Fidel had not fired his shot
that "History will absolve me,"
and had not climbed up into the Sierra
and if there were no scholarships
and no talk of dialectic
and Marxism,
if we were to blame for the hunger we suffer,
I would probably decide
to go with you on that trip
(the palms are still here and the sun and the green always).
That trip that's not yours,
that doesn't interest you,
it's your daughter-in-law and my brothers,
it wasn't your idea
but you go along with it
because you know they can't earn their living.
Because your problem, old woman,
is always to be looking for another problem.
Now that you didn't have to put up with
my drunken father
shitting on your dead mother
(you remember that we had to leave the house).

If things had been as they are not
I would go away with you,
if only for the sharp memory that I have
of those bellyaches
that left me
when I saw you with
the manicure set,
because the old man wouldn't give you a nickel.
So that you wouldn't go off frightened
at me

who didn't want to work in the sausage factory
and then you would catch me
writing on bits of paper
things about love and men.

If they weren't as they are
I'd go with you to save you from the weeping
at night.

If Lezama explained to you
that the family after it's made is scattered
and you decided not to go anywhere
and you lived for your own sake the years
you wouldn't have to be desperate thinking
how you're going to get along in that strange land,
that you know nothing about,
beginning all over again at forty-odd.

If that's the way it was,
I wouldn't be crying alone on the bench
in this park,
the tears would not be falling down
my face.

Because it's not a question of the family
going off
and O.K. so what?
It's a fucking mess, old woman.

»»»

And other sentences noted down:

Be wary of that one. He was the one who took
Lezama Lima's *Paradiso* out of the bookstores. Until Fidel
and Dorticós found out and ordered it put back on the
shelves.

The Cuban Revolution has cost less blood and has
been more successful than the Chinese Revolution, just
as it cost less blood and was more successful than the
Russian one. The new Latin American revolutions could
also be better than this one, and with less bloodshed.

When Khrushchev took the nuclear weapons out of
Cuba, Fidel was so furious that he punched the walls of
his room.

As the Revolution became gradually more Marxist the enemies of the Revolution became more Catholic, right? No opposition was permitted, so then they went to church to demonstrate their anticommunism, right? Many Marxists then viewed going to Mass as an antirevolutionary activity, right? And many Catholics stopped going to Mass so as not to be confused with the others, right?

I was in a town when Fidel arrived at nine in the evening; there were meetings and discussions until breakfast time; after breakfast, we were about to go to bed, Fidel took us to another place where they were going to open a dairy; a total of thirteen hours, and Fidel was fresh as a daisy, ready to make a speech in the square. The speech went on for three hours. I fell asleep on the platform.

»»»

In *Juventud Rebelde,* in big green letters, the headline: ONCE UPON A TIME THERE WAS A REPUBLIC. A photograph: black, disheveled mothers carrying squalid, naked children. Another photograph: a naked child, scrawny buttocks, asleep on a carpet of garbage.

"This is the story of the recent past: children who, with a lost look and tottering little steps (drinking perhaps twice a day blackish sugared water), follow the handcart pushed by the father, with the little crib and the baby, grandmother's armchair, mother's brazier, the boilers to cook meals, the one bed. Where are they going? . . . They are the defendants. The Justice of the Laws of the Republic is throwing them out in the street." The text goes on to describe the starved little face of that homeless child who sleeps in the storm, the undernourishment that is as bad as starvation, the sickness, the prostitution, life spent huddled in archways. . .

Beside it, in a chestnut-colored picture, some words of Fidel, in his speech defending his attack on Moncada, *History Will Absolve Me:*

I AM GOING TO TELL YOU A STORY. ONCE UPON A TIME THERE WAS A REPUBLIC. IT HAD ITS CONSTITUTION, ITS LAWS, ITS FREEDOM: A PRESIDENT, A CONGRESS, COURTS OF LAW. . .

(I thought: a newspaper that seemed to have been written by Isaiah or Jeremiah or any of the prophets.)

With Young Catholics

"It was quite startling to see the *Populorum Progressio* published by Communists." It was a young Catholic who was talking. We had gone to the Malecón pier for a talk, but as it was drizzling we took shelter in one of the cabins which had just been erected for the carnival. These were some young Catholics with whom it was really worthwhile to talk.

One of them commented on how little interest Catholics had had in the cane harvest. The other spoke of the slight interest they had had in aid to Peru. To help Peru they took one bottle of olive oil away from each Cuban, and that week they got only one bottle instead of two. "And would you believe it? It was the Catholics who protested. The only ones I heard protesting were Catholics."

They were students. We talked of the difficulties that Catholics have at the University. One of them said: "They have good reason to distrust us." I asked them about the JEC. In *Mensaje* ["Message"] I had read a very fine statement of theirs, in which they gave the Revolution their support. But in Cuba nobody had been able to tell me about the JEC. Oliva had said: "Such an organization does not exist in Cuba, unless it's underground." Now I cleared up the mystery of the JEC (Juventud Estudiantil Cristiana) [Christian Student Youth]. Those boys told me that the movement was not Catholic but Protestant, and besides it was a very small group, splintered, and not really revolutionary.

One of those young men belongs to the Parish of San Juan de Letrán, and he told me that the only reason that more people hadn't walked out on me when I preached there was that they had to hear Mass, and if they left my Mass they would have to go to another Mass. A couple was sitting next to the young man while I was talking, and the lady said to her husband: "That priest is a communist. The Church has gone to hell."

I told them what the other ex-seminarist from San Juan de Letrán said in front of a group of people: "There is hunger here. For example, I went to bed last night without supper, and I haven't had any breakfast yet." "It's a lie," said one.

"He probably hadn't had supper or breakfast just as I've not had breakfast yet: not because I didn't have money for food but because I left home early and I wasn't hungry. Here everyone has enough to eat. Why wouldn't he? But housekeepers have to plan their food for the whole week, because since everything is rationed, if they don't plan well they'll run out of food before the week is over and there'll be no place to buy it."

The young poet Eduardo Lolo came to see me. He had written me several letters at Solentiname. "What do you do for a living?" I asked him. He was an educational supervisor. He worked from nine in the morning until two in the morning, as a rule. When did he write? He made his poems during the trips, when he went from one place to another in buses, in jeeps.

»»»

A VISIT TO THE TRENCHES

—Samuel Feijóo

The evening is dark purple
like yesterday. Gray blue
is the sea that can no longer cope
with the evening and the star
of Venus.
        The militiaman
looks at the horizon. He waits for
the invader who is coming for his houses,
his farms, his oil,
his prostitutes, his slaves.
He waits. The mangrove swamps grow black.
In the middle of the dense night
if we are to die, let it be
next to the poor; if we are
to live, let it be
next to the honorable poor.

A Religious

They told me that near Güines there were two French members of the Order of the Little Brothers of Jesus, founded by Charles de Foucauld, and I wanted to go to see them. The Little Brothers of Jesus have no mission, their goal is simply to live the life of the poorest people. In the Sahara they live the life of the desert Bedouins. In Peru they live among the Indians up in the Andes. In Spain there are some who work in the mines. In the Near East they are shepherds. In the United States they are hoboes. In Santiago de Chile they live in the shanty town and in Venezuela among the lay brother Indians. In Cuba? In Cuba they work on a people's farm, I was told.

I told the House of the Americas that I wanted to visit some French religious, and they sent me a car from ICAP (Instituto Cubano de Amistad con los Pueblos). I was accompanied by two Chileans, a priest and a student leader in Cuba with tourist visas, and a Cuban friend, Enrique López Oliva.

López Oliva is an ex-Catholic who had studied at the Jesuit School in Belén where Fidel had once studied. In his time there, he said, there was still a picture of Fidel in a frame of honor as a Distinguished Student. Fidel had been president of the Literary Academy, which met Sundays after Mass to discuss "contemporary problems." But these meetings, said López Oliva, were led by a reactionary priest, Father Rubino, who was also a director of the *Diario de la Marina*. López Oliva had already talked about the luxury of that Belén school ("A profusion of marble. Stained-glass windows that had cost a fortune, a library of shocking ostentation, very expensive uniforms for the students. . .") The school was only for the sons of the very rich. Beside it, the Jesuits had a little school for the poor. Now there are no Jesuits, and the Belén school is filled with workingmen's children.

On the way Oliva said that the Church served the counterrevolutionaries as a trench. The enemies of the Revolution became militant Catholics to fight, according to them, against "atheistic" communism, but in reality it was to defend capitalism. Many of them went to church, he said, as if to a kind of counterrevolutionary club. The young revolutionaries then gradually stopped going to church in order not to be confused with the counterrevolutionaries. Also, he said, because they were rejected by the others. One Sunday when he went to Mass, he went up to some friends who were talking in the vestibule, and he heard one of them say to the others: "Careful, here comes a tainted one." He never went to Mass again. Oliva, who used to be a devout Catholic and is now a devout Marxist, is an expert on the revolutionary tendencies of the clergy in Latin America. We call it renewal, and he calls it "the crisis of the Catholic Church in Latin America."

In Güines we enquired at the parish church for the People's Farm, and some young Catholics who were with the priest went with us. First we took a bus, and then we walked. We found one of the Little Brothers of Jesus, shirtless, cooking his lunch. The other one wasn't there. Their hut had walls of boards, whitewashed, a palm roof beautifully thatched, a cement floor. He told us his name was Brother Henry; he was a priest but he didn't want to be called Father. He worked on the farm as a carpenter and mason; he had built this house and many others like it for the workers on the farm, and he also made carts. His comrade, Brother Humberto, ran a tractor and worked twenty-four hours in a row on the tractor, one day on the job and the other day off, because the tractors have to be kept going all the time. "That twenty-four hour stretch is a tough one," he said. Brother Humberto had won the distinction of "Outstanding Worker" on the farm. The normal work day is eight hours, but beyond this there is voluntary work, and there is voluntary work Sunday morning, generally. They have been here five years, and he came from Chile, where he had worked as a laborer.

In the hut they have a tiny chapel. The altar is made of a thick palm tree trunk; the floor and the walls are covered with matting. The hut has in addition two little rooms, a tiny kitchen and a little reception room where we talked. The furniture is country-style. They don't have electric light, just a Coleman lamp. On the walls there are no pictures or any other decoration, just a map of Cuba.

Brother Henry was frying some potatoes when we arrived, and to serve us lunch he mixed them up with some noodles and with all the eggs that he had in the kitchen (three), and so he invented a new dish which turned out to be delicious for hungry people (and we were hungry). We added to the lunch some ham sandwiches that we had brought from Havana.

Before the Revolution, most of the farm workers did not have work all year round, said Brother Henry. There was a part of the year that they called "dead time," and the farmers still remember it. A neighboring carpenter, who took part in forty cane harvests under capitalism, says that he never lacked work, but the great majority say that they didn't have work for the full year. Now there is work for everyone all year long, although they cannot always choose the work that they want. They don't have too much food, but they have enough—and that is very important. The food that the farmers have is the same that any person in Havana has, whether he is an architect, a doctor, a top manager. This food he finds similar to that of a well-paid worker in Chile where workers eat well, he told us. But he added: "Of course I eat a lot because I'm quite tall. This State Farm used to be an estate, and the mansion of the estate's owner was given to his cook. Afterward the army took over the mansion, but they built another house, of cement and very fine, for the former cook, and they gave her the former owner's furniture."

I asked Brother Henry if they had been treated badly because of their religion, and he said no. Father Voillaume, the General of the order, had come several times to Cuba to visit them, and he had no trouble getting in. And what about Catholicism in Cuba? He said: "They really believe in God. They have their children baptised, and they celebrate certain feast days: Christmas Eve, Good Friday, Our Lady of Cobre. Their morals are natural, with certain deviations. There is practically no Christianity."

Oliva asked him what moved him to forsake his comfortable life in France and the intellectual profession that he had, to lead this harsh life, and he answered: "To imitate the secret life of Jesus of Nazareth, to share the life of the poorest, to atone for the sins of the world." I thought he might have used a more revolutionary language to describe his revolutionary form of life. But that's what he said.

The Little Brother of Jesus took us to see the house that the army built for the one who had been the cook of the owner of the estate. She showed us the owner's furniture that they had given her. On a handsome double bed were displayed the provisions that she had just received for the "Christmas supper" of the 26th of July: a bottle of rum, a jar of pickles, a Rumanian wine, a box of Spanish Christmas nougat—the same things that all the people in Havana were getting and that all the farmers were getting out here. The farmers had just received free whitewash for their houses, as they always do at Christmas time all over Cuba.

The lady told us she would not go to the mass meeting in Havana to hear Fidel. She would hear the speech on the radio. But her husband would go, he was "on the list." "He was on the list?" we asked. "Are they forced to go?" "Oh, no. They're not forced. They go because they enjoy it. He's on the list to get a seat on the bus, because they take them there in a bus." The Little Brother of Jesus also said: "No, they are not forced to go."

A Reformed One

We were at the People's Farm where the Little Brothers of Jesus worked, and the Chilean Father said: "Listen, it seems that everything is not rose-colored, and that there are horrible things in the Revolution. Go talk with Alberto, that fellow over there, who spent five years in jail for taking part in a Good Friday procession. That's all I know." When we left the farm I questioned Alberto, one of our companions. We were walking along a muddy road, bordered by fields of sweet potatoes.

"Yes, I was in jail, not for five years but for four and a half. Yes, I was in jail for taking part in a performance of the Passion, one Good Friday. Not the four and a half years, but less, the last time I was in jail: because really those four and a half years were various sentences. It was Good Friday of '61, which fell on the 31st of March. We performed the Passion in the square of Güines, before fifteen thousand people; I played the role of Pilate. Militiamen and a lot of other people arrived to attack us, shooting bullets. Some of them hit the Cross. They took about fifty people to jail. They let them go except four, and I was one of the four." "No, it was not a political demonstration," he protested. "It's true that on Palm Sunday we had converted the religious procession into a political demonstration, but not on Good Friday. . . Why were there fifteen thousand people there? Because in Güines the performance of the Passion attracts a lot of people every year. . . Yes, there's no doubt that they were alarmed at the number of people. And it must be admitted that those were nervous times."

I remembered 1961. The 31st of March. The bombardment of Havana was the 15th of April, and two days later came Playa Girón. Alberto continued: "I was a student leader. I organized demonstrations and strikes at the University. . . No, not against Batista, but at the time of the Revolution, against Fidel. I had been in jail before. This time they sentenced me to nine years. But I was a prisoner only three years. In fact I was in jail only one year; the other two I spent on a rehabilitation farm, and I got reformed. . . The treatment in jail? Yes, it was tough. They hit us with bayonets, they punched us. But I want you to know that they don't do that any more. On the rehabilitation farm they treated us well."

I asked him what persuaded him to get reformed. "The horrible things I saw in jail. . . No, not the treatment by the jailers, although, as I said that was tough, but the things that the others did." "What others?" "Why, the Batista people. First, I saw that while the Revolution outside was making all men equal and had suppressed social classes, inside the jail the prisoners were keeping right on with class differences. There was a very marked difference between rich and poor. The rich did not mix with the farmers and workers, who were really in jail for having defended the interests of the rich. They used to get very good meals brought in, and they didn't share them with the poor who were right beside them, in spite of the fact that outside the jail the whole nation was being divided up in a spirit of equality. Besides which they wanted everything to go back to where it used to be." "As it was in Batista's time?" "Exactly. We Catholics had a social studies group with Father Laredo, who was in jail with us for having hidden a man who had tried to hijack a plane. And the Batista followers said we were Reds because we had social studies. They were always quarreling. Because many wanted to be President. All the future Presidents of Cuba were in that jail. One time two of them were fighting over an estate that belonged to the State, because each one wanted it for himself, and they even came to blows, and we had to separate them. I said to myself: I don't want to have anything to do with these people. And then I decided to reform. Those of us who asked to be reformed got all kinds of insults from the Batista people. The worst insults that I got in jail came from them. I got out after two years of work on the farm, and now I work as an electrician. At first they wouldn't give me work because I'd been in jail, but the Department of the Interior intervened to get me accepted. And they gave orders that I was not to be bothered because of the past. And they really haven't bothered me. Each month I have to report to the Department of the Interior to sign a form (I've just been there), and each month they ask me if anyone has bothered me in any way. I always say no, because they really haven't bothered me."

We were coming to the end of the potato fields, and a wheat field was next. Looking at the sown fields, Alberto said that the last time they had sown sweet potatoes all through there, and that nobody remembered to harvest them and they had all rotted in the field. At times, he said, there is gross carelessness like that, and many people, in order not to be conspicuous, don't dare to denounce it. I asked him if he was "integrated" into the Revolution, and he said he wasn't, but that he did all the voluntary work.

"The 'voluntary' work is really voluntary?" "It's voluntary. Although it may happen that sometimes they call it voluntary and it's something else." "And what about what some Catholics have said, that the Communists now are living better than the rest of the people and that they enjoy privileges?"

"There are cases. But when they're discovered they're punished. Here in Güines there were leaders who had their houses full of things that they had taken out of stores. Since the ration books are quite complicated, when simple people arrived and presented their ration books, they would put down that the people had taken things, shoes, clothes, whatever, which they hadn't taken, and then they would keep all that. They were discovered, and they were tried in Güines Park, before the whole town. And they showed the things that they had found in their houses, furniture and other things. A captain's wife had been found with a great number of pairs of shoes and dresses in her closet. They were condemned. Not to jail, but to work on a farm. Five months, for example."

We were approaching Güines. It was Sunday, and a lot of homeowners were working in the street in front of their houses, planting little trees, digging drains, cleaning the street, whitewashing their houses, putting up Christmas decorations for the 26th of July. "All this work is voluntary, and people really enjoy doing it," said Alberto. We walked to Güines Park, where the public trial had taken place, and there he took leave of us.

Back in Havana I told the Chilean priest that the Good Friday story was a bit different from the way it appeared at first sight, and I told him the details. He said: "I'm so happy. Because whenever I hear a good thing about the Revolution I feel a great satisfaction, and when I hear something bad it hurts me deeply. One would wish the Revolution to be something perfect, impeccable."

»»»

"We have been too ethereal," said the parish priest of Güines, a young man, when we asked him his opinion of the situation of the Church in Cuba. In the past six years church attendance had diminished fifty to sixty per cent. At the beginning there was a movement of rapprochement with the Revolution, he said, the Revolutionary Catholic Youth. "Before I was ordained a priest I was one of them." The rich made use of religion, he said. "Years before, in a plane going to Miami, a rich man spoke to me, complaining that the Church was not fighting. I said: 'You want the Church to fight for your interests while you leave Cuba.'"

He told us that a young man of his parish saw an issue of the *Osservatore Romano* and was surprised to find it so advanced. He advised the young people who became integrated with the Revolution to go and cut cane, to do voluntary work, to become militiamen.

»»»

I opened the paper and was surprised by some headlines:

IN SANTIAGO DE CUBA 45 CHILDREN DIE
VICTIMS OF ACIDOSIS
ACTING MINISTER OF LABOR DECLARES
THE GOVERNMENT WILL NOT ALLOW
ANY MORE WORK STOPPAGES

and in a little box: an eighteen million dollar drop in the wages of public employees as the government readjusts the national budget. The cuts will range from eight per cent to seventeen per cent.

It seemed to me that I was reading the papers of my own country. Then I understood that it was a joke. They were commemorating the assault on the Moncada Barracks with headlines from the newspapers of that period.

In one corner of the page there was an ad that said: APPLE CLUB (with a goblet) and in another, the results of the races at Oriental Park, Havana: "First Race: Horses: Boo Script, Ships Pass," etc. . .

»»»

LET'S GO, FOR THIS IS THE YEAR

—A Protest Song of Noel Nicola

Listen, everybody,
this is the moment to take photographs
because at the end of a few years
there'll be nobody who'll recognize our picture.

Let's
change the face of this earth where we are
Let's go,
it won't be easy
but there'll be lively spirits to help us
Let's
push neck and neck and everywhere
this stone of backwardness that jams us
Let's get our hands on it, let's go

As always
some skeptic will come to say we're raving mad,
but people are awake:
he's going to catch his fingers in the door
Let's get our arms into it
and let's get our arms into it
and let's get it all going
and let's go, for this is the year
let's go, for this is the year!

A Television Program

In a room at the hotel we saw a television program on which Haydée Santamaría and Melba Hernández talked about Moncada. The Bulgarians who had come as an official delegation for the 26th of July and were staying at the hotel protested because they didn't want to see this program, they wanted an American movie. In the program Haydée and Melba were seated on a sofa:

Haydée: "We always knew that our comrades had great fortitude, but tortures are tortures and sufferings are sufferings. And Melba and I both had great affection for Gómez García because he was a very sensitive person. Poor fellow, he never had time to. . . Everything that was in him. You know that he wrote some poems. He was very young and he had no time to develop all that he would have been today. But he was very sensitive. He was a little fellow, very gentle, very sweet, and always concerned about us.

"Gómez García had a really infinite sweetness. He was a boy of such integrity, but with boyish characteristics, with that angelical childlike quality, with that purity. And when we were on our way from the hospital to the barracks, I thought of everyone, but I thought especially of Gómez García, because it seemed to me that he was going to suffer more than the others because of all those things. And I thought: 'Oh, if they would only shoot him quickly, not to let him suffer.' And he was one of the comrades whom we saw suffer most, and we didn't see. . . In his eyes there was only a worry for Melba and me.

"I remember now that we were sitting like this. . . Was it on the floor? We were sitting on the floor in a half circle, I think. And Melba said: 'Yeye, look: Gómez García.' And I looked for Gómez García there and I couldn't see him, because I knew what he looked like. She said. 'Look at Gómez García,' and I didn't recognize him. I said: 'Which one?' She said: 'That one.'

"Then, when I saw those eyes—because he had such eyes, with a deep and very gentle look, melancholy but extraordinarily beautiful—and when I looked at him then and realized that he was Gómez García, it seemed as though he saw in my face that I hadn't realized that it was he, and he smiled as if saying: 'Don't you worry about me.' He smiled like that. And really the condition that Gómez García was in was terrible.

"And he was one of the comrades of whom we were most afraid that things might hurt him, all that, because he would suffer not just for himself but for all the others. He was extremely gentle. And there you could see what he was: in that moment when he was so frightful, so frightful that I didn't know him, when I looked right at him and said: 'Melba, but where is Gómez García?' And she said: 'Look at him right there', and I looked at him like that, and I sat there thinking if that was Gómez García, and he smiled. He smiled with his eyes, because he couldn't smile with anything else. . . The only part of his face that I recognized were his eyes.

"That's the way Gómez García was. Not to speak of Abel, right? for at any moment. . . It didn't seem to him as though he were going to have a bad time. So much so that at one moment, I don't know if Melba said to me or I said to her—because in those things there are times when thoughts get confused if we both think alike at a given moment—well, we said: 'But Abel doesn't realize what is going to happen.' Do you remember, Melba?

"And when I'd say to him: 'But look, Abel. . .' trying to see if we could do something to save him, he would calmly say not to worry about him, that we should worry about ourselves. And that's the way all the comrades really were."

The Bulgarians went on protesting. They said that was enough of that program. They wanted to see an American movie. Haydée went on:

"I spoke of Gómez García because I never thought that he could endure all that without a complaint. Not through cowardice, because if he had been a coward he wouldn't have gone there, but because he was so sweet and so concerned for others. So concerned that he finally managed to send a note to his mother, to say: 'Your son is alive. I am a prisoner, your son.'

"I think that Gómez García knew that he was not going to live, but he wanted to give his mother the joy of knowing that he was there. A few minutes more of joy for his mother. That was Gómez García."

Melba: "Remember, Yeye, we must be honest. We were

trying to evade that part a little. When they took us out of that place where we were arrested, as you said, sitting on the floor, the last thing we saw there was precisely the horrible tortures that they were giving to Gómez García in a little cubby hole next to the big room, and we both left with the feeling that Gómez García could not survive that monstrous treatment. And we were quite right, because soon after we left prison they brought us some films that were taken just then, and it was Gómez García whose death was shown, but he didn't die of any gunshot wound or any bullet: Gómez García was tortured to death.

"Yeye talks of Mateo. Mateo was the first wounded man on our side, a shot in the stomach, which didn't at first seem serious; Yeye herself gave him first aid, and we made him one of our group, and we dragged him along. We didn't know if he was dead or alive, we just didn't know. He couldn't even sit up. Yeye and I tried to protect him, to shelter him, because when they sat him down he fell over. It was horrible."

Haydée: "But he didn't utter even a sigh. It was really. . . I think that if it happened again I would scream, because why not? Why shouldn't we scream?"

Melba: "Besides, how did we find out that Boris was in prison, too? By the comments that all that pack of hounds came and made there in front of us."

Haydée: "That was when Boris's nature appeared."

Melba: "I remember that when they came in they talked about 'that one with the two-toned shoes.' And that showed up Boris's true character, and, besides, the great integrity of the comrades. Boris had bought those shoes to wear into action. They were his new shoes, he was like a child with new shoes, and he went with his new shoes into action. When Yeye and I heard them talking about 'that one with the two-toned shoes' we looked at each other. We knew it was Boris. Then they explained how, no matter how violent the tortures, they couldn't break Boris. And then we learned more when they took him out in the night and already half dead he went on insulting them, and in the jeep they also tried to break him."

The Bulgarians tried to change stations to see the American movie. They protested saying that the interview was very boring.

Melba: "What happened to Mario Muñoz was in front of us, right in front of our eyes."

Haydée: "Yes, But he was one comrade who didn't suffer."

Melba: "Yeye is quite right. There was a moment when we felt something, a peace, when we learned, for example, how Gildo Fleitas fell in action, because we thought that he had been spared all that tremendous martyrology. And Mario Muñoz was one of those comrades murdered while a prisoner but who in fact didn't suffer so much. Mario was walking a few yards from us. We could see that Mario was arguing with the soldiers, and suddenly the shot came. Mario fell. And I grabbed Yeye, and as we walked by him we leaned over as far as we could to see if he was still alive and if we could do anything for him. But I don't think so, I think we couldn't do anything. I think he died at once."

Haydée: "Now, notice, Melba: at those moments we would have wanted all our comrades to have died like that. Because I often thought in those moments: 'If Abel could have died fighting at the hospital.' And two years later I am glad that it didn't happen that way. Because it is sad to die quickly and thoughtlessly, today I almost prefer to know that Abel had time to think, to analyze, to know that he was going to die, even, if you wish, to be happy in the knowledge that he was going to die for a cause."

Melba: "And to organize, Yeye, to organize. Because remember how Abel, as soon as he realized that they would murder us, warned us that we had to defend our lives without giving up our principles, our dignity, or our honor, that it was absolutely necessary for somebody to be alive to tell people about what was going on. It is not easy for us to talk about this. We really didn't want to talk about it. We are revolutionaries. And today we are close to the people of Vietnam, and we say to them that we give our blood for them, and it is true, and we are on the side of any people who struggle for. . ."

Haydée: "It is easier to do it than to talk about it."

Melba: "It is easier to do it than to talk about it. I said a few days ago that it's been seventeen years. I thought it was a unique situation for Yeye and me. We know very well what all this means to Fidel. But, for example, I was much moved that night when I heard Comrade Aguilerita talk about Abel, because a few days before we were saying that in seventeen years we had not let a single day go by—no matter how urgent our task—without remembering our comrades, and first of all Abel, Boris, those who were closest to us, Raúl Gómez García, and it is not easy to talk of that. Now, Yeye is right: when one starts along the road to Revolution, on top of everything is the basic objective: the liberation of the peoples. The sacrifices are, indeed, hard. . ."

Haydée: "I tell you I don't know why it is so hard for us to talk about things that it's not at all hard to have done, so hard to talk about things that we would do again and that we have done again, besides. The fact is that when we begin to talk by ourselves we talk about the good things. But we just have to be in a group, on television or something, and it's all different."

The program ended. The Bulgarians rushed at the set to look for the cowboy picture.

»»»

Roque Dalton and I were waiting for lunch in the dining room of the hotel, and he asked for a double rum on the rocks, and they didn't bring it. He finally got up impatiently to talk to the waiter, and he got the drink. The communist poet said to me laughing: "There are still some remnants of clericalism in Cuba. You know what I did to get them to bring my drink right along? I said: 'Really, the Father asked for a drink some time ago, and he hasn't got it, and he's thirsty!' "

With the Foreign Secretary

At a reception at the House of the Americas, the Foreign Secretary, Raúl Roa, said: "Don't believe that this people is not religious. The Revolution is also a religious phenomenon. We have had some very difficult times. Without the Revolution's religious and mystical element it would not have survived."

I told him that as a priest and as a revolutionary I wanted to see the conflict between the Revolution and the Church in Cuba disappear, and that I wanted the Church to be revolutionary. This would be good for the Revolution and good for the Church. For the Church, because it was a return to the evangelical substance of primitive Christianity. For the Revolution, because it would greatly accelerate the revolutionary processes in Latin America. Revolution in Latin America will not occur without the Church. And it will not be made without Cuba. Cuba is a model for Latin America, but revolution in Latin America would be easier if there were also the model of a revolutionary Church in Cuba. (Not a Church in power: neither Christians nor revolutionaries can want that, for it would be antievangelical and also antirevolutionary.) It would not be difficult to create a revolutionary Church in Cuba, but to do this Cuban Catholics would have to stop being isolated from revolutionary Catholicism in Latin America. The government should encourage the circulation of Catholic leftist publications among Cuban Catholics. It should bring to Cuba revolutionary priests, from among those being expelled (exiled) from Brazil or Colombia, for example. And Roa said: "That would be to divide Catholicism." I said: "As a priest, I believe that it is necessary to divide Catholicism, to separate true Christianity from false Christianity." He said: "But we don't want to fall into the error that others have committed by creating a national Church. We don't like the creation of a national Church."

I said: "This would not be a national' church separated from the Church of Rome, because the revolutionary Church of Cuba would be that of the Council, that of Medellín, that of the Gospel, and the Church of Rome itself. Whereas the other one is the dissident one, the heretical one, the one that

Fidel has rightly called the 'Church of Washington.' The selection of priests who are to come to Cuba should be made not through nuncios or bishops but from the clandestine movements that are fighting for the liberation of those countries, movements with which you are in contact, as are also the revolutionary priests. I'm talking about importing to Cuba the revolution of the Latin American Church."

Roa told me I should talk with Fidel. (They told me about the time that Raúl Roa, who is a great orator, shouted in the United Nations: "Fuck your mother!" And while they were ringing the bell on him: "Fuck your fucking mother!!")

»»»

We were in the parish office of a church near Havana. Several young people, blacks and whites, came up to me. They recognized me by my beard. They had wanted to go to my poetry reading at the University of Havana. They asked me if I didn't think it was the duty of a Christian to become a part of the Revolution. I said I did think so, that Christians ought to take part in all the great tasks of the Revolution, in voluntary work, in the sugar cane harvest. They jumped with joy when I said that, they clapped their hands and hugged one another. They said they'd have to come to Havana to talk with me. (But I never saw them again.)

»»»

I told Lezama Lima the incident concerning the Bulgarians in the hotel, and he answered, in his slow asthmatic speech: "Those Eastern countries . . . it seems . . . are not communist. The Revolution did not surge up . . . from the people . . . as it did in Cuba. . . It fell on them . . . a system from on high like a circus tent."

»»»

It was said that the Revolution would enter into a new period with the speech of the 26th.

»»»

Other slips of paper:

Haydée Santamaría talking in the House of the Americas: "Fidel is timid. He gets nervous when he's going to talk with someone. When he went to talk for the first time with the mother of Camilo Torres, he said: 'What will I say to her?'"

A rainy afternoon. The sea around Havana the color of asphalt.

On the radio: "Here is left the clear / the lovable transparence / of your beloved presence / Commander Che Guevara."

The voice of the hotel receptionist talking on the phone: "Comrade. . ."

Havana as serious as a reformed prostitute. It doesn't have the joy that it used to have, but it has another joy.

And far off against the black sky the red neon lights, not announcing a Nicaraguan beer but saying WE SHALL OVERCOME.

Fidel has just been on the pier (during the carnival). A great many people crowded around him, and he had to escape by jumping on a passing bus.

There are automobiles that seem to have been pulled out of a car cemetery and set going by a miracle. The automobile of the poet Eliseo Diego is a skeleton of an automobile. Cintio said to me: "I don't understand why he hasn't thrown it out. Most of the time it stops on him, and he has to leave it in the street. He spends much more time walking home (and then trying to get someone to fix his car and bring it home) than we do riding the buses."

After my poetry reading at the National Library, some poets invited me to have a drink with them. Where could they get a bottle of rum? We went to my hotel to discuss the matter. "Let's use our imaginations," Pablo Armando Fernández kept saying. Some of them went to the telephone. One had a bottle at home but he lived too far away. Padilla said: "Let's not be Utopian. The same thing has happened to us countless times, and we always end up by each of us going home." In fact, it wasn't possible.

"Statistics in Cuba are always correct." (Cintio)

Communist Parties

At the start of the attack at Playa Girón, Fidel declared Cuba a socialist country, and the Party of the Revolution was at that time called the Communist party. But little by little the old communist leaders were replaced, and of them only Carlos Rafael Rodríguez is left—the only one of the communists to get to the Sierra (and besides, one of the bravest and most capable men in the government). The revolutionaries had been against the communists because the latter had supported Batista. The communists were the first anti-Castro group. They condemned the assault on Moncada, saying that it was a "rash attempt" and that its heroism was "false and sterile," "guided by false bourgeois concepts."

Fidel Castro had written in *Bohemia* (in 1955) against Batista: "What right does Mr. Batista have to talk against communism if he was the Presidential candidate of the Communist party in the 1940 elections, if his electoral satires took shelter under the hammer and sickle, if he had his picture taken with Blas Roca and Lázaro Peña, if a half dozen of his current ministers and close advisers were outstanding members of the Communist party?"

"Fidel has never denied his non-Marxist past," said Debray. And Fidel, in an interview: "If you ask me if I considered myself a revolutionary when I was in the Sierra, I'll say yes. If you ask me if I considered myself a classic communist, I'll say no." The communists also condemned the uprising in the Sierra. And Che said: "In Cuba, the Communist party did not lead the Revolution. It was incapable of recognizing modern methods of fighting, and it was mistaken in its estimate of the opportunities for victory." They also said that at the Punta del Este Conference in Uruguay, Che said to some Argentine communists: "Well, what are you doing here? Have you come to start a counterrevolution?" As is well known, Fidel is at odds with all the Communist parties in Latin America. He has often said: "Our country will always maintain its own seal."

»»»

275

At breakfast some Marxists asked me about our community at Solentiname. I explained that we try to lead a life in common, with no "thine" or "mine," a life of voluntary poverty—free from the desire for money and from the demands of a society of consumption. We live in brotherly union, all working for the community. We are all equal. And then I stopped. I understood that what may seem very novel in the capitalistic world is a daily reality in Cuba. (I couldn't talk to them about prayer because it would be misinterpreted, and I wouldn't know how to explain mystic union to people who don't believe in God.) I was afraid that they were going to ask me what need there is for such communities in a socialist society. At that moment I would not have known what to say.

I kept thinking of the question that the young Marxists might have asked me. It seems to me that in a perfect socialist society it would not be necessary to "flee from the world" in order to live the Gospel. In any case, the material life of those communities would be the same as that of all the others. And I remembered what St. John Chrysostom said (in a letter to a rich man): "If cities were Christian, monasteries would be unnecessary."

»»»

On the first page of *Juventud Rebelde* I saw a photograph of some women in rags and some naked children at the door of a miserable hut. In another picture a young mother with her naked son asleep on a sidewalk. In another, a district of shanties made of cardboard and planks. And below these another photograph with a circle of gentlemen in tuxedos and ladies in long dresses and necklaces. It seemed to me again that I was looking at a capitalistic newspaper. I read under a photograph: "In Cuba there are 200,000 huts and hovels: 400,000 families in the country and the city live in slums lacking the most elementary hygienic conditions. . ." (Again commemorating the assault on Moncada.)

»»»

A young Catholic (a supporter of the Revolution) told me that they can't get Catholic books in Cuba. He asked me to send him some. He wanted modern Catholic books to be up to date. "Social books?" "No, I don't need those. In that field we're more modern here than elsewhere. Nothing from outside could make me more revolutionary. I want books on mysticism. To learn how one can be a mystic and also a revolutionary."

»»»

FOR THIS FREEDOM

—Fayad Jamis

For this freedom to sing beneath the rain
we'll have to give everything
For this freedom to be tightly tied
to the firm and gentle heart of the people
we'll have to give everything
For this freedom of a sunflower open in the dawn
          of lighted
factories and shining schools
and rustling earth and waking child
we'll have to give everything
There's no alternative to freedom
There's no other road than freedom
There's no other fatherland than freedom
There'll be no more poem without the violent music
          of freedom
For this freedom that is the terror
of those who have always raped it
in the name of vain miseries
For this freedom that is the oppressors' night
and the final dawn of the whole people now invincible
For this freedom that lights the way for sunken eyes
for bare feet
for riddled roofs
for the eyes of children who wander in the dust
For this freedom that is the empire of youth
For this freedom
as lovely as life
We'll have to give everything
if necessary
even the coolness of shade
and it will never be enough.

A Catholic Leader

Raúl Gómez Treto is one of the brightest Catholic leaders that I met in Cuba. We met with him at the home of a communist, Enrique López Oliva. There were Brother Roberto of Taizé, the two Chileans, and I. The house was in a section that used to be upper middle class. They had lived in the same house before the Revolution. Oliva told us that some of the neighbors were workers or farmers who now occupy the houses of doctors and lawyers who had left. Other neighbors had lived there since before the Revolution; many of them are antirevolutionary and are annoyed by their new neighbors. In the living room of the Oliva house was a Sacred Heart that belonged to the grandmother. She took us to her room to see her other saints: a Saint Anthony with the Infant Jesus in his arms, another smaller Saint Anthony, the Virgin of Cobre in a glass niche, Saint Francis. She said she had not been able to persuade her grandson to bless himself before he went to bed; perhaps we, who were priests, could persuade him. The grandmother brought us coffee in the living room, while we began to talk with Gómez Treto. Afterward we had some glasses of Caney rum. Gómez Treto said:

"The Revolution was a completely new thing in Cuba. It did not follow preconceived plans. Many powerful elements did not see it that way. A pity. . . First, there was the anticommunist prejudice. Then there was the problem of the schools. The opposition to this Revolution was very great. So great that I believed it could not last. I believed that it would break down.

"The well-to-do workers reacted against the Revolution more strongly than the aristocracy. The employees and the top workers who wanted to become rich. They were stuck here, with no way of getting to Miami, with no income from abroad. That's why they were getting more and more bitter. The others cared less because they could get on a plane or a yacht at any moment and go off and live in any country they wanted.

"The executions? They were for robberies, murders, and other such crimes. Very rarely for political crimes. I calculate that there were about eight hundred to a thousand executions in the course of three years, which was the time of the shootings. And that doesn't seem much to me. You have to bear in mind that in Batista's time there were twenty thousand murdered."

I asked him about political prisoners, and he said: "A friend of mine was in jail. He was a leader of the Catholic Gentlemen of Cuba. I asked his wife how they treated him, and she said: 'My husband is just great. On a farm. They don't make him work in the fields. He gives classes. He has to take walks so he won't get fat. He eats meat twice a week.' As you know, the rest of us only get meat once a week. She told me also that he was eating better than she was. Well, he got out of jail, and I went to visit him to find out if what his wife had said was true, or if he had been deceiving her, or if she had deceived me. He backed her up. He said they wouldn't let him work in the fields because of his age, but that he taught, and that's why he had to take hikes, and that at first his wife used to send him food, but he refused it because he was eating better than she."

We talked about the Church. "The Masses are for people who don't work, at five in the afternoon. For old people or for the few bourgeois that are still here and are living on income. Imagine in a socialist country, where everyone works except children and the aged, they say Mass during working hours.

"Militiamen in church? Never. The militia are a civil reserve national defense, and almost all the revolutionaries are militiamen. Some Catholics are, but not many. But I couldn't imagine anyone with a militiaman's uniform in a church.

"The Nuncio told us in 1963 that a Catholic could collaborate with the Revolution, and that it was not a sin. Also that one could join the militia. And that made a scandal. People said that the Nuncio said that you couldn't be a Catholic without joining the militia; in his opinion, to be a Catholic you had to be a communist. . . The Nuncio also told us that this was a good Revolution, that this change was beneficial for the people, and that it was necessary. Marxism replaced material stimuli with moral stimuli. And the Catholic Church protested because the material stimuli had been suppressed. It's a paradox, isn't it?"

I asked him if Fidel could be a Christian at heart, and he answered: "Fidel studied with the Jesuits, don't forget. And there's a lot of Jesuit about him. The Christian upbringing that he got from the Jesuits must not have been superficial. He was a good pupil. The Jesuit pupils, besides, do a spiritual retreat every year. Fidel must often have done the Saint Ignatius Retreat."

"Can a Catholic be admitted to the Communist Youth or be a Model Worker?" "Yes, but he can not proclaim his faith." "And in the University?" "It's hard in the University." We knew that he had been a leader of Catholic Action, although he was not one then. We asked him about the organization, and he answered: "It's a corpse." I wanted to know about the Barefoot Carmelites, and he said:

"They are an anachronism, museum pieces. We don't know why Fidel hasn't said to them: You get out of here! A two-story building on a whole block of land for only twenty nuns. . . They're supposed to be contemplative nuns? Well, I don't know their hour for contemplation, because they talk all the time and they're up on all the gossip of Havana and Miami. . . The Dominican contemplatives? Other museum pieces. They have placed their altar facing the congregation, but only provisionally, waiting until Rome decides to turn them back the way they were. The prioress is ninety. The nuns of the Precious Blood? Their contemplation must be mostly of the Beatific Vision, because there are more of them in the other world than in this one. The youngest is eighty."

And he said finally: "And the worst of all is that if a revolutionary becomes a convert there is no priest to take him to. I try rather not to let him see a priest. I tell him: Kid, let's go on being friends, and let's see what comes out of here."

»»»

Two-page spread in *Bohemia:* An infant (as though advertising a talcum powder):

I WANT TO BE A HEALTHY CHILD
BOIL MY WATER!
GASTROENTERITIS CAN BE AVOIDED

»»»

We were in a Czechoslovak bus going from the Cuban

Institute of Friendship with Peoples to Old Havana, and one of the girls who was going to show us the museum told me that she had been a friend of very important revolutionaries at the time when they were conspiring against Batista. She had not been a conspirator, just a sympathizer, and now she felt remorseful about it. I enquired about those friends, and she said: "Now they are top leaders in Cuba. They have high positions." I asked her if she saw them. "I see them very little, because our work is different, but we continue to be great friends."

»»»

With regard to the privileges of the leaders, at Paz Espejo's house I was told about the great campaign that Fidel launched against what he called the Dolce Vita (at the time when the film *La Dolce Vita* reached Cuba). Commander Ifigenio Almejeiras, Chief of Police of Havana and in addition a hero of the Sierra Maestra, a hero of Playa Girón, and a hero of the War of Algiers, and with four brothers killed in the Revolution, was stripped of his position and deprived of all his ranks because he had taken advantage of his position to lead a life of luxury. And young Raúl Roa, the son of the Foreign Minister, was sent to a rehabilitation farm for the same reason. He's reformed now.

»»»

A Cuban friend told me that he had attended a trial at La Cabaña where a man was condemned to death. There were about twenty accused persons, and he was there because a friend of his was one of the accused. She was not a counterrevolutionary; her only crime had been to collect clothing and blankets for the prisoners on the Isle of Pines. She did this solely for humanitarian reasons, but her action was enough to have her viewed as suspicious and linked with a group of counterrevolutionary conspirators, with whom she had nothing in common. At the trial nothing could be proved against her, and she was freed. The leader of the group was a physics teacher who had brought in arms and conspired with his students. He courageously assumed all the blame and said that his students should not be punished. He was condemned to death, and the others in the group were given long and short sentences. What's a short sentence? I asked. "About five years."

My friend finally said: "We, the relatives and friends of the girl, were happy because she was freed. But it was a terrible experience to see a man condemned to death and to know that two hours later he would be facing a firing squad. I can still see that man when they led him out of the courtroom: he turned around and raised his handcuffed hands above his head to say good-by to his family and his friends."

Waiting for a Bus

In that big park, I forget its name, near Revolution Square, we were waiting for my bus, and we waited a long time. The buses were filled with people, and we were standing in line under the midday sun. I was the only one who was going to get on the bus, the rest were friends who were keeping me company, while I stood in line. In the square they were erecting gigantic portraits for the 26th of July, for Fidel's speech: CAMILO, ABEL, CHE, VIETNAM, THE SUGAR HARVEST, THE SIERRA MAESTRA (with Raúl and Fidel).

Paco made us laugh a lot telling us about the bombs that he planted in Batista's time. They weren't bombs that killed people, they were bombs that made noise. One was made of phosphorus, and it threw out a lot of smoke. Once he set one off in an apartment, and the whole building filled with smoke. A young man leaves us; he can't go on waiting for my bus because he has things to do. When he has gone, Paco says:

"That young man is a movie critic. And now he is beginning to make his own film. He has begun it, with twenty minutes of film that he found somewhere. And four years ago I was head of a school—imagine me as head of a school—well, I've seen many things. So I was head of a school, and in the school they were trying a boy in the Disciplinary Court, and it was this boy. They were trying him because one night he had escaped from the dormitory and had returned at one in the morning. All he did was stare at his shoes. He didn't say a word. Then it occurred to me to ask him where he had gone. Because, goddamnit, they were going to send him to a farm for problem youngsters, and he would never do any more studying. The woman in charge of the dormitory was determined that he should be sentenced, and I said to myself: This is very serious, first a question should be asked. So I asked him where he had gone. He said, still staring at his shoes: "To the movies." It occurred to me to ask him: "To see what?" "*The Trial.*" "So you like Kakfa," I said. On hearing Kakfa he raised his eyes quickly, it was the first time he had done so, his eyes were brilliant. I said: "Leave me alone with him, I have to talk with him before I reach an opinion." Because I thought: I want to know who he is, what he thinks, what kind of a person he is. I talked with him for twenty minutes. About the movies. And while I was talking with him I said to myself: This fellow does not leave here on any account. I also said it to him: "Young fellow, don't you worry, you're not leaving here." I told the other people on the court that I had found out he was a fine young man. And in fact I had learned that he was. He liked movies. And I said to myself: The Revolution can not condemn to a lifetime of work on a state farm a young man who has gone to such extremes to see Kakfa. And the fact is that you have to be careful with the Revolution, because the Revolution can destroy a life. But the woman in charge of the dormitory said: "The truth is that there is something else that you don't know: he is from a bourgeois family. If you knew that family!" "So what? The families of Marx and Engels were bourgeois."

"You saved him," Fina said. "He has said that he would have been destroyed on that farm." "Completely and hopelessly destroyed." We said good-by. My bus arrived.

»»»

EVERYONE TO REVOLUTION SQUARE THE 26TH OF JULY!

Frank

"The first days of the Revolution were incredibly euphoric and disorganized. I came from the United States, soon after the triumph of the Revolution, to be of help to it. They gave me a room in the Hotel St. John, and nobody gave me another thought. Time went by, every day interesting things happened, and I went on living in the Hotel St. John, without doing anything and without anyone thinking about me. I had spent more than a month living in the St. John, and I said to myself: Well, I've come to Cuba to join the Revolution, not to spend my whole life in a room in the Hotel St. John. And then I heard about a forestation plan: the Forest Militia; and I got romantically enthusiastic about that forestation plan, to plant little trees. I went there, and they accepted me at once, and when I was enrolled I saw that I had fallen into a trap; the trap they had laid for the bandits and for people who set bombs. The rifles they gave us had no bullets. And we were watched all the time. I realized that some of my companions were serving thirty-year sentences. Imagine what those people were like: Commander Universo Sánchez, the great hero of the Sierra Maestra, once came to see us, and they threw rocks at him. I said to myself: The best thing to do here is to keep to myself and not to talk to anyone.

One day a lieutenant said: "Young fellow, why do you take a different road than the others?" Then I explained my life and my ideology to him. He said: "You're going to be a political instructor." And so I became a political instructor. In April, at the time of Playa Girón, all the barracks were bombed and burned. We got out of there. I wound up being responsible for all the Forest Militia. In the Revolution each one has his personal experiences; some have moved ahead, others have fallen.

"It turned out that I organized a library in the camp. Outside it was a hut, inside were books, with rustic lamps, tables, ash trays, everything very pretty, and eighty readers a day. A leader saw it and said to me: 'Make us a plan to create libraries in all the military bases in Cuba.' That filled me with enthusiasm. I imagined myself creating libraries all over Cuba.

Fidel discussing the plan with me ('Listen, kid. . .') and all that. But what they wanted was only a few fish crates with three books inside. I quit, and I went back to the company to be in charge once more of the Forest Militia. When I reached my barracks I found a woebegone man: he saw me and began to make a caricature of me. About ninety-five per cent were blacks, and he was blond. I asked him: 'What are you doing here?' He said he was being punished. He was Masíquez, the great painter. He said: 'I was in China, and I had a problem.' In China he had fallen in love with Chinese women, and they had injected him. Yes, some injections that the Chinese use to produce temporary impotence. The effect of the injections was only for the time that he was going to be in China. He protested, he raised a diplomatic scandal, so now here he was being punished. 'You're not going to plant trees,' I told him. 'You're going to set up an art school.' And we set up an art school, a library, a lecture hall, an exhibit hall. We began with twenty-five women students, very pretty mulattoes. We also built a pottery kiln.

"The farmers were very religious (Protestants), and they didn't take to our political orientation. Then we organized the lecture hall just like a church, just as the Pentecostals did (but we did it to talk about Marx and Lenin). We also picked up the music of their hymns and with religious music we would sing: 'We are / we are communists.'

"We taught them that religion was the opiate of the people. And that it had been invented to exploit them. And you won't believe this: the Party condemned all that because it said that it had a religious character. (What I'm telling you about was in the time of communist sectarianism.) We noticed that the pastor shook hands with everyone as he left church, so we also shook hands with everyone at the end of the dialogue (only the leaders spoke in those dialogues), and the Communist party viewed as religious that idea of shaking people's hands. Those of the 26th of July Movement pulled one in one direction, and 'sectarianism' in another. That was in Pinar del Río. We planted twenty-two million eucalypus trees. Afterward Masíquez left there.

"And one day I broke a leg, and they had to put me in a cast, and in the church the Catholics were praying for me and, Christ, how could I be ideologically opposed to these people when they were praying to God for me. . ."

Frank was now working to invent an automatic baseball catcher to train pitchers. They asked him: "Isn't there already an automatic catcher?" "No, what we have is a pitcher. I've been working on this invention for three years." He told us that he was a farmer. He had gone to the United States to study physics and had concentrated on electricity.

A Gathering of Poets

We were in a penthouse that had belonged to some rich man. From it you could see the bay of Havana, dark except for the lights of some ships moving up slowly, not many. The apartment without any decorations, almost unfurnished. We were sitting on a couch, on some chairs, and on the floor. From time to time we would sip a little glass of rum, parsimoniously, because there wasn't much. And, as everywhere in Cuba, we were talking about the Revolution. (Cintio had said: "Cubans not only like to make their Revolution, they like to talk about it. In Cuba, for eleven years there has been almost no talk of anything except the Revolution.")

One person said: "The Revolution is traumatizing many, and it seems to me that five years from now this Revolution will be understood only by a psychiatrist. Perhaps instead of developing man what we are going to do is confuse him."

We laughed. And he went on: "Yes, this Revolution is a real revolution of the neurons. It can create a trauma! Because they destroy one's defenses. One is naked in the midst of society. Fidel said that the Revolution was a social cataclysm. I would say that it is also a psychological cataclysm. . . Our social unbalance is also increased by the obsessive propaganda that we have. For example, that 26, 26, 26, that is seen everywhere now, on all the walls, in all the streets, in all the towns, in all the cities, 26, 26, 26, 26. Or those other slogans: LIKE IN VIETNAM . . . or now, with the failure of the sugar harvest goal: CHANGE DEFEAT INTO VICTORY, which are obsessive.

"If I were Fidel," said one of the poets present, "I would say to the people: 'Now don't repeat even one word of what I have said.' "

"Here the people live on slogans. And the bad part is that at times you have to change the slogan for the people, because conditions are different, and people have to make a new psychological readjustment. One then has to enter into a new fervor."

"And one suddenly thinks," said the poet again, "that perhaps we are, without realizing it, evolving toward primitive communism. . ."

"That's what the enemies say: that the country is under-developing," said one fellow laughing. "And the truth is also that some of our Party leaders are craps."

I then asked them: "Is there any fear? Some people have said that there is fear in the factories, in the work assemblies. Others have said that people can speak freely. Is there or is there not fear?"

Everyone talked at once, saying contradictory things: "There certainly *is* fear." "There is and isn't fear." "What fear?" "In the assemblies, in certain places, there is fear. . ." "Yes, in certain places, not in all. . ." "And also sometimes we too can be afraid. But I have often tried to analyze what this fear is. Is it because something can happen to you?" "No, nothing happens to you." "Because they're going to throw you in jail or throw you out of your job? No, one can criticize and nothing happens. I have analyzed it many times, and I'm going to tell you the reason for the fear: one has a certain moral fear, a kind of human respect that they are going to think that one is not a revolutionary; not because something is going to happen to one but because he could be looked down upon by the others. One does not wish to suffer the shame of being confused with the enemy."

Again several people spoke at the same time: "Yes, of course." "That's the truth." "Now the thing is very clear." And one of them, turning to me: "Besides, you ought to know this: here everyone is armed. This is the first government in the world that gave arms to the people and taught them to use them. Here anyone can be a militiaman. They accept anyone into the militia, practically without question. If the people were counterrevolutionary they would already have revolted."

We left at one-thirty in the morning. We walked in the middle of the street in a little group. No one was in the streets except a militiaman here and there guarding the main door of some building. I was instinctively frightened by the green uniforms, and it seemed to me that they would be listening to what we were saying, in loud tones, but none of them paid us the slightest heed.

I walked in front with the poet Padilla. I asked him if it was true that among the workers joy existed, the euphoria in manual labor described by the newspapers and some magazines like *Bohemia*. He said. "Euphoria in work? Nonsense. Euphoria like that of the fans at a prizefight, no. There's no such euphoria in competition on the job. The modest satisfaction of winning a medal, yes. Work is always hard, even in socialism. I believe that man's ideal should not be work but leisure. Work is hard, and anyone who doesn't think so ought to read Marx!"

»»»

They told me that a few days ago Fidel told some University students that his speech was going to "make the earth shake."

»»»

From my notebooks:

With a young Marxist. I said to him: "What is needed here is to *split* the Church" (which is what I had said to Roa). He answered: "I'll be reconverted on the very day that the division is made. I'll become a Catholic again."

Benedetti was surprised that we hadn't talked with Fidel. Almost all members of the House of the Americas' juries have had an interview with him. And besides: "Any stupid journalist can get to see him and have an eight-hour conversation with him."

I read in the paper: About forty young musical groups will take part in the carnival. One of the groups, playing modern music, is called "Los Golpes Duros" (The Tough Blows), and they sing in English and Spanish. Their name, the paper said, comes from the blows that the Cuban Revolution gives to imperialism.

Haydée Santamaría said that only in 1962 when the School City was opened in the Moncada Barracks did she realize that they were making a Revolution.

An opinion: "The failure of the sugar harvest was a good thing, because this way Fidel will see that they had been deceiving him. This will help to improve a lot of things, because the harvest's not the only thing that's gone badly."

Che Guevara: "And also banish completely everything meant by the thought that to be elected a member of some mass organization or the party that leads the

Revolution entitles these comrades to have the slightest opportunity to achieve something more than the rest of the people."

Pablo Armando: When the Nuncio was newly arrived, a commission of Catholics went to ask him for "orders and orientation to throw out the regime." The Nuncio said that he asked them in amazement: "Are you crazy?"

Jehovah's Witnesses: They have been practically exterminated. They were the religious group most antagonistic to the Revolution. Someone said to me: "These people have been treated with no compassion. They are all on farms." Another one said: "It's because most of them were agents of the CIA."

Rosi: On an inspection trip from the Department of the Interior in Ciudad Sandino she saw how they were punishing some imprisoned farmers (of the mutinous ones in Escambray), making them eat grass on all fours. She reported the act.

In no newspaper have I seen attacks on religion. It is merely ignored.

The whole hotel is filled with Christmas decorations, now that the 26th of July is near: Christmas trees, tinsel, crowns, little bells, mistletoe.

Cintio told me that, according to Paco, Fidel's speech on the 26th will be a new assault on Moncada. Because "over and over again Fidel keeps assaulting Moncada."

More than two thousand foreigners are arriving for the festivities of the 26th of July. It will be harder to see Fidel.

Three Friends

Three young revolutionaries: a Marxist, a Catholic, and a Protestant. And three very close friends. "How prejudices disappear among friends!" said the Marxist. "Friendship comes first. We began as friends, not arguing over ideological questions. Now, being friends, we think and feel alike, without this one ceasing to be a Catholic or that one a Protestant or I a Marxist. I used to be very suspicious of Christianity, but now I'm not after being their friend, because I have confidence in them. And they have confidence in me, with all my ideas, including my atheistic Marxism. The three of us are twenty-five years old. I get along better with them than I do with many other Marxists, and they get along better with me than with people in their churches. We believe that that's the solution for Cuba. A socialist democracy has to be pluralistic. This is a necessary condition."

We were at the Marxist's house. The Dean of Theology at the Catholic University of Chile—a Jesuit—and two other Chileans, had come with me. A bottle of rum and some ash trays were on the floor. Some of us chose to sit on the floor. It was the night of July 25th, which was now Christmas Eve and New Year's Eve.

Eugenio, the Catholic, told us about being in the UMAP (Unidad Militar de Ayuda a la Producción), which means Military Unit for Aid to Production, but which really means concentration camps, and how he had become a revolutionary in the UMAP. "They began to take people off to the UMAP. There was no beer in those days, so they would put a barrel of beer out on a corner and pick up some strange guys, not part of the Revolution. Especially homosexuals. The homosexuals were quite happy in the concentration camps, because a place where they would be concentrated must be like a paradise for them. There the homosexuals became more homosexual; some began to paint their faces. Other people were sent there for other reasons. They sent me because I was a Catholic. And there I became a revolutionary, together with other friends. Not the Baptists, on the contrary, they became more antirevolutionary. There were horrible scenes."

"What scenes?" I asked. "Deaths, for example. Because they committed suicide. I once saw a homosexual who had hanged himself. The Jehovah's Witnesses were treated worst of all. I remember, for example, that they were digging latrines. The latrines were holes filled with water, and there were those Witnesses with water up to their waists. The work was hard. We used to work twelve to sixteen hours a day. On Sundays we had to work only twelve hours. We were surrounded by a barbed wire fence two and a half yards high."

"In '65 I was amazed at the great number of homosexuals in front of the Habana Libre," said the Marxist. "They were allowed to hang around there. And it was there that they picked them up. And the massive purges at the University began. The methods were those of fascism. They accused them of anything at all, and they couldn't defend themselves. They presented a series of charges against them. They convicted them. And the public approved the convictions wholeheartedly."

"The fear of communism has gradually left us. But at that time this was not so. I was a counterrevolutionary because I was faithful to myself."

"Then they imprisoned you as a counterrevolutionary and not as a Catholic?" I asked, remembering the story of Good Friday in Güines. "No, they tailed him for being a Catholic," said the Marxist. The Catholic nodded, and went on: "There were thirty-five thousand of us, about two thousand were Catholics. The parish would send us a leaflet and the communion wafers in a little box. But that didn't solve the problem. Instead it aggravated it. I was a counterrevolutionary, and I was planning to leave Cuba before they sent me to UMAP. Afterward, I had the chance to leave and I didn't. In the concentration camp I realized that I ought not to leave. That to fight to make the Revolution better you had to be a revolutionary. The bad things and the abuses seen in the concentration camp converted me to the Revolution. Because they were caused by those who were in charge of the camp, and they were farmers from the Sierra Maestra, who had been good guerrilla fighters and good rebels, but they had not been previously trained, and the Revolution hadn't yet had time to train them. And the society to which I had belonged was responsible for their ignorance and for their stupidity. Besides, I saw the living conditions of the farmers around us, and they were almost like ours. Their huts. Just the way our jailers lived: in other huts. The living conditions in the concentration camp which seemed horrible to us were almost normal in the huts facing us. And they had always lived like that. I was from a petit-bourgeois family. The document of the bishops of the Third World fell into my hands, and that made me think. I said to myself: the Church approves of the socialism that attacks me, and it is glad that I am attacked. I realized that, to live my faith, I must change my life. My former life had been merely pious. Some people would begin to weep, and I would encourage them. At times I would even ask myself: Why don't I weep? I myself did not know. . . At the same time, many opportunists in the University approved of the UMAP. They supported the Revolution and the UMAP. We who were in the UMAP discovered that the Revolution and the UMAP were separable. And we said to ourselves: We won't leave Cuba, we'll stay and make what is bad not bad. I came to Havana four times, and I found the parish incomprehensible. The liturgy, the gestures, the words, the thoughts, we found it all empty of meaning and removed from reality. After three years the UMAP ended with Fidel's speech. But our camp did not end at once. The day after the speech they took a yard off the two-and-a-half-yard barbed-wire fence. They made us take down the barbed wire. That was the only change, except there were attempts at afternoon study."

"Study?" I asked. "Or attempts at study?" "Attempts at afternoon study. At the end of six months the whole thing stopped. And we got out." "From this time on, Raúl has not spoken in public," said the Protestant. "Raúl is given credit for UMAP." I asked the Marxist: "Is that true?" "Like all Cuban data it is inflated. All Cuban data are inflated."

The Catholic continued: "Many of us left the camp anticlericals. At the same time, the Church rejected those of us from the UMAP because we came out revolutionaries, and it wasn't expected that anyone who had been in the UMAP would support the Revolution. We came out with a revolutionary attitude, one of compromise. And that was very strange: 'We must not leave Cuba' was the phrase we repeated to the Catholics. We criticized the priests who approved the idea of leaving Cuba. At that time we formed an ecumenical group: Catholics and Protestants who dissented from the official positions of our churches. At first it was just to pray. That was our only action. We had a pietistic attitude. Then we began to change. We began to work in the parishes. A work of conscientiousness, a word that is not common except among you. And then came the irritation of the people. And at the same time our great offensive. That's where we are. We think that Archbishop Oves will support us, because he is a revolutionary. When he was appointed we felt as though one of us had been appointed."

We spoke of other topics, always dealing with the Revolution. They said that at carnival time there were humorous criticisms of Fidel. Blacks danced in the street singing: "Fidel can shout / the ten million are out," and that in Santiago de Cuba the blacks had paraded in front of Fidel singing to a conga tune: "The blacks of today / are the blacks of Batista."

Suddenly there were cannon shots. Rifle fire all over the city. Firecrackers. The 26th of July had begun. It is well known that in Cuba the people are armed. And with these arms everybody was shooting into the night. If they were not shooting against the Revolution it was not because they couldn't but because they didn't want to. The Catholic said with sparkling eyes: "The Cuban Revolution is a revolution in depth." The Protestant said: "If moral stimuli were abandoned for material stimuli the Revolution would be put back fifty years."

The Marxist had been in the communist countries of Europe, and he told us that the Cuban Revolution seemed to him much better than the communism of those countries. I asked him if he thought that the Cuban Revolution was communist, and he answered: "I think that this is something more advanced than what there is in communist countries." He added: "After fifty years this Revolution can't be on the level of the Russian one. If after fifty years, that is, in the year 2000 more or less (I'll be . . . how old? seventy-five years old), the Cuban Revolution has not produced a situation better than that of Russia (and I'm not referring to economics and techniques), I'll revolt. I'll revolt in the Sierra Maestra!"

We said good-by close to dawn on the 26th of July. Eugenio walked with me to the National Hotel. He said, as we walked: "Father, when you write about Cuba, say that there are Christians among us who are happy to live in Cuba. We are going through a fascinating experience, and not for the world would I wish to have been born twenty-five years earlier. I believe it is a great gift of God to be living in Cuba right now."

»»»

26

—A Protest Song by Noel Nicola

A question of more or fewer Julys?
it's always July
A question of more or fewer men?
there they go
A question of more or fewer decisions?
It happens that "moment" plus "human being" adds up
    to 26.

A question of superior beings?
I don't believe it
A question of men with a capital M?
yes indeed
If a human being could have more than one heart
each one of them would surely have 26.

It dawns
and at any hour one can feel it
(but now it is dawning).

A question of plans and values?
I don't doubt it
A question of having been born in time?
maybe
A question of seeming to be the same?
There is always time, there is an almanac filled with
twenty-sixes.

(It dawns)

The 26th of July

At eight in the morning on the 26th some people were beginning to arrive in the square for Fidel's speech, which would
begin at six that afternoon. I was invited to the house of
Cintio and Fina for the Christmas—26th of July—dinner that
would be at noon; from there we would go to the speech. To
reach their house I went through Revolution Square, about
noon, and a lot of people were already there.

Before the meal we celebrated the Eucharist at the dinner
table with a little bread and wine. Cintio thought it was the
first time that a Mass of that sort had ever been celebrated in
Cuba. I told them that I approved of the shift of Christmas to
the 26th of July, even though many Catholics thought of it
as a profanation. The primitive Church celebrated the birth of
Christ on the 6th of January (as it is still celebrated in the
Orient), and the feast was later moved to the 25th of December
because on that date the Romans celebrated the birth of the
sun. Even now—I said—some think that Jesus was born in or
near August . . . and that is close to the 26th of July. Wasn't
it better to celebrate the birth of Jesus on the birthday of the
Revolution than on the birthday of the sun? "And this *is* the
birth of the sun in Cuba," said Cintio. He recalled that it was
also the feast of the harvest in Cuba: on that day the great
harvest officially began. Cintio read his poem, "Los peregrinos
de Emaus" [The Pilgrims of Emmaus], in which the pilgrims
discover that the intimate supper, the bread shared with
friends, was not enough. The bread was not faulty, but it was
not complete. It was necessary to go out, to find the stranger,
to share with him the mystery of the others:

> We had to see the stranger,
> not to know his name, to converse
> with the suspicious brother, perhaps the enemy,
> to walk with him, perhaps never to arrive.

We shorten the liturgy of the Word, I said, because today
on the Square we are going to have a long liturgy of the Word
which will also be part of this Mass of the 26th of July.

When we offered the bread and the wine at the offertory I said we were presenting to God the distributed bread of Cuba and the equally fraternal wine (because the Rumanian wine they had given Cintio for the 26th of July was the same as the wine I had seen on the double bed in the People's Farm), and with it we offered all the fruits of the earth and the labor of man: sugar, rum, citrus fruits; the effort of the long sugar harvest, and in the factories and workshops, in tractors or with the F-1s, in schools, polyclinics; in short, we presented to God, to be consecrated, the Host of human solidarity and the Revolution. Let us remember the dead: Abel, José, Antonio, Frank País, Camilo, Che, and all the other martyrs of the Revolution. Seated at the table with us was the servant. They didn't call her "servant" but "comrade," and Fina introduced her as "the comrade who helps us in the kitchen." She was one of those old servants who have stayed on in some homes out of affection for the family, and she ate with them. Their two sons, sixteen and twenty-one, were also there. Some ten years ago, in Mexico, Cintio had told me that he was worried because atheistic education was being introduced, and he had two small children. When I came to Cuba I asked Cintio and Fina about them; the younger one was a fervent Catholic. The older boy was an atheist ("He's at the age when many boys feel the need to be atheists," said Cintio). At this Mass they both took communion.

The meal included the traditional Christmas suckling pig (a very small quantity, almost symbolic, but one given to every home in Cuba), rice, and kidney beans. Spanish nougat (the same as I had seen at the People's Farm), a bottle of rum, and the Rumanian wine.

»»»

THAT WE SHALL SEE ABLAZE

—Roberto Fernández Retamar

In the beginning Abel shed his blood.
Only the humble, the forgotten ones followed him.
And, after walking upon the sea,
Twelve were left, and all began again.

They came down bearded as the year broke,
And they had disciples upon the vast earth.

This the book already knew.

But the symbols that they made
Had no book: those who made the things
Had no names, or at least no one
Knew their names. The dates that they filled
Were empty as an empty house.

Now we know the meaning of Moncada Barracks, 26.
The meaning of Camilo, Che, Girón, Escambray, October.
The books gather it up and propound it.
The immense wind that affirms it sweeps the mountains
        and the plains
Where those who have no names,
Or whose names no one yet knows,
Prepare in the shadow flares
For empty dates that we shall see ablaze.

The Speech

The Christmas meal did not last long. At three o'clock Cintio and I went off to Revolution Square, and it was already a sea of people: the great square and also the nearby streets. We members of the jury of the House of the Americas had reserved seats on the platform, very close to the small rostrum where Fidel was going to speak. The platform was a terrace raised quite high above the square and at the foot of the gigantic monument to Martí, and on the platform were places for about two thousand special guests. Below it was another larger terrace for five thousand guests. Below that, the square with a half million people.

About thirty yards from where I sat was the rostrum with four microphones. A murmur as from a rough sea rose from the square. The people were in constant motion, and many protected themselves from the sun with parasols, plastic sheets, newspapers, hats. At intervals there were stands offering water, refreshments, food, some booths used as latrines, and first-aid stations and ambulances.

The façades of the largest buildings around the square had enormous portraits. (Stylized photographs with a few massed shadows.) Che on the Department of the Interior building, in blue, with his beret and his bush jacket, a little star on his beret, youthful and romantic. Camilo Cienfuegos on the Armed Forces building, in red, with his flowing Nazarene hair, his happy smile, his wide-brimmed hat. Abel, to whom this July 26th was dedicated, sad, in red, on the Communications Headquarters, his blurred student identity card snapshot (which they had apparently taken at a moment when he had a premonition of his torture and death—covering seven floors of the building. On the National Library, Fidel and Raúl and other guerrilla fighters, the historic photograph taken at the peak of the Turquino, in green. Two other great panels: Vietnamese fighters (in lilac), and a worker cutting cane (yellow and brown). A huge banner: ABEL, YOUR EYES ARE THE BEACON OF THIS REVOLUTION.

Enormous numbers of people came through all the streets, although it seemed that there wasn't room for one more person in the square. "Entire towns are arriving," Cintio told me. Professor Paz Espejo sat down next to me. Behind the microphones where Fidel was going to speak, in the place of greatest honor in the whole square, were the men who had cut the greatest amount of cane in the sugar harvest, the biggest "millionaires." They were the aristocracy of today. (I remembered a sentence of Fidel's: "The idle person used to occupy a place of honor in Cuban society; now that place is occupied by the workingman, and that is what the Revolution has meant.")

Behind the cane-cutters, although we couldn't see them from where we sat, were Dorticós, the ministers, the diplomatic delegations. A little below us were the families of those who had died in the assault on the Moncada Barracks. Abel's parents were there. The mother of Frank País ("That's she," said Cintio). Frank, a devout Protestant, was twenty-three when he was killed. "The bravest, the most useful, the most extraordinary of our fighters," Fidel had said. Farther down, in the second platform of five thousand people, was another large contingent of cane-cutters.

A large number of movie and TV cameras were already in front of the microphones. Many people on the platforms had earphones for simultaneous translation: Vietnamese, Russians, Bulgarians, Mongols, North Americans, Congolese, Chinese. Debray's mother had her hearing aid. A girl was going around in circles near the place where Fidel was going to speak. She was Celia, the daughter of Che. Opposite her, on the other side of the crowd, was the huge portrait of her father, and perhaps at this moment she was remembering, as I was, the farewell letter. ("Above all, be capable always of feeling to the depths any injustice committed against anyone in any part of the world. That is the finest quality in a revolutionary. Farewell, children. . .")

Next to the microphones, giving instructions to the cameramen, was Commander Almeida. He was a black. He had been a bricklayer before the Revolution. He was one of those who had attacked Moncada seventeen years ago today, and he was one of the twelve survivors of the landing from the *Granma*. It was close to six o'clock. Along all the streets that empty into the square more people kept coming, but by now they couldn't get into the square. The crowd was tightly packed even several blocks from the square. Paz Espejo said to me, as we watched the crowd milling around below us:

"These people are not Marxists. If Fidel now, in his speech, says that Marxism is no good, that we have to throw it out, that it didn't work, the people will at once turn anti-Marxist. What these people are is Fidelists. Their fidelity is to Fidel." It was curious that she, a Marxist, should say this.

This was the General Assembly, called into session by Fidel. Here it was, gathered together. He no longer engages in dialogue with the people, as he used to: only an occasional question or a vote on an important matter that he requests of the Assembly. This speech would be a long one, said Cintio, because it was known that it would be important, one of those speeches marking an epoch. Although Fidel no longer spoke for five, six, or seven hours. This speech, Cintio calculated, would last only three or four hours.

"It's a great experience to be down in the square with the people," said Paz Espejo. "People sit on the ground on news-papers, they stand up at the climactic moments of the speech or when there is tension. The comrades don't spend all their time listening to Fidel: they eat, drink refreshments, chatter, go off to urinate, they listen for a while and discuss among themselves and then listen some more. They can't keep their attention fixed for so long a time, and besides they don't understand all that Fidel says. Mothers suckle their children, the boys play." "After the speech there will surely be an official reception for the delegations," said Cintio, "but Fidel will not go to the reception. He always goes off to the editorial offices of *Granma* to talk over the speech with report-ers and stays there until dawn. He corrects the proofs himself; he wants to make sure there are no errors, especially in the figures—his latest speeches are full of statistics, and he doesn't leave until the edition is printed."

It was threatening to rain, and Paz told me that Fidel goes on talking just the same, the same number of hours, even though it is pouring, and he is never willing to put on a hat. Once he had laryngitis, and he was talking to a crowd; it began to rain, and he didn't want to put on his hat, and everyone began to shout: "Put on your hat! Put on your hat!" and they wouldn't let him talk until he agreed to put his hat on.

Near us was the beauty star chosen in the carnival (in socialist Cuba they are not called queens), a very classic beauty, blue-green eyes, and a pony tail. In the competition they take into account not only physical beauty but moral qualities (and above all revolutionary zeal). It had just struck six, Cintio was talking about the sugar harvest and was showing me the callouses on his hands, when a thunderous applause broke out in the square. Fidel, all in green, was at the microphones.

Applause, applause, applause. At first there were scattered bursts of applause. Then the applause became rhythmic, with shouts of: Fi-del, Fi-del, Fi-del. . .

He was quite near us, but we didn't see him appear. He was greeting the cane-cutters, while the applause went on. Pants, jacket, kepi, all olive green. The beard very black and the eyes clear, fine skin, hefty, smiling, very youthful. I remembered the verse of Michael McClure: "The eyes in your lion's face are gentle." He looked very happy. Next to him was Raúl, also dressed in green, also smiling. And the applause went on, diminished a bit, and then new waves of applause began. I also applauded under the influence of the two beside me (Cintio, Catholic, and Paz, Marxist) who were frantically applauding. About eight minutes of applause, perhaps ten.

When the applause finally stopped, the master of ceremonies went to the microphones and said a few words to open this ceremony in which we would listen to the speech of the Commander in Chief, Fidel Castro. . . A new ovation. But Fidel hadn't begun. Some decorations arrived. Fidel decorated the cane-cutters. Applause. Then Fidel was decorated for his cane-cutting (he cut 15,085 *arrobas* of cane in seventy-four days). Again great applause. But Fidel didn't speak. There was a speech by the Bulgarian Minister, in tie and jacket, somewhat fat and bald. In a monotonous voice he read a speech in Bulgarian and received a big round of applause when he finished. But he hadn't finished. Next came the translation. ("We express once more our solidarity in the struggle against imperialist domination. . . Our common cause, the cause of liberty, national independence, and socialism. . . Forward for the victory of this ideal, for liberty, and for human progress. . . And the other peoples who struggle against oppression, for liberty and independence. . . The ideas of friendship and fraternity among the peoples and of proletarian internationalism.") Great applause when he finished, but, a disappointment, that was only the first part. Another part followed in Bulgarian. And then in Spanish. Another part in Bulgarian, and again in Spanish.

Paz Espejo said to me, smiling and winking: "That's like

all the speeches of the communist leaders: 'War to the death on capitalist imperialism, etcetera.'" Most enthusiastic applause when the Bulgarian at long last left the rostrum. Again the master of ceremonies. He announced that now we would hear the Commander in Chief, Fidel Castro. An ovation almost as prolonged as the first one, while Fidel smiled, loaded with papers, in front of the microphones. I don't see how the people can bear to applaud so much (I thought). My hands were burning, and I had applauded only moderately, and Fidel's speech hadn't even begun.

"Comrade Todor Yivkov, First Secretary of the Bulgarian Communist Party. . ." (Great applause.)

"Cane-cutting comrades, heroes of labor. . ." (Another burst of applause.)

Then he turned to the diplomatic delegations. The Soviet Union (great applause). North Vietnam and the Provisional Revolutionary Government of South Vietnam (an even more prolonged applause). I noticed that the crowd did not applaud mechanically. The delegation of the Tupamaros received a very special applause. Laos, the delegation of the Palestinian guerrillas, the People's Republic of the Congo: very warm applause. But even warmer was the applause for the delegation of Brazilian guerrilla fighters and for the Secretary of the Communist party of the United States. (There was no delegation from any of the Latin American Communist parties.) Fidel went on naming people who were present: Che's father (applause). The parents of Tania (applause). The mother of Inti and Coco Peredo (applause). The mother and the wife of Debray (applause). The mother of Camilo Torres (applause). Then the representatives of the foreign brigades who had come to cut cane: The Latin American (applause). The Swedish one (applause). Vietnam (applause). Korea (applause). USSR (applause). Japan (applause). . . The final one received the greatest applause: the "Venceremos" Brigade, from North America, which could not be present but sent a letter (which Fidel read). And at last!

"Honored guests and comrade workers: . . ." (*Now* the speech was going to begin.) "The class is beginning," said Cintio.

In a calm and measured tone Fidel said that this would not be a commemorative speech, to recall the successes and achievements of the Revolution, nor would it deal with international problems.

"Today we are going to talk about our problems and our difficulties." (A round of applause interrupted him.) They had told me to expect that the speech would criticize the leaders because of the failure of the sugar harvest goal and because of all the other things that were not going well. The applause showed me that the people were hoping for that criticism. And also that they were paying attention to what Fidel was saying and that they were having a dialogue with their leader. More applause when he said that he had had to bring many papers, because there were lots of data and figures.

And he began to quote data and figures. Without any frills, like a teacher in a class. Without any oratorical devices. Without seeking applause. Enunciating with great clarity so that they could understand the figures. The population had increased one million seven hundred nine thousand since the triumph of the Revolution. Of this, eight hundred forty-four thousand were infants or children too young to work. One hundred eighty-eight thousand were people beyond working age, because they were women over fifty-five or men over sixty. Therefore sixty per cent of the increase in the population had no part in production. The situation would not improve but would get worse. Between 1970 and 1975 the population would increase by six hundred sixty thousand persons, and of those, two hundred eighty thousand would be young people, not old enough to work. That was the structure of the population. And it would improve only between 1975 and 1980. This meant that now only thirty-two per cent of the population would be occupied in economic activities. And out of that thirty-two per cent one had to deduct people performing services that were not productive but investments for the future: health services, education, defense of the Revolution. In this population structure the Revolution had given pensions and retirement allowances to three hundred seventy-nine thousand eight hundred forty-two people. And one hundred ninety-eight thousand and two hundred sixty people got increases in the ridiculously small pensions or retirement allowances that they had had before the Revolution. Fidel continued to analyze how with the Revolution the costs of social security had gone up . . . public health . . . education. . . Before the Revolution there were nine hundred thirty-six thousand seven hundred twenty-three pupils in the schools. This year there were one million six hundred fifty thousand one hundred ninety-three. Before the Revolution there were twenty-three thousand six hundred forty-eight teachers: the past year one hundred twenty-seven thousand five hundred twenty-six. The number of scholarships before the Revolution, fifteen thousand six hundred ninety-eight; now, two hundred seventy-seven thousand five hundred five. . . The figures continued, he went on enumerating the costs. There was a need for eighteen thousand eight hundred new teachers per year; sixty-four thousand in the next five years (they were needed, but they couldn't graduate that many). The number of families that had received free housing: two hundred sixty-eight thousand and eighty-nine. Those who stopped paying rent for their land, over one hundred thousand. The people listened to the figures and the comparisons between them in complete silence. With no applause. The money in cash and the people's savings accounts, three billion *pesos*. A policy of prices to make up for those imbalances between goods and services and money would have been, he said, a heartless sacrifice for the people. Devaluation is proper when it is applied to the bourgeoisie, but it would be repugnant to do this to the savings of the workers (here there was applause). And he continued to analyze the problems.

Fidel did not read his speech, except when there were figures (some of which he knew by heart). The speech was improvised and spontaneous, but the words flowed with amazing ease. His enunciation was very clear, each word stressed each letter, always with impeccable syntax, and although at times the paragraphs were long no sentence was badly constructed, never a stammer or a failing of voice; at times there were digressions, parentheses within parentheses, and it sounded as though he had lost track, but he came back to the initial idea, tied all the loose ends together, and ended the sentence perfectly.

"Because I do not believe that anyone doubts how indispensable it was to give the right to an old-age pension to the men and women who labored and were exploited all their lives. And what kind of a people would this people be if, filled with egotism, it failed to make reparation for such an injustice; what kind of a people would it be if it had remained unfeeling toward the cane-cutter who after thirty years of work gets a pension of seven dollars a month?"

The sound of that voice, the repetitions, the gestures, said Dorothy Day, reminded her of Peter Maurin. The sky was getting dark. Night was falling.

And the medical services established by the Revolution could not be reduced—"a tragedy familiar to millions of people in this country, families who watched the death agonies of thousands and tens of thousands and hundreds of thousands of their children." And education could not be restricted. . . Nobody could say that we should make a little less effort in education, to give a somewhat smaller number of scholarships, to create fewer places for teachers, to build fewer schools. . . Sixty thousand were graduating from the sixth grade each year. In the near future a hundred and fifty thousand ought to be graduating. And the destiny of the children of these people was not just to get to the sixth grade. "Because today a simple sixth-grader is practically an illiterate." And the expenses for the Armed Forces could not be reduced with an extremely powerful enemy only ninety miles away. To these realities one more must be added, he said afterward: "Our own inefficiency, inefficiency, our inefficiency in the general work of the Revolution." He went on enumerating the difficulties of development (he gave as an example the manufacture of hydrogen fertilizers), and he said again afterward . . . "added to the unquestionable inefficiency of all of us."

He had been talking about an hour, almost all of it figures and data. And the people were silent. No applause. We sensed the attention of the masses.

"At that time there was no talk of production—production is what concerns capitalists—or of figures or of statistics or of structures. There was talk of the necessities piled up by unemployment, exploitation, abuses, injustices of all kinds."

Fidel was standing in front of the statue of Martí. From where we sat Fidel's face was about the size of Martí's mustache. And the white body of Martí is small before the immense obelisk, also white, that rises behind it like a spirit. From the square Fidel must look like a little dot. And I remembered that once from the National Library when I looked with Cintio at this Martí Monument, and the place where Fidel was going to speak, he said: "Fidel has a lot in common with Martí. Martí overflowed in writing, just as Fidel overflows in speech. Martí said that it was a weakness of his to publish newspaper articles as if they were books. He wrote until he got writer's cramp. Fidel talks until his voice gets hoarse. Martí, like Fidel, was a person who had scarcely any private life. They are both men with a cause. Martí said: 'Nobody has a right to sleep peacefully as long as there is a single unhappy man,' and this seems to be a sentence of Fidel. Martí also spoke of a 'radical and solemn redemption,' imposed by force if necessary. It was not in vain that Fidel called his movement the 26th of July. He had always said that Martí was the initiator of this Revolution. Their two glories were different: Fidel won success, Martí won martyrdom."

Martí with his big moustache. Fidel with his big beard. And now Fidel was talking about the imbalance in the foreign debt. The debt with the Soviet Union, especially over the petroleum imports. "We import all the energy for those lights that dazzle us. . ." Fidel turned toward the powerful reflectors, because it was now night and the reflectors were lit. "We have not yet encountered a single citizen who has said: 'Why so much light? why not a little less light?'"

Fidel fondled a microphone. He leaned over it as though he had a great weight on his shoulders. His voice was filled with sadness when he said that the heroic effort to raise production was interpreted as a breakdown of the economy.

"It is clear that the enemy made much use of the argument that the ten million harvest figure would create some of these problems. Our duty was to do all we could to prevent this. And the truth is that we weren't able to do it."

A pause. The great square was in deep silence. Fidel bent over the microphones again and went on: "Our enemies say that we have troubles, and in this our enemies are right. They say that we have problems, and our enemies are really right. They say that there is unrest, and our enemies are really right. They say that there is friction, and our enemies are really right. As you see, we are not afraid to admit it when our enemies are right." And here there was applause, which surprised me. Not great applause, moderate. The people were corroborating their leader, as to there being friction.

Everything that he had with him, Fidel said—and he indicated the great bundles of paper—was a top secret economic document (and here another round of applause), was one of those things that governments keep secret so that their enemies will not find it out.

And he stretched up and raised his arms to the sky while his voice increased in intensity: "And if some of these things that we say are exploited by the enemy and bring us deep shame, we welcome the shame!" Applause, and he said, now shouting above the applause: "Welcome to misery if we can change shame into strength!" And shouting even louder, his face to the sky: "If we can change shame into dignity." ("The poor man, he is weeping," exclaimed Paz Espejo.) And the last words can scarcely be heard because of the strength of his shouting: "If we can change shame into morality!" Applause, applause, and shouts, all the people standing, raising their arms: "Fi-del—Fi-del—Fi-del / Fi-del—Fi-del—Fi-del / Fi-del —Fi-del—Fi-del. . ." From where we sat we can see a bright spot on his cheek. He must surely be weeping, as Paz had said. And she again said: "Oh, the poor man, he is suffering!" And she joined in the chorus of: "Fi-del—Fi-del—Fi-del. . ." The ovation was almost as great as at the beginning. I thought: the people at first showed that they were unhappy, and now they are showing that they are not unhappy with him.

When the ovation ended Fidel continued smiling and calm: "So here are the secrets for the people" (more applause). He laughed. And the figures and the data followed. Pages were turned. He leafed through a document, put it aside, and continued with another. At times he stopped because he couldn't find a statistic, and he went back to previous pages. In rice there was an increase, but they were very far from feeling satisfied. Milk, from January to May, 71.3 million quarts, which meant a 25 per cent reduction from the previous year. Cement: production up to June slightly below that of 1969. Steel bars: deliveries have been down. . . Nickel. . . Fishing. . . Fertilizers. . . Electric power: it had increased 11 per cent but demand had increased 17 per cent. Shoes have been of very poor quality. Textiles: there is a backlog of 16.3 million yards of cloth. Bread: a shortage in Havana of 6 per cent. He analyzed transportation. The great delays in ships in ports because of lack of storage. Delays in cattle cars coming from Camagüey. . . Breakdown in transport of raw material for soaps and detergents. . . Cutbacks in vegetables and fruits. . . The rice quota was raised to 6 pounds. . . Fresh fish: the delivery to the people was increased beginning in January. . . The consumption of beef and poultry was restricted. . . Fats and beans: a delay in delivery. . . Refreshments: a drop in quantity because of a lack of bottles. . . (He leafed through papers, looking for new data, new figures.) Beer and alcoholic beverages: consumption reduced because of the nonreturn of containers, owing to limitations in the system of consumption and a storing up of stocks for the July festivities. Cigars and cigarettes:

it was necessary to ration these products. . . Some difficulty in the distribution of industrial products such as detergents, tooth-paste, textiles, clothing, and underclothes. . .

He devoted another hour to these figures. The people completely silent. No applause. "This is shattering," said Cintio. "Outside Cuba, at this moment, our enemies will be amazed. They are probably thinking that Fidel has gone crazy. But that's the kind of thing that Fidel does."

"Only some of the causes appear in this statistical enumer-ation. One must point out the inefficiency . . . [Someone behind us muttered: "Where is all this getting us?"] . . . One must point out the inefficiency, that is to say, the subjective factor among the causes that have been influencing these problems. There are, to be sure, objective difficulties. But we are not here to point out the objective difficulties. Our task is to point out the prob-lems concretely. And they are man. Man is here playing a role of fundamental importance. And it is fundamentally [his voice sounds like thunder] men who are charged with leadership." The people burst into deafening applause. I wondered what the leaders and the sugar cane cutters sitting behind him were thinking about. When he mentioned the leaders, the applause was very loud.

But Fidel changed his tone and began a new sentence with a very soft voice: "We are going to begin by indicating in the first place that all these problems are the responsibilty of all of us (here his voice was almost sobbing) and mine in par-ticular." Perhaps he was weeping again. His face was bent over in the shadows. People could be heard exclaiming. Paz, with tears in her eyes: "Oh, no!" "I do not claim, far from it, to point out responsibilities [and here his voice went up and up until it became a shout, a shout that seemed to end in weeping] or to claim that such responsibilities do not fall upon me and all the leaders of the Revolution." Applause. A wild applause, mixed with shouts. It was not an ovation. I didn't know what the people wanted to demonstrate with this ap-plause. Everybody was standing up again. They were waving flags. "Lamentably these self-criticisms can not be accompanied by solutions." The sentence was spoken with a trembling voice. And then in a broken voice he said: "It would be better to tell the people to seek another leader." And then shouting, above the shouts of the people: "Just that: to seek other lead-ers!" The square exploded in shouts: "No! No! No! No!"

Fidel had stepped back from the microphones. It seemed as though he was going to leave the crowd, and the immense chorus of shouts and no's grew louder and louder, everyone with arms in the air, waving flags and banners. "No! No! No!" Fidel approached the microphones, and when the crowd calmed down: "It would be better. But in truth on our part [he smiled a little] it would be hypocritical." He paused. "I believe that we, the leaders of this Revolution, have had a too costly apprenticeship. And unfortunately our problem—not when it is a question of replacing the leaders of the Revolution [now he was shouting and getting more and more excited, and at the end of the sentence his voice was shaking the whole square]—for this people can replace them whenever it wishes, at the moment that it wishes, and right now if it wishes!!!" Again he stepped back, and the ovation was gigantic, the square shook with applause, applause prolonged many minutes, perhaps as much as ten minutes, with shouts of "No! No! No! No!" and all the hands in the air signaling "No!" and the shouts of "FIDEL!" everywhere, and then a chorus like a chant: "Fi-del—Fi-del—Fi-del. . ." Fidel had risked rejection by the people right there. If the square had been silent, he would have fallen. But the people gave their vote to him, and to him alone, in a form that could not have been more eloquent.

And again, with the square silent: "One of our most difficult problems, and in this we are paying for a fine inheritance, is precisely that of our own ignorance." The sky had become dark and was filled with stars. The spotlights above the heads of the people were more brilliant. The portraits of the dead lit up against the black sky looked more ghostly.

Fidel's voice, amplified by the loudspeakers all over the square, was powerful enough to match the portraits. And his voice bounced off the buildings opposite and echoed back to where we were as though the portraits were repeating each word of Fidel. The echo from Che, the echo from Abel, the echo from Camilo. Down below the sea of people under the spotlights, behind him the cane-cutters serious, priestly.

All the movie and TV cameras were at work. Many photographers came close or stood to one side to take snapshots. At times Almeida gave instructions to the cameramen. At one point he went down a few steps, where he too took a picture with his little camera. And Fidel told how in the past few days he had gone around visiting all kinds of factories and had talked with everyone. I remembered what on another occasion Paz told me: "He mingles with everyone in a crowd, and that frightens his bodyguards." (Che's little daughter appeared again and circled around Fidel.)

Fidel said that in Santiago de Cuba he had been analyzing the problems with a great many workers. The Titan factory: how did it fail to produce some fifty thousand tons of cement . . . The flour factory that failed to produce six thousand tons because they didn't take away the flour that it had produced, so that there was no space to store more flour, while the people had no bread for breakfast because there was a lack of flour. . . He had seen how they had failed to produce some three hundred thousand barrels of beer and malt, which the people could have drunk. . .

"And production today is not for profit, it's for the people. Production is for need. And if production can be increased so that more workers, more young people, more students, more families can drink more malt and can drink more beer, at relatively slight investment, why not do it?"

In the bus workshops he had found many workers with ragged clothes and broken shoes, but they didn't talk to him about this: they talked to him about production problems. He made a passing remark about the bad quality of the shoes. The cane-cutters know, he said, that sometimes after ten days, or even five days, the soles will fall off new shoes.

"If we could solve problems simply with a change of men!" There had to be changes, he said, many leaders were tired and worn out, and it would be necessary to replace them, but it would be demagoguery and a deception of the people to claim that the problem is only about a group of men. "We believe that this is a problem of a whole people!" The solution was to have the masses make the decisions. "Because where the decision is administrative it will always be subject to a heap of contradictions and even to the risk and the danger of favoritism." (Applause.) There always had to be someone responsible, but the management of the factories would be composed of a collective organism in which everyone would be represented. (A poet had told me: "When Fidel is making a speech, what is present in front of you is the whole supreme government gathered in plenary session. Whatever he says at that moment—and at times it can be a sudden inspiration that comes to him during the speech—will be the new guidelines he follows until he makes a new speech.") And now the guideline is decentralization. "Why does an administrator have to be the only responsible one? Why not introduce representation for the collective workers in the management of the factory? Why not have more confidence? Why not believe in that formidable proletarian spirit of men who, even though at times barefoot and with ragged clothes, maintain the production there?" (Applause.)

In the night that was blacker and blacker the spotlighted Fidel stood out more and more. All eyes were fixed on him up there, alone, in dazzling light. And now Fidel was talking about himself, about his cane-cutting, but at first I didn't realize that he was talking about himself because he said "we" and this "we"—I later noticed that he never said "I"—gave his words a modest tone: it seemed that he, uneasy at that height, shining above the multitude, wanted to diminish his pre-eminence. "That cane-cutting had no merit for us: it was just a distraction. And perhaps the most difficult thing for us in cutting cane is not really cutting cane but cutting cane while we are thinking about problems. And during the first days what was most difficult for us was to get those problems out of our head, until we gradually learned more or less to control our thinking. But we would like to have cut a little more sugar cane. We had created an illusion—and that's the word for it—that we were going to be able to cut cane four hours during every day of the harvest, that we were going to live the Utopia of being able to alternate manual and intellectual work, and to do something as healthful as that. And so you see that that was a good rhythm, but the whole thing stopped on the 9th of January. The truth is that we were not thinking of a certificate. We were thinking of the tens of thousands of men who were making that same effort, and we wanted somehow to have a part in the effort that they were making. And therefore it was our desire, and also our illusion, to cut cane during the whole harvest. And afterward the problems began to appear. . ."

And he talked on and on. His Greek profile stood out in the night. His green uniform, his green kepi very brilliant under the floodlights. "Notice that even in a speech as long as this one, there is no demagoguery, no cliché," said Cintio.

Now Fidel was saying that a million houses were needed.

From where we were we could see very clearly his big bright eyes. He leaned back. He raised his arms to the sky. He adjusted his kepi. He hugged a microphone. He rubbed his beard. And he touched the microphones again. He was saying that a mother could be living in one room with twelve children and that they could all have asthma, and that he saw people suffer, ask for things, and that he would like to be a magician to take all those things out of his pocket and give them to them.

"The road is hard. Yes. Harder than it seemed. Yes, lords of imperialism, the building of socialism is hard." His head raised, he was talking now, above the crowd, to other hearers. I was moved when he began to speak, modestly, talking confidentially, simply: "When we tried to take the Moncada fortress seventeen years ago it was not to win a war with a thousand men but to begin a war and to wage it with the people and to win it with the support of the people. Years later, when we returned with a group of expeditionaries it was not to win a war with a handful of men. We had not had the marvelous experiences and the marvelous lessons that we have had in these years, but we already knew that war could be won only with the people." The battle that had to be won now, the battle of economic development, was much more difficult.

"It was relatively easy. We knew nothing about war. And there the apprenticeship was swift, and men came out of it who knew how to command a squad, a company." And he alluded in the same modest, familiar tone to the most glorious day of his life: "Ah, it is not the first time that we say this. We said it when we arrived here on January 6th or 7th. . ." [and I thought: can it be possible that he doesn't remember the exact date of his entrance into Havana?] ". . . and we said that we were conscious that the task was great and that we had much to learn."

Camilo Cienfuegos was laughing down from his portrait, as he laughed on his white horse when he entered Havana, surrounded by banners, and mothers lifted their children up to let them see him. When Fidel turned to the right, to speak to the crowds on that side, it seemed that he too was looking at the great red portrait in back of them, and it seemed to me that he might be saying to himself: "Am I on the right track, Camilo?" And Camilo was laughing—I was told—a week before his death, listening to Fidel telling tales of the Sierra, and he was saying that many years later he would still be telling stories "and Camilo had died long ago." And I thought how painful it must have been for Fidel to have to refer in a speech—surely in that very square—to the slander of the enemy, slander declaring that he had killed Camilo. A slander that the people never believed. "What a lovely little tailor!" Che had said to a woman writer from Argentina.

And now Fidel was talking of sad, painful things, in the same confidential tone, addressing the crowds as though they were close friends, and the crowds were still, perfectly silent: "It is seventeen years, or a little more, seventeen years since Moncada. Before that it was necessary to work hard organizing, preparing. Eighteen years ago we began this struggle, eighteen years of our lives, a part of ourselves that we have invested in this: eighteen years, a part of our youth that we have invested in this." ("We have invested in this," the echo repeats.) "And what can we do today?" ("And what can we do today?") "What can we desire today more than ever? The energy that is left to us, whatever energy may be left to us, to the very last atom, to devote to this task. To settle our debt with so many enemies—objective, subjective—with the imperialistic enemies who hope for the failure of the Revolution; with the accumulated poverty, with ignorance in general, with our own ignorance—" ("Our own ignorance.")

Opposite, from the Ministry of the Interior, Che looks with a serious look, perhaps sad, perhaps tragic also, but at the same time serene; like a slightly embittered Christ; a slight frown on his brow; his beret in the shadows—with the little star shining on it—and his long hair also in the shadow, blown by the wind. A questioning look fixed on the void, as if he were peering at the horizons of Latin America or contemplating death (he was watching the explosion of the French ship laden with munitions in the port of Havana when they took that picture of him). It's curious, I thought: Fidel here in this square in front of the giant picture of Che, recalling Moncada. And in the cafés of San José de Costa Rica some Cubans told Che the story of that assault and about the exploits of Fidel, and Che didn't believe them and said: "And now why don't you tell me the plot of a cowboy movie?" Afterward Che met Fidel. ("I met him on one of those cold Mexican nights, and I remember that our first discussion was about international policy. A few hours later the same night—at dawn—I was one of the expeditionaries.") And it was in this same square, I was told, that Fidel announced officially, before a million silent people, the death of Che. When he was going to speak his name, I was told, he faltered, he could not call him Che (too painful) but Ernesto Guevara.

"Facing the defeats of the 26th of July, right away, instantly, we thought only of beginning again, we thought only of the hour when he would return to the fight, we thought only, when we heard the horrifying news of the murders committed, that a day would have to come on which we would settle accounts with them. Today we are not fighting against men—unless perhaps the men whom we are fighting against are ourselves—we are fighting against obstacles of all kinds. This is truthfully the greatest challenge that we have had in our lives and the greatest challenge that the Revolution has ever had."

And there was Abel looking down with his sad eyes, while Fidel spoke of the "horrifying news." I've been told that, just before the assault on the barracks, Fidel had told Abel that, even though all the others died, he must not die, he was young, he must survive to carry on the Revolution; and Abel had told him that he who was young must die, and that Fidel must live to complete the Revolution. And Haydée said that, at the time of the shooting, Abel said to her: "Well, they are going to kill us here, but Fidel is the one who must not die. Will those who are with him understand that Fidel must not die?" When she talked of Moncada, Haydée never mentioned her brother's eyes or her fiancé's testicles. "The rest was a cloud of blood and smoke," she said, "the rest was won by death. Fidel would win the last battle, he would win the Revolution." It was Abel, they told me, who thought that all the barracks in Cuba should be converted into schools, and it was in his memory that they did this. I thought that Fidel's thoughts must be sad as he looked at that portrait covering the Central Post Office from the first floor to the top. Shortly before the speech Paz Espejo told me that Haydée had said that since the assault on the Moncada Barracks, Fidel never again said the name of Abel. He always called him "your brother." But only a few days before, Fidel had again spoken the name of Abel; looking at Haydée's son, Fidel said: "He has the eyes of Abel."

The green figure of Fidel was stirring up there like a palm tree swayed by the wind: "We do not seek glory, we do not seek honors!" (And here the first person plural was again "we," but the "we" seemed to erase the distinction between himself and the people; he was himself in the plural: Fidel and the people.) "We serve a cause that is worth more than all the glories in the world, which—as Martí said—would all fit into a grain of corn!" Here there was great applause. "In his great speeches there is always a quotation from Martí," Cintio told me, as the applause continued. Below Fidel was the multitude, facing him were the portraits, and above him the starry sky.

"We do not seek honors! We do not seek power!" (And one felt that he was being deeply sincere, his voice was husky and came from his heart.) "Of what use is power if we cannot win the battle against misery. . ." (His voice was now a piercing shout, almost tearful) ". . . against lack of culture, against all those things?" There was a pause. He looked down upon the enormous crowd at his feet (a half million or maybe seven hundred thousand, said Cintio), raised his eyes to the sky, and exclaimed: "Power! What is power?" He shook his arm with a violent gesture of scorn, his face upraised as if he were also addressing more distant listeners, outside Cuba: "What is this power without power?"

We looked at him all alone up there, between the crowd and the sky, like a god. But he gave the impression that he did not feel himself deified on that height but perhaps diminished instead: one individual facing a multitude.

I had read an interview published in *Playboy,* shown me in the House of the Americas, in which Fidel said that he did not at all enjoy the adulation of the newspapers, that he had never enjoyed it even for a second, that he knew that any individual had few merits, that circumstances always determine what he does, and that the masses project a heroic stature on certain men because they feel the need to create symbols on which to concentrate their own feelings, and that they attribute to one individual the work not of him alone but of many others. "Gratitude is not distributed equitably, and it would be an error for anyone—I say this sincerely—not to be conscious of this, to believe that one really deserves all that gratitude, and all that affection." And he also said that nothing satisfied him more than to see that things depended less and less on him, because the work of one man could have no importance if it were to last only as long as that man. And that he thought it was a good idea to retire relatively young; it was not only a duty it was a right, he had other things that attracted him besides government. It was not retirement that was going to be difficult for him, it was old age; because he would no longer be able to do so many things that he liked: climbing mountains, or swimming, or scuba diving.

"None of us, as individuals, are in any way interested in honors or glories. They have no interest, no value. If we are worth an atom of anything, it will be that atom representing an idea, that atom representing a cause, that atom in union with a people."

"He is in one of his poetic moments," said Cintio beside me, and Fidel was saying, with his face raised to the starry sky: "And we men are of flesh and bone, incredibly fragile. We are nothing, yes, we can say this. We are something only as we exist to carry out this task." We looked at him all alone up there, between his people and the night. "Incredibly fragile," repeated Cintio. He told me that he had once heard Fidel say in a speech: "What is man? A desolate nothing!"

Fidel was now thanking the public; he had been talking for three and a quarter hours, and the back of my neck ached, but I wanted Fidel to go on talking. Suddenly he said: "Fatherland or death—we shall overcome." He stepped back. A great ovation. What a pity: he had stopped. Almeida approached him and whispered something. Fidel went back to the microphones, and the ovation was interrupted. He had forgotten something:

"Of course, while we were expressing these ideas, of course, we forgot something that we wished to communicate to you on this day. . ." His voice was tense. He was clearly trying to control his emotion. "There is something more, something that we wish the people to take with, let us say, a certain serenity. After sending us Che's diary, Doctor Arguedas struggled and strove to bring to our country the death mask of Che, the death mask that they took of him there, the day that they murdered him, and he also brought to our country the hands of Che." Applause, lengthy applause. I looked at all the faces filled with emotion. We could sense Fidel's grief. His words were slow, trembling slightly, but serene. "This is part of Che's body, all that is left to us. We do not even know whether some day we shall be able to find his remains. But we have his hands practically intact: and that's why we want to ask the people what their judgment is." "Keep them. Keep them. Keep them. Keep them." A multitude of cries from the multitude.

"Then we want to submit this project for your considera-
tion . . . to keep, in a crystal urn, and to place here on the
statue to Martí . . . the death mask and the hands. The hands
with which he grasped his liberating weapons, the hands with
which he wrote his brilliant ideas, the hands with which he
worked in the cane fields, and in the ports, and on the buildings." (A great ratifying applause.) Many of us were looking
at the great illumined blue portrait, which seemed now erected
not against the Ministry of the Interior but erected against
the night. It also seemed that the photograph of Che looking
at the explosion of "The Copper" was now a photograph of
eternity. "Che does not belong to our country! Che belongs to
America! And one day those hands will be where the peoples
of America want them. Meanwhile our people will keep them
and will watch over them. . . Some day everything we may
have will belong to all the peoples. We are the primogenitors
on this revolutionary road, the first but not the only ones!
And some day we shall be the peoples of Latin America. And
not in order to impose a powerful imperialism but to live
together united also to a great people, the day when the imperialist yoke has been shaken off and the Revolution has happened in its own country: the people of the United States."
(Applause.)

"So then we shall dedicate this place where his mask, his
hands will be, and where the people can see them. Although
we confess that it will always be hard for anyone when that
instant comes. I know that for many comrades the very idea
has been overwhelming." A great number of people were probably weeping. Beside me, Paz Espejo's eyes were filled with
tears. I too was moved. Fidel controlled himself, his voice was
serene but incisive, slow, trembling. "Here, when we began
the ceremony, was Aleidita, and I talked with her, and I told
her, so that she would not be taken by surprise. Her eyes red-
dened, a few tears, but she said: 'Yes, it's fine.' So that Che's
companion knew it, his father knew it; and only a few of us
knew it; the children did not know it. This was what I needed
to tell you." The ovation was endless; it was as if the whole
square were sobbing.

We went to look for the bus of the House of the Americas
—the square still applauding—and to make a shortcut they
made us go up the other platform, going around the statue of
Martí. As we went by we saw the place where Che's mask and
hands would be. "All the glory of the world is in a kernel of

corn." But I thought, Martí knew what a kernel means. ("If the kernel does not fall into the earth and die. . .") And he had said that to die is to sow. And while we went down the steps on the other side, silent, among a multitude visibly moved, I thought that Martí's speeches must have been something like these speeches of Fidel. (A farmer had said that when Martí spoke they hadn't understood everything he said, but they wanted to die for him.) And I remembered also that for Martí the imperfection of human language was proof of the need for a future life.

When we were on the bus, and the crowd was scattering in all directions, Cintio said: "I was deeply impressed to see Fidel so alone in his speech. I felt more than ever that the whole weight of the government rests on him. And I was very sad to see him so alone. His best friends are dead: Abel, Frank, Camilo, Che. He was surrounded by those portraits of the dead, he was the only one alive. Of course, he has very good friends around him, but he has no close friends. So now he is alone. But he has the people with him."

Airport

The Cubana de Aviación plane delayed its departure a few hours, and so my last conversation in Cuba was unexpectedly continued at the airport. It was with Cintio and Fina, who had come to say good-by to me at dawn on the 27th of July. And so we talked again about what everyone talks about in Cuba at all hours, the Revolution.

Cintio remembered the entrance of the bearded ones into Havana: "There was a sharp contrast between the city with its skyscrapers, its luxury hotels, and all its capitalist splendor, and the ragged clothing of its new owners. Because, just imagine, they came in tatters, filthy, with very long hair. It was a shock, people didn't know that the guerrilla fighters went around like that—up until then they had never seen them—and nobody expected that they were going to come in looking like that."

And Fina: "I remember, during the parade, a TV interviewer, very elegant, very powdered, as pink as a suckling pig, interviewing, with the servility toward the powerful to which he was accustomed, the new lords of the city: evil-smelling, long-bearded, and disheveled. And it was very amusing to see him so elegant, I remember that he was very powdered, bowing down before his new masters, dressed worse than beggars. The contrast even appeared in his language. The interviewer with the language of commercial television: And now we present to you distinguished televiewers. . . And the person being interviewed was a farmer, and he spoke with great gentleness of how he had knocked down a light plane with his carbine, and he described the movements of the plane, without saying her name, he just said 'she'; 'she' went up and down and turned . . . and he said it with a country gentleness as if he were describing the flight of a butterfly."

And Cintio: "And then Fidel's entrance into Havana: a tremendous thing. Because Fidel came much later, he had moved in triumph through all the towns, and he delayed a long time before entering Havana. And when he came he occupied the Habana Libre Hotel, which then was the Havana Hilton, he made it into his headquarters. The whole hotel was occupied by him and his guerilla fighters. It was a marvelous spectacle, and I used to go every afternoon to stand in front of the hotel, for the joy that I got out of seeing the bearded ones instead of the rich Yankees. Those were the finest days of our lives, for all of us who lived through that time."

Fina: "And those days were like the Last Judgment because each one got what he deserved: some, punishments, others, prizes. And everything that had been hidden came out into the light. The good and the bad. And everything that people had endured during the Revolution was made public: the death of a son, imprisonment, tortures. And one wanted to have suffered something then; but one who had not suffered at all," Fina complained gently, "was worthless."

Cintio remembered Fidel's first speech in Havana. It was on the 8th of January at Columbia Field. "And it was curious that the cheers of the crowd should have brought to Fidel's mind the day of his death. He said: 'Never in our lives will we again witness such a spectacle. Except on another occasion on the day when we die, for we shall never defraud the people.'"

And Fina said that a dove whirled above Fidel's head, and they looked at it as if it were the Holy Ghost. It even seemed to them that the Father also had appeared at that moment to say: "This is my beloved Son. . ." Cintio added with a smile that when Fidel declared himself a communist many Catholics no longer believed that he had the Holy Ghost. In his speeches Fidel was very hard on the bishops. Once he said a sentence that sounded harsh: "Let them excommunicate me if they want to." Afterward it was clear that Fidel had a clearer idea of authentic Christianity than the bishops had. He said that the Cuban clergy, allied with the rich, had prostituted the essence of primitive Christianity. Which was true. And that Christianity had been able to exist in Imperial Rome, in feudalism, in absolute monarchies, in bourgeois capitalism, and why would it not now be able to live in a regime that had much more social justice than the preceding ones?

And Fina said: "I believe that the patron saint of Cuba, the Virgin of Charity of Cobre, has had to do with this Revolution. The Charity of Cobre has been a great Cuban devotion, and that was why Cubans had always practiced charity. To be *nice people* has always been very important for Cubans; here there has always been a lot of talk about being *nice people*—it meant being nice to other people. And the Revolution has made us all *nice people.* I believe that this Revolution, atheistic and Marxist-Leninist as it is, came to us from heaven; it is a gift from the Charity of Cobre: she is the patron of the Cuban Revolution, although this is not known."

And Cintio: "The Cuban has never had much religious faith. What Cubans have always had, more than faith and hope, is charity. Charity, that was Martí: a flaming love. And if you analyze Fidel's speech of last night, you will find no religious faith in it. Do you remember that he mentioned the word 'miracles'—but it was to say that miracles were made by the people? Hope, there was some, but not much. He left a certain hope. But above all the speech was filled with charity, with a great love, wasn't it?"

I commented that for St. Paul the greatest virtue was charity; the two other virtues would disappear and charity would stay eternally. And I recalled Father de Lubac's phrase, very appropriate in Cuba today: "Love, and believe what you want." The Revolution sums up all the Law and the Prophets. The Christians should have been the first to love this egalitarian distribution of consumer goods. And I also told them that I had seen here in Cuba, more than anywhere else, what Camilo Torres had said of all Latin America: "Those who love have no faith, those who have faith do not love."

They brought us coffee and sandwiches because we had had no breakfast, and the flight was still delayed. Cintio said: "It's a shame you didn't talk with Fidel." Raúl Roa had offered to arrange an interview, but many delegations had arrived for the 26th of July and, in addition, during the days before the speech Fidel had spent almost all his time visiting factories in Santiago de Cuba. Cintio also said: "You didn't cover the island from one end to the other, but you got to know the Revolution in depth, talking with very dissimilar people. You must have many things in your notebooks that even we Cubans don't know."

(I was leaving without notebooks, because in Mexico they take papers away from anyone coming from Cuba. I had given my notebooks to the House of the Americas and asked them to mail them to me. In the notebooks was all that I had heard, both good and bad. What those ladies in the sacristy had said to me: "Father, this is horrible," "Worse than what we had under Batista," "We've been putting up with this man for eleven years!" Or else: "This is the criticism that we young people make of this Revolution. . ." Or: "I was in the UMAP. . . ," etc. In Mexico a friend said: "Say good-by to those notes, they'll never get to you." All the notes reached me.)

I told Cintio and Fina that my trip had been too short: I knew this Revolution only superficially. Yet a great change had taken place in my life; it was the most important experience since my religious conversion. And it was like another conversion. I had discovered that now, and in Latin America, to practice religion was to make revolution. There can be no authentic Eucharist except in a classless society. St. Paul reproached the Christians of Corinth for being divided into classes, and he told them that this was not the Lord's Supper. The Church, to correct the abuse of inequality in meals, suppressed the feasts and instituted Eucharistic feasting, but the solution resulted in the suppression of the classes. Ration cards made feasts possible again. Also in Cuba I had seen that socialism made it possible to live the Gospels in society. Earlier it had been possible to worship only individually, or in the bosom of convents and monasteries. Fidel had reconciled us with communism. And I also said that this island had returned to what it had been before, because Pedro Martir tells us that for the Indians of Cuba the earth was as common as the sun and the water and that there was between them no *meum* or *tuum,* seeds of all evils: "By their nature they venerate the one who is right; they consider bad and perverse the one who takes pleasure in insulting anyone." The announcement of the plane's take-off was sudden, and we scarcely had time to say good-by.

The airport was filled with sun when I went out onto the runway. The palm trees very green in the sunlight. I remembered again another time that I was there, a dark airport, a rainy Havana afternoon, a dreary day—although for me the happiest day in my life. Some euphoric Yankees had come aboard loaded with bottles of Bacardi. At that time Ernesto was a bootblack here. I might have seen him, and he would have meant nothing to me. My heart sank at the thought that by dusk I would be in a capitalist city: ENJOY ORANGE CRUSH . . . DRINK COCA-COLA. This time I was leaving a bright and gleaming Cuba.

Epilogue. A Conversation with Fidel

The next year I made another visit to Cuba, a much shorter one, the main object of which was to talk to Fidel. One night I was in my hotel room—this time the Havana Riviera—and suddenly the phone rang. "Cardenal, this is Celia Sánchez. We have just received your message, and Fidel wants to see you. Stay right there in the hotel. Don't leave your room."

It was then about eight o'clock. At about nine the telephone rang again. "Cardenal, this is Celia. Fidel says to go down to the main entrance to the hotel. He'll come by and pick you up." When I got off the elevator I saw two young soldiers; one said: "Follow us." At the hotel door was a small black car with the door open, and from a distance I could easily recognize the figure inside with the green suit and the black beard. I sat down beside him, and the car took off. Two very young soldiers in front, one of them driving, and the two of us in the back. Between us a great pile of papers, on which Fidel was resting his elbow. The moment I got in the car, he began to talk to me as though he were talking with a lifelong friend:

"I have a terrible cold. . ." (putting his handkerchief to his nose) ". . . I caught it Tuesday, with Kosygin; we got soaked. I don't know how I'll get along in southern Chile . . ." (lowering his voice, with the air of one revealing a great secret), ". . . *because I am going to Chile.*" And it *was* a secret; there had been speculation in the international press about a trip to Chile, but it had not been officially announced. He told the chauffeur to drive around the streets, and he continued:

"I received your note, very terse. I said to myself: if it is brief it's probably important. It aroused my interest. That's the advantage of being brief. Your message was right to the point; it was written in revolutionary style. Tonight I had been going to go to Oriente; I didn't go because of the cold, that's why I am able to see you; otherwise it would have been impossible because I now have only three days left in Cuba. We'll talk while the car drives around, all right? Afterward, if you want, I'll take you to the University, because I want to see the students, we'll be there only ten minutes. I was with them several hours last night, and I was very tough with them, I was quite severe, and I'm sorry about that. I want to go and make amends; I should have sugar-coated the pill a little. You can also come with me for a moment to the Habana Libre where I have to see some sugar cane technicians."

We went swiftly through the empty streets. I broached the subject that I wanted to discuss: the religious question in Cuba. I said: "The situation in the rest of Latin America has changed; there the Catholic Church is obviously moving toward Marxism." I told him that in Chile I had seen many Marxist priests, and some of them were openly Marxist-Leninists. Fidel listened very attentively. Many, I told him, find that Marxism is a science and Christianity a faith. I was about to say that others went further, but he tapped me on the shirt and interrupted:

"And not only Marxism as a science. Also as a philosophy. Look: Marxist philosophy and Christianity coincide ninety per cent of the time. Right?" He talked excitedly. He seemed happy. His tone was very confidential, like that of an old friend. Tapping my shirt again: "And dialectical materialism is more spiritual than positivism. Isn't that so?" I told him it was, and that dialectical materialism was not opposed to spirituality but to idealism. We came back to the case of Cuba, and he said: "Look, I know Christianity as you know it. And I know that the authentic Christianity is revolutionary. Why, it was the religion of the poor and the slaves in the Roman Empire. But here not everyone knows Christianity that way, and there are certain prejudices against it which one must count on, and which are explained, besides, by the way that the Cuban Church behaved here."

I said that I was aware of how the Cuban Church behaved, and Fidel continued: "The Church here, you know, was very bad. It was not the Catholicism that you have had in the rest of Latin America, which has worked with the poor and the Indians. Catholicism here was not out in the country; it was town-centered; it was class-conscious. It was the religion of the rich. What was really popular here was the African religions. And the Protestants too had more ties with the people."

I said: "And I've been told that they had less conflict with the Revolution." "They did have less conflict." He kept changing gestures as he spoke: he put his chin in his hand; he lifted a finger for emphasis; he leaned his right side against the window, or his left side with his elbow on the pile of papers between us, and he cupped his chin in his hand. "Here we had a revolutionary priest. It's too bad you never met him. He died. He was a good friend of ours. . ." "Yes," I said, "Father Sardiñas. And he was a Commander. . ."

"He was a Commander. He was a good priest. And a good revolutionary. And a good guerrilla fighter. We baptised many children in the Sierra Maestra, he and I. At that time there was a lot of belief in that. He and I would go to see which children were not baptised, and we would baptise them. We baptised more than a hundred. I was the godfather. I have more than a hundred godsons in the Sierra." (He laughed.)

I spoke about the importance of the Church's collaboration, for the triumph of the Revolution in Latin America, and he said: "Not only for the triumph. Also for afterward: to consolidate socialism." He told me that he had heard that the seminarists were now revolutionaries. They had gone to cut cane. And he had told the Nuncio that one of these days he'd like to go and see them, to encourage them: "Poor fellows. They must be encouraged. When they are priests they'll have a hard job: to make revolutionaries out of Cuban Catholics. A great responsibility."

I said that true religion, according to St. James, comes to the aid of widows and orphans and that I had said in Latin America that that was the religion that Fidel practiced: day-care centers, polyclinics, schools. . . It seemed to me that he was moved. And he said: "It's true, we have practiced that kind of religion a good deal here." I repeated to him what the Nuncio had said to me: "You can be a communist if you want, as long as you don't lose your faith!" And Fidel said: "Good for the Nuncio. It's quite clear. You can be a communist without ceasing to be a Christian. Why not?" Our car was far out in the suburbs. We passed a construction site. ("Here we are building a hydroelectric plant.") He said it was time to go to the University.

Speaking of the union of Christians and Marxists in Latin America, I said it was a split union: a union of the revolutionary Christians and Marxists, separated from the reactionary Christians and Marxists, as were most of the bishops and the Communist parties. "Because in Latin America all Communist parties are reactionary." And he said: "You mustn't generalize. Many are bad, but they aren't like that everywhere."

And about the collaboration of the Church he again said: "Not only for the triumph of the Revolution. It's important for that, as you say. But a revolution could also triumph without the Church. And this might be more important in the long run. To avoid certain conflicts. And to encourage the sacrifices that socialism demands." We reached the University about ten o'clock. Two other small cars had followed us, with two or three soldiers in each, very young (no machine guns). A girl came up: "Commander!" Five or six other young people saw him from a distance and came running up. The Student Council was meeting with the Rector in the building opposite us, and we went there with the students and the escort. They were surprised when we entered the room: "Commander!"

We sat at a long table with the others. More students arrived. Fidel told them that the night before he had been very harsh, very negative. All he had talked about were bad things. Now he was coming to say good things, too. . . He smiled: "Of course, everything I said last night against the technicians is true, but I said only the bad things." Now he would be with them only fifteen minutes, because he had to talk with me (but he stayed about an hour). The University had trained good technicians, but there was also the danger of falling into technocracy. It was also necessary to avoid creating an intellectual elite. Then he began to analyze with them a new educational plan: education would always go along with work, and work with education. The University would be brought to the factory, and the factory to the University. Students were going to be workers, and workers would be students. It was not fair to have one man devote all his life to intellectual work, and another man to manual work. In the society of the future all men would be intellectual workers and also manual workers. For now, while there are still only a few intellectual workers, they should be as much like the rest of the workers as possible. A factory educates better than a university, although the universities are also necessary because they give theoretical instruction. That's why we must combine the factories with the universities. People in his generation didn't get educated. What education could a society of wolves give? A little academic training in school; but in the street children were taught to deceive, to be exploiters, to be thieves. Teaching today was to prevent the existence of laziness, parasitism, deceit, egoism. Capitalism created the concept of the exploitation of labor, not the concept of labor for the material and spiritual well-being of man. Schools have to educate children in the discipline of work. Not educate them like children of the rich. Young people now have better schools than rich children used to have. But education has to be different. The children of the rich didn't know how things were produced, and they squandered them. A child must be taught from an early age to produce some goods. Children in the fourth or fifth grade should have a garden, a vegetable garden. There the children see how the little seeds are sown, how to fertilize, how to water, how to pull up the weeds. They will value everything more. And better than seeing all the food come in a truck and not knowing who grew it. And they will learn about plants. From his earliest years the child will learn how to participate in production, how to contribute to society. . .

The Rector spoke of a technical school in which the workers in a factory could now study, while the students would go to work in that same factory. Fidel said at once: "How many buses will be needed? Figure out how many buses. And we'll build them. We already have a small bus factory."

Fidel again said that every man ought to do intellectual work and manual work; if he didn't they would be going back to a class society. If they were not careful about that the whole Revolution could collapse on them. Capitalism was very dangerous because it was very attractive. It favored all man's instincts: egotism, covetousness, sensuality, laziness, prostitution of all kinds, usury. Whereas socialism was anti-instinct. The position of socialism as opposed to capitalism was disadvantageous, because socialism was sacrifice. They should not aspire to create a consumer's society: the true name of that society is not "consumer's" but "squanderer's." Things were manufactured to be thrown away. A hundred, a hundred fifty million automobiles in the United States: and with them they were exhausting all the oil reserves in their territory and in most of the rest of the world, contaminating the atmosphere, making traffic impossible. One automobile for each person: that was madness! Socialism was food for everybody, housing for everybody, clothing for everybody, health for everybody, education for everybody.

From the University we went to the Habana Libre. On the way, Fidel said: "You know? Socialism is not abundance, it is distribution, sharing, and therefore sacrifice. Socialism is brotherhood, right?" I said: "Yes, it is love." A bit later he said: "Look, all the qualities that make a priest are the qualities needed in a good revolutionary." I said: "That makes a good priest."

Suddenly the car stopped inside a basement. "And this, what is it?" I asked. "It's the Habana Libre." The soldiers' movements were rapid, but Fidel's were leisurely. We went up to the apartment where the sugar cane technicians were. They had just arrived from the United States where they had created an international problem by making an unexpected landing in New Orleans without any landing permit. Fidel made them tell the whole story, and he was delighted. They told him of the confusion of the American authorities when the plane landed, and he laughed heartily. They explained that they were arriving for an international congress to which Cuba had been invited—more laughter from Fidel. "Did they accuse you of violating their air space?" "No, they didn't," and that also amused him. He knew they wouldn't do that, he said. He turned to me and said: "Every day they violate Cuban air space with their U-2s." They told him about the headlines in the United States press, and he laughed again. The head of the delegation of technicians was a black, and that was a sensation in New Orleans, and that also amused Fidel. Some technicians from the Dominican Republic said that the Cubans were not known internationally and that instead of technicians they were probably spies. Fidel laughed and told me that the head of the delegation, who was one of the great Cuban technicians, had been a mason before the Revolution and that was why he did not have an international reputation. He said to them: "And did you know that just then a hijacked plane arrived here with a hundred and twenty passengers? So that unexpectedly we had some hostages." This also amused him. "They'll always believe that we hijacked the plane." More laughter. "But we returned the plane there before you returned here. That was a very graceful gesture on our part."

That unexpected landing had been a brilliant idea, he said. He spoke confidentially about other conflicts between Cuba and the United States—and always in a joking tone. He ordered a round of daiquiris to celebrate the return. ("But only one round.") He served himself last. And he really had only one drink. Afterward, turning serious: "Tomorrow, when you're interviewed on television, don't tell only the bad things. Tell the good things, too. Don't you agree? That gives us moral strength."

Fidel asked if there were representatives of the three universities among the technicians. They said only Las Villas and Havana. "Who represented the Las Villas University?" And afterward, turning to one: "Aren't you the Vice-Rector?" "Yes." "And who represented Havana?" "Suárez." He then asked: "Which are the agricultural engineers?" And then, to the black who had been a mason: "One thing I want to tell you: while you were away, people made an effort to finish the winter sowing. Notice: now after accomplishing this mission, you have to bring yourselves up to date quickly in order to see how all the provinces are in sugar cane sowing. Las Villas is up to date, and it will pass the mark. Oriente is well along. In short, we're making an effort. I think they are quite on time for the preparation of the spring sowing."

Fidel asked if they had brought newspapers. He looked at the headlines. He was much amused by a cartoon showing him with Nixon. They told him there was also an article in Spanish, by a "worm," full of horrible things about him. "Let's see, let's see it!" He read in a declamatory tone: "The reign of terror of the Communist tyrant Fidel Castro. . ." (A burst of laughter. And they all laughed with him.) ". . . the Caribbean jackal. . ." (More laughter.) ". . . the bloody Castro dictatorship. . ." (More laughter, by Fidel and the others.) ". . . the oppression affecting the unhappy island. . ." He read to the end with much laughter. As he left he again advised them not to tell just the bad things. ("This gives us moral standing.") He must have been very tired because he yawned between laughs. His voice was hoarse. Who knows how many hours or days of unending conversations he had had. His clothes were rumpled.

Back in the car, I asked Fidel: "And now where do we go?" "We're going to your hotel, but I'm not going to leave you yet; I want to talk more with you." Near the Havana Riviera he said to the driver: "Just drive up and down along the wharf." It was near midnight, and we had been driving back and forth in the car about an hour. Great waves were crashing on the pier, they shot up as white foam two or three yards, and fell back as rain upon the street. The car went as far as the Miramar tunnel and returned to the National Hotel and back again to the tunnel. Fidel asked me about the revolutionary priests of Latin America. Would any of them be interested in coming to Cuba? What was I writing? What new things was I planning to write in the future? I told him that I was about to publish a book on Cuba, which I was going to dedicate to the Cuban people and to him. ("Many thanks. I shall read it with interest.") He asked me lots of questions about our community of Solentiname. What our life there was like. What was the meaning of the name, 'Solentiname'? What were the islands like? How many inhabitants? How long was the lake? How deep? What breeds of cattle did we have? And he gave me advice on cross-breeding. The lake fishing: why wasn't it commercialized; the fresh-water sharks. . . "And tell me: is it true that they are very ferocious?" "They are not all that ferocious." "Well, then, why did my technicians say they were?" "Are the lake fish tasty? I like salt-water fish better than fresh-water fish. Are there sailboats? Is the lake beautiful? Those islands must be wonderful!"

The car went from the Baltimore to the National and the Coppelia, and from there it approached the Havana Riviera, and back again, and once more we would pass by the great hotels: Capri, Habana Libre, Presidente, Saint John. We would go by the white skyscraper that was once the embassy of the United States, and the House of the Americas, and the State Department, and we would reach the tunnel, and at times the car would go through the tunnel and head for Miramar, and then come back past all the hotels and the tunnel once more and Miramar.

Fidel questioned me at length about Peru and Chile, where I had just been. I told him about my interview with Allende. With the Peruvian military. ("That one is also an authentic revolution," he said. "The far-left students ought not to fight it. Do you think they would listen to me if I spoke to them? I'd like to talk with them.") I spoke to him about the socialist priests of Chile. He told me that they had planned an interview for him with the Chilean Cardinal. ("It's a good thing for me to see him, isn't it?") He asked me about the area where Sandino had waged his guerrilla war. Were there many followers of Sandino? What possibilities did I see for the liberation of Nicaragua?

Fidel finally told the driver to go to my hotel, but not to stop at the front entrance but at the rear entrance. The car went around back where the service wing was, and Fidel went on talking with me for a long time inside the car. He would have liked to talk with me about four hours longer, he said (we had already been talking for four hours), not only about Christianity and the Revolution, but also about Nicaragua and my island and agriculture and many more things, but it was not going to be possible because the next day the Hungarian Prime Minister was arriving, and the day after that he had to go to the doctor's and get vaccinations for his trip, and the next day he was going to Chile; and he had mountains of papers to look at before the trip (he lifted the pile between us), a hair-raising quantity, horrifying. We could talk some more in Chile; when I arrived he would be in Antofagasta . . . (he did some calculating) . . . afterward, until the 20th, in the South of Chile . . . but no, we wouldn't be able to do any talking there, that trip was going to be a whirlwind. We went on talking for a while, out of the car, in the rear patio, deserted at that hour (it was one in the morning) with the escort cars some distance away. "So the lake sharks are not so ferocious? Those technicians! They told me they were fiercer than the Caribbean ones!" And then, smiling: "Perhaps I'll drop in on them one day at your island. . ." We embraced. We waved to each other. He dashed off in his little black car and was lost in the night.

Some People, Places, Dates, and Other Data

Note: *In Cuba* is filled with names, places, acronyms, and other allusions. When I was able to clarify the allusion, from internal or external evidence, I attempted to do so for the curious reader, and I apologize for the allusions that remained elusive.—D.D.W.

Abel: see Santamaría, Abel.

Allende Gossens, Salvador (1909–73): Marxist President of Chile, killed during a right-wing coup d'état.

Althusser, Louis: Marxist philosopher.

Antofagasta: seaport in the north of Chile.

arroba: measure of weight, about twenty-five lbs.

Barbusse, Henri (1874–1935): French novelist.

Batista, Fulgencio (1901–73): ruler of Cuba, legally or illegally, from 1934 to 1959.

Benedetti, Mario: Uruguayan author, editor of the Montevidean weekly *Marcha,* and cultural adviser to Cuba.

Blas Roca: Secretary General of the Cuban Communist party.

Borges, Jorge Luis (b. 1900): Argentine poet and short-story writer.

Boris: see Santa Colona, Boris.

caballería: three hundred thirty acres.

Camilo: either Camilo Cienfuegos or Camilo Torres.

Castro, Juanita: Fidel's "worm" sister, who fled from Cuba when her brother became Premier.

Castro, Ramón: Fidel's nonpolitical older brother.

Castro, Raúl: Fidel's younger brother, Vice Premier and Minister of the Armed Forces.

CDR: Comité por la Defensa de la Revolución.

Celia: see Sánchez, Celia.

Céspedes, Carlos Manuel de (1819–73): Cuban patriot who organized the 1868 insurrection, was named President of Cuba in 1868, and in 1873 was ambushed and killed by Spanish troops.

Che: see Guevara, Che.

Cienfuegos, Camilo (d. 1959): a tailor who became a guerrilla leader and one of Castro's chief lieutenants. He was killed in a plane crash at sea.

Cintio: see Vitier, Cintio.

Cobre, Nuestra Señora de, or La Virgen de: Cuba's patron saint.

Cohen, Robert: American poet living in Cuba, present husband of Margaret Randall.

Corno (El Corno Emplumado) (lit., "The Plumed Horn"): a bilingual literary journal edited (1961–69) by Sergio Mondragón and his wife Margaret Randall.

Coronel Urtecho, José (b. 1904): a Nicaraguan poet, Cardenal's cousin and literary collaborator.

Cortázar, Julio (b. 1914): Argentine novelist and poet, author of *Raya (Hopscotch,* 1965).

Dalton, Roque (b. 1933): Salvadoran poet and political exile. His *Taberna y otros lugares (Tavern and Other Places)* won the House of the Americas Prize in 1969. He served with Cardenal on the 1970 poetry jury.

Darío, Rubén (1867–1916): Nicaraguan Modernist poet, one of the greatest and most influential in Spanish America.

Day, Dorothy: cofounder of the radical journal, *The Catholic Worker.*

Debray, Régis: French Communist who fought with Guevara in Bolivia. He was captured there and imprisoned for a time.

Diario de la Marina (Coastal Daily): conservative Catholic newspaper published in Batista's time.

Diego, Eliseo: Cuban Catholic poet, member of the *Orígenes* group, teacher at the University of Havana.

Dorticós, Osvaldo (b. 1919): President of Cuba under Castro's premiership.

Echeverría, José Antonio (d. 1957): Catholic student leader, early *fidelista,* killed leading an attack on Batista's palace.

Ernesto: 1) Ernesto Cardenal, or 2) a bootblack in the Havana airport whom Camilo Cienfuegos encouraged to seek an education. He now teaches philosophy at the University of Havana.

Escambray: see Sierra de Escambray.

Espejo, Paz: Chilean Marxist who teaches philosophy at the University of Havana.

Felipe, León: pen name of León Felipe Camino García (b. 1884), Spanish poet, political exile in Mexico.

Fernández, Pablo Armando: Cuban poet and mystic. Editor of *Lunes de Revolución,* founded in 1959. His *Los niños se despiden (The Children Say Good-by)* won the 1968 House of the Americas Prize.

Fernández Retamar, Roberto (b. 1930): Cuban poet and essayist. Editor of the literary review *Casa de las Américas.* Professor at the University of Havana.

Fidel: Fidel Castro; a *fidelista* is a follower of Fidel.

Fina: see García Marruz, Fina.

Garaudy, Roger (b. 1913): French Marxist teacher and writer.

García Márquez, Gabriel (b. 1928): Colombian novelist, author of *A Hundred Years of Solitude.*

García Marruz, Fina: poet married to Cintio Vitier.

Gethsemani, Kentucky: Trappist monastery where Cardenal studied with Thomas Merton.

Ginsberg, Allen (b. 1926): beat-generation antiwar poet, author of "Howl" (1956).

Girón: see Playa Girón.

Gómez, Máximo: (1833–1905) Cuban general in the insurrection of 1868 and (with Martí and Maceo) in the 1896 revolution against Spain.

Granma: 1) the ex-capitalist yacht that was Castro's navy in the 1956 invasion of Cuba; 2) the Cuban morning paper, official organ of the Communist party.

Guantánamo: Cuban city, part of which is the site of a U.S. naval base.

Guevara, Ernesto (Che) (1927–67): an Argentine doctor who became Castro's right-hand man. He tried to foster a peasant revolt in Bolivia, was captured and executed. Che is the common Argentine greeting, like "Hi."

Guillén, Nicolás (b. 1904): a black poet and leading twentieth-century writer. Director of the Cuban Writers and Artists Union.

gusano ("worm"): an anti-Castro Cuban.

Hart, Armando: Castro's Secretary of Organization, married to Haydée Santamaría.

Hernández, Melba: fiancée of Abel Santamaría.

A Hundred Years of Solitude (Cien años de soledad): famous novel by García Márquez.

ICAP: Instituto Cubano de Amistad con los Pueblos (Cuban Institute for Friendship with Peoples).

Ingenieros, José (1877–1925): Argentine socialist philosopher.

Isle of Pines: an internment center for political prisoners under Batista and Castro.

JC: Junta Comunista.

JEC: Juventud Estudiantil Cristiana (Christian Student Youth).

José Antonio: see Echeverría, José Antonio.

Juanita: see Castro, Juanita.

Juventud Rebelde (Rebellious Youth): the evening paper in Havana.

Lezama Lima, José (b. 1910): Cuban poet and novelist, a director of its Union of Artists and Writers, one of the founders of the literary journal *Orígenes*.

López, Rosi: Nicaraguan painter, friend of Cardenal, now living in Cuba.

López Oliva, Enrique: Communist who studied with Castro at the Jesuit school in Belén.

Lupin, Arsène: chief character in the detective novels of Maurice Leblanc (1864–1941).

Maceo, Antonio (1848–96): Cuban patriot killed during the 1896 revolution.

Macondo: the remote and imaginary locale of *A Hundred Years of Solitude,* by García Márquez.

Managua: capital of Nicaragua.

Mariátegui, José Carlos (1895–1930): Peruvian writer, founder of the Peruvian Communist party.

Martí, José (1853–95): Cuba's greatest hero, poet and journalist, killed in battle during the War of Independence.

Mártir, Pedro: Pietro Martire d'Anghiera (1457–1526), Italian geographer and historian, author of *De orbe decades octo* (1530).

Maurin, Peter (1877–1949): cofounder with Dorothy Day of *The Catholic Worker.*

Melba: see Hernández, Melba.

Merton, Thomas (1915–68): American poet, a convert to Catholicism. In 1941 he became a Trappist monk at Gethsemani, Kentucky.

Miller, Henry (b. 1891): American writer of such well-known autobiographical works as *Tropic of Cancer* (1934) and *Tropic of Capricorn* (1939).

millionaire: someone who has cut a million *arrobas* of cane in a year.

Moncada Barracks: Castro's unsuccessful attack on this Batista strongpoint in Santiago on July 26, 1953, was the start of the Revolution.

Mondragón, Sergio: Mexican poet, former husband of Margaret Randall. With her he edited the bilingual quarterly *El Corno Emplumado* (1961–69).

Montecristi Movement: an anti-Batista and anti-Castro Catholic democratic group, led by Justo Carrillo.

Neruda, Pablo (1904–73): Chilean poet and Marxist who won the Nobel Prize in 1971. The poem referred to on p. 35, "La carta en el camino" ("Letter on the Road") is the final poem in *Los versos del Capitán (The Captain's Verses)*.

Oliva: see López Oliva, Enrique.

Ordoqui, Joaquín: Cuban communist leader put under house arrest in 1964 for allegedly being an "imperialist agent." His son is a friend of Cardenal.

Oriente: the westernmost province of Cuba. In it is the Sierra Maestra, where Castro's rebellion began.

Pablo Armando: see Fernández, Pablo Armando.

Padilla, Heberto (b. 1932): Cuban poet and translator. He was not allowed to receive the poetry prize of the Writers Union in 1968 because a poem of his, "Fuera del juego" ("Out of the Game") was considered "insufficiently committed" politically.

País, Frank (1930–53): a Baptist schoolteacher and one of Castro's early lieutenants. He was murdered by the Santiago police.

Parra, Nicanor (b. 1914): Chilean poet, author of *Poemas y antipoemas (Poems and Antipoems)*.

Peña, Lázaro: Secretary General of the Confederation of Cuban Workers.

Peru: a terrible earthquake in June 1970 took 30,000 lives and left 400,000 homeless.

peso: the unit of Cuban (and most Spanish-American) currency. The Cuban *peso* was at one time worth a dollar.

Playa Girón (Girón Beach): one of the landing places in the

abortive Bay of Pigs invasion on April 17, 1961. In 1965 Holy Week was renamed Playa Girón Week.

Populorum Progressio: an encyclical of Pope John XXIII.

Ramón: see Castro, Ramón.

Randall, Margaret (b. 1936): poet, editor, translator, born in the United States, now living in Cuba.

Retamar: see Fernández Retamar, Roberto.

Roa, Raúl: Dean of the Faculty of Social Sciences at the University of Havana, Cuban Ambassador to the OAS, Foreign Minister of Cuba.

Rodo, José Enrique (1872–1917): Uruguayan essayist, author of *Ariel* (1900).

Rolland, Romain (1866–1944): French biographer and novelist, author of *Jean Cristophe,* who won the Nobel Prize in 1915.

Rosi: see López, Rosi.

Sánchez, Celia: Castro's secretary.

Sandino, Augusto César (1893–1934): Nicaraguan revolutionary and political leader. He opposed the U.S. invasion of Nicaragua. The Marines withdrew in 1933. A year later Sandino was murdered in Managua.

Santa Colona, Boris: fiancé of Haydée Santamaría and a martyr of the Revolution. Captured in the 1953 assault on the Moncada barracks, he was castrated and executed.

Santamaría, Abel: Castro's second in command during the attack on the Moncada barracks in 1953. Brother of Haydée Santamaría. His captors tore out one of his eyes before executing him.

Santamaría, Haydée: an ardent *fidelista,* married to Armando Hart, Castro's Secretary of Organization. Director of the House of the Americas. Her brother and her fiancé were executed in 1953.

Sardiña, Father Guillermo: a priest who was a commander and chaplain in Castro's guerrilla army.

Sierra de Escambray: a center of pro-Castro guerrilla action and later of anti-Castro military action. Farmers were evacuated from the mountains to prevent food from getting into anti-Castro hands.

Sierra Maestra: a chain of mountains in Oriente Province, the scene of Castro's first victories.

Skármeta, Antonio (b. 1940): Chilean member of the poetry jury. His collection of short stories, *Desnudo en el tejado (Naked on the Roof)*, won the House of the Americas Prize in 1968.

Smith, Octavio: Cuban Catholic poet.

Solentiname, Nicaragua: an island community where Cardenal and friends have built a school and a medical center.

Sue, Eugène: pen name of Marie Joseph Sue (1804–57), French Romantic novelist.

Tania: the professional name used by the communist composer Zoila Castellanos, married to Lázaro Peña, Secretary General of the Confederation of Cuban Workers.

Torres, Camilo: a Colombian guerrilla priest, killed in action.

Tupamaros: Uruguayan radicals and kidnappers who took their name from Tupac-Amaru, a descendant of Peruvian Incas who proclaimed himself sovereign in 1781. He was drawn and quartered by the Spanish.

Turquino: Cuba's highest mountain, in the Sierra Maestra.

26th of July: birthday of José Martí (July 26, 1853). A century later Castro chose this date to open his war against Batista with the attack on the Moncada Barracks (July 26, 1953). It is now the Cuban national holiday, and Christmas is "officially" celebrated then.

UMAP: Unidad Militar de Ayuda a la Producción (Military Unit for Aid to Production), which was for some time Castro's concentration camp.

Vallejo, César (1892–1938): Peruvian poet, a Catholic and communist, and an ardent supporter of the Spanish Republic during the Franco rebellion.

Vargas Vila, José María (1860–1933): Colombian novelist.

Venceremos ("We Shall Conquer" or "We Shall Overcome"): a revolutionary slogan and also the name of a brigade of Americans who went to Cuba to help with the sugar-cane harvest.

Vitier, Cintio (b. 1921): a Cuban Catholic poet and a founder of the journal *Origenes*. Director of the Martí Room in the National Library.

Walsh, Rodolfo: Argentine essayist and sociologist.

worm (*gusano*): an anti-Castro Cuban.